This 3rd edition of Lonely Planet's *Polish phrasebook* is based on the previous edition by the Lonely Planet Language Products team and Piotr Czajkowski, who provided the translations and pronunciation guides as well as cultural advice.

Piotr works in Lonely Planet's Melbourne office as a senior GIS analyst. He hails from Gliwice and Kraków and studied in Wrocław before migrating to Australia to further his education at the University of Melbourne and Swinburne University of Technology. He's adapted well to life in Australia but still pines for Polish *piwo* peevo (beer). Piotr would like the world to know that, contrary to popular opinion, Polish is not difficult to pronounce. It has, in fact, one more vowel than English.

Piotr would like to thank his wife Gosia and his daughter Aleksandra for their help, and little Karolinka for her patience.

Thanks also to James Howard, English teacher and long-time resident of Kraków, for contributing his insights into Polish language and culture, and to Yukiyoshi Kamimura and Wendy Wright for the inside illustrations.

Thanks to the Lonely Planet Language Products team who produced the 2nd edition of the *Polish phrasebook* on which this one is based: Vanessa Battersby, Steven Cann, Francesca Coles, Adrienne Costanzo, David Kemp and Karin Vidstrup Monk.

acknowledgments

make the most of this phrasebook ...

Anyone can speak another language! It's all about confidence. Don't worry if you can't remember your school language lessons or if you've never learnt a language before. Even if you learn the very basics (on the inside front cover of this book), your travel experience will be the better for it. You have nothing to lose and everything to gain when the locals hear you making an effort.

finding things in this book

For easy navigation, this book is in sections. The Basics chapters are the ones you'll thumb through time and again. The Practical section covers basic travel situations like catching transport and finding a bed. The Social section gives you conversational phrases, pick-up lines, the ability to express opinions – so you can get to know people. Food has a section all of its own: gourmets and vegetarians are covered and local dishes feature. Safe Travel equips you with health and police phrases, just in case. Remember the colours of each section and you'll find everything easily; or use the comprehensive Index. Otherwise, check the two-way traveller's Dictionary for the word you need.

being understood

Throughout this book you'll see coloured phrases on each page. They're phonetic guides to help you pronounce the language. Start with them to get a feel for how the language sounds. The pronunciation chapter in Basics will explain more, but you can be confident that if you read the coloured phrase, you'll be understood. As you become familiar with the spoken language, move on to using the actual text in the language which will help you perfect your pronunciation.

communication tips

Body language, ways of doing things, sense of humour – all have a role to play in every culture. 'Local talk' boxes show you common ways of saying things, or everyday language to drop into conversation. 'Listen for ...' boxes supply the phrases you may hear. They start with the script (so a local can find the phrase they want and point it out to you) and then lead in to the phonetic guide and the English translation.

CONTENTS

5

social 105

CONTENTS

7

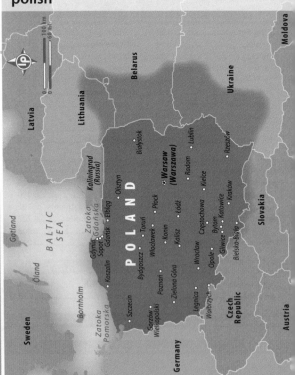

100 km
60 mi

Moldova

Latvia

Lithuania

Belarus

Ukraine

Gotland

BALTIC SEA

Öland

Zatoka Gdańska

Kaliningrad (Russia)

• Białystok

• Lublin

☆ Warsaw (Warszawa)

• Rzeszów

• Radom

• Kielce

Olsztyn

• Elbląg

Gdynia• Sopot •Gdańsk

•Koszalin

Zatoka Pomorska

Bornholm

• Toruń

•Włocławek

Bydgoszcz

P O L A N D

• Płock

•Konin

• Łódź

•Kalisz

Częstochowa

• Kraków

Bytom Katowice

• Poznań

Wrocław•

•Gliwice

• Opole

Bielsko-biała

Zielona Góra

• Legnica

• Wałbrzych

Slovakia

Czech Republic

Austria

Germany

Szczecin•

Gorzów •Wielkopolski

Sweden

official language

generally understood
(areas are approximate only)

minority language

Poland
EUROPE

For more details, see the **introduction**.

Ask most English speakers what they know about Polish and they will most likely dismiss it as an unpronounceable language. Who could pronounce an apparently vowel-less word like *szczyt* (meaning 'peak'), for example? To be put off by this unfairly gained reputation, however, would be to miss out on a rich and rewarding language. The mother tongue of illustrious personalities such as Copernicus, Chopin, Joseph Conrad, Marie Curie and Pope John Paul II has a fascinating and turbulent past and symbolises the resilience of the Polish people in the face of domination and adversity.

The story of Polish begins with the arrival of the Polish tribes who occupied the basins of the Oder and Vistula rivers in the 6th century AD. These tribes spoke a range of West Slavic dialects, which over time evolved into Polish. The closest living relatives of Polish are Czech and Slovak, which also belong to the wider West Slavic family of languages.

Polish reached the apex of its influence during the era of the Polish Lithuanian Commonwealth, which was formed in 1569 and lasted until 1795. The Commonwealth covered a swath of territory from what are now Poland and Lithuania, through to Belarus, Ukraine and Latvia and part of Western Russia. Polish became a lingua franca throughout much of Central and Eastern Europe at this time due to the Commonwealth's political, cultural, scientific and military might.

When Poland was wiped off the map of Europe from 1795 to 1918 after three

at a glance ...

language name:
Polish

name in language:
język polski jen·zik pol·skee

language family: Slavic

key country: Poland

approximate number of speakers: 45 million

close relatives:
Czech, Slovak

donations to English:
horde, mazurka, vodka

introduction

9

successive partitions in the second half of the 18th century (when it was carved up between Russia, Austria and Prussia), the language suffered attempts at both Germanisation and Russification. Later, after WWII, Poland became a satellite state of the Soviet Union and it came under the renewed influence of Russian. Polish showed impressive resistance in the face of this oppression. The language not only survived but enriched itself by borrowing many words from both Russian and German. The works of Poland's greatest literary figures who wrote in exile – the Romantic poet Adam Mickiewicz, and, during Communist rule, the Nobel Prize winner Czesław Miłosz – are testament to this fact.

Today Poland is linguistically one of the most homogeneous countries in Europe – over 95% of the population speaks Polish as their first language. There are significant Polish-speaking minorities in the western border areas of Ukraine, Belarus and in southern Lithuania, with smaller populations in other neighbouring countries.

Getting acquainted with Polish is easy. It's not difficult to pronounce and the coloured pronunciation guides in this book are designed to help you say any Polish word with ease. This book gives you all the practical phrases you need to get by, as well as all the fun, spontaneous phrases that will lead to a better understanding of Poland and its people. Local knowledge, new relationships and a sense of satisfaction are on the tip of your tongue. So don't just stand there – say something!

abbreviations used in this book

a	adjective	loc	locative
acc	accusative	m	masculine
adv	adverb	m pers pl	masculine personal
dat	dative		plural
f	feminine	n	neuter
gen	genitive	nom	nominative
general pl	general plural	perf	perfective
imp	imperfective	pl	plural
inf	informal	pol	polite
inst	instrumental	sg	singular
lit	literal	v	verb
	translation	voc	vocative

BASICS > pronunciation

Although written Polish may seem a bit intimidating, with its apparent excess of consonants, pronouncing Polish isn't hard at all. Many of the sounds also exist in English and each Polish letter is generally pronounced the same way wherever it occurs. If you listen carefully to native speakers and follow the coloured pronunciation guides in this phrasebook, you'll easily get your message across.

vowel sounds

Polish vowels and diphthongs (vowel combinations) are quite similar to those found in English. Vowels are generally prounounced short, giving them a 'clipped' quality.

symbol	english equivalent	polish example	transliteration
a	cut	*tak*	tak
ai	aisle	*tutaj*	*too*·tai
e	get	*bez*	bes
ee	feet	*wino*	*vee*·no
ey	they	*kolejka*	ko·*ley*·ka
i	bit	*czy*	chi
o	not	*woda*	*vo*·da
oo	put	*zakupy, mój*	za·*koo*·pi, mooy
ow	cow	*migdał*	*meeg*·dow
oy	toy	*ojciec*	*oy*·chets

nasal vowel sounds

One distinctive feature of Polish (which it shares with French) is nasal vowels. Nasal vowel sounds are pronounced as though you're trying to force the air out of your nose rather than your mouth. It's easier than it sounds! English also has something similar to nasal vowels – when you say 'sing' in English the 'i' is nasalised by the 'ng'. Nasal vowels are indicated in written Polish by the little hooks under the *ą* and *ę*. Depending upon the letters that follow these vowels, they're pronounced with either an m or an n sound following the vowel.

symbol	english equivalent	polish example	transliteration
em	like the 'e' in 'get' plus nasal consonant sound	*wstęp*	fstemp
en		*mięso*	myen·so
om	like the 'o' in 'not' plus nasal consonant sound	*kąpiel*	kom·pyel
on		*wąsy*	von·si

consonant sounds

Most Polish consonant sounds are also found in English, with the exception of the kh sound (which is pronounced as in the Scottish word 'loch') and the rolled r sound. Consonants are sometimes grouped together without vowels between them where in English you'd expect one, as in the word *pszczoła pshcho·wa* (bee). With a bit of practice these 'consonant clusters' will roll off your tongue with ease. The apostrophe is used in transliterations (as in the word *kwiecień kfye·chen'*) to show that the consonant before it is produced with a soft y sound.

In our pronunciation guides you'll notice some syllables made up of the single consonants f, v, s and z. These represent the prepositions *w* and *z* ('in/on' and 'with'). When pronouncing them, just run them into the word that follows them.

symbol	english equivalent	polish example	transliteration
b	bend	*babka*	*bap*·ka
ch	child	*cień, czas, ćma*	chen', chas, chma
d	drum	*drobne*	*drob*·ne
f	friend	*fala*	*fa*·la
g	grass	*garnek*	*gar*·nek
j	jar	*dzieci*	*je*·chee
k	kiss	*kac*	kats
kh	loch	*chata, hałas*	*kha*·ta, *kha*·was
l	lever	*lato*	*la*·to
m	milk	*malarz*	*ma*·lash
n	noon	*nagle*	*na*·gle
p	prone	*palec*	*pa*·lets
r	rolled, as in Spanish *arriba*	*róg*	roog
s	scatter	*samolot*	*sa*·mo·lot
sh	shallow	*siedem, śnieg, szlak*	*shye*·dem, shnyek, shlak
t	tank	*targ*	tark
v	violet	*widok*	*vee*·dok
w	welcome	*złoto*	*zwo*·to
y	yield	*zajęty*	za·*yen*·ti
z	zoom	*zachód*	za·khoot
zh	leisure	*zima, żart, rzeźba*	*zhee*·ma, zhart, *zhezh*·ba
'	like a soft y	*kwiecień*	*kfye*·chen'

pronunciation

word stress

Stress almost always falls on the second-last syllable. In our pronunciation guides, the stressed syllable is italicised.

reading & writing

The relationship between pronunciation and spelling in Polish is consistent. This means that a letter or a cluster of letters is always pronounced the same way. The Polish alphabet is presented in the table below. It has 32 letters – all the letters of the English alphabet except 'q', 'v' and 'x' (which only appear in some foreign words and names), plus nine letters with diacritical marks (marks above or below the letters). For spelling purposes (eg when you need to spell your name to book into a hotel) the pronunciation of each letter is provided.

polish alphabet					
A a a	Ą ą on	B b be	C c tse	Ć ć chye	D d de
E e e	Ę ę en	F f ef	G g gye	H h kha	I i ee
J j yot	K k ka	L l el	Ł ł ew	M m em	N n en
Ń ń en'	O o o	Ó ó oo	P p pe	R r er	S s es
Ś ś esh	T t te	U u oo	W w voo	Y y* i	Z z zet
Ż ż zhyet	Ż ż zhet	*note that the letter y is not a consonant but a vowel pronounced i			

In addition to the individual letters of the alphabet above, Polish spelling combines pairs of letters to form a single sound. These are ch (pronounced kh), cz (ch), dz (dz or j), dź and dż (both roughly pronounced j), rz (zh or sh) and sz (sh). Also, when the letter i follows s, z and c these letters are 'softened' to sh, zh and ch respectively.

a–z phrasebuilder

contents

The list below shows which grammatical structures you can use to say what you want. Look under each function – listed in alphabetical order – for information on how to build your own sentences. For example, to tell the taxi driver where your hotel is, look for **giving instructions** and you'll be directed to information on **case** and **demonstratives**. A **glossary** of grammatical terms is included at the end of this chapter to help you. Abbreviations like **nom** and **acc** in the literal translations for each example refer to the case of the noun or pronoun – this is explained in the **glossary** and in **case**.

adjectives & adverbs

Adjectives usually come before the noun, and change their gender, number and case endings to agree with the nouns they describe. In the **dictionaries** and word lists in this phrasebook, adjectives are given in the masculine form and nominative case (see **case** and **gender**).

The most common endings in the nominative case for singular nouns are -y -i for the masculine, -a -a for the feminine and -e -e for the neuter gender.

This is a beautiful forest!
   To jest piękny las!   to yest *pyenk*·ni las
   (lit: this is beautiful-m-nom forest-m-nom)

This is a beautiful river!
   To jest piękna rzeka!   to yest *pyenk*·na *zhe*·ka
   (lit: this is beautiful-f-nom river-f-nom)

In the plural, Polish distinguishes only between masculine personal adjectives (those describing men only or mixed groups of men and women) which end in -*i* -ee or -*y* -i, and a general class of adjectives (encompassing women, children, animals, objects and abstract nouns). The general class takes an -*e* -e or -*ie* -ye ending in the plural.

good lads   *dobrzy chłopci*   *dob*·zhi *khwop*·tsi
   (lit: good-m pers pl lad-m pers pl)

good girls   *dobre dziewczyny*   *dob*·re jev·*chi*·ni
   (lit: good-general pl girl-general pl)

Adverbs are generally formed by removing the final letter of an adjective and replacing it with -*o* -o or -*ie* -ye. Their position in the sentence is fairly flexible but they mostly come before the verb.

He played beautifully.
   On pięknie grał.   on *pyenk*·nye grow
   (lit: he beautifully played)

a-z phrasebuilder

articles

Polish doesn't have an equivalent for 'a' and 'the' – *dom* dom can mean both 'a house' or 'the house' depending on context.

be

describing people/things • making statements

The verb *być* bich (be) takes the forms shown in the table below in the present tense.

być – present tense			
I	am	*jestem*	yes·tem
you sg	are	*jesteś*	yes·tesh
he/she/it	is	*jest*	yest
we	are	*jesteśmy*	yes·tesh·mi
you pl	are	*jesteście*	yes·tesh·chye
they	are	*są*	som

I'm here for a holiday.
 Jestem tutaj na wakacjach.   yes·tem too·tai na va·kats·yakh
 (lit: I-am here for holidays)

In the past tense, the forms of *być* change to match both the gender and the number of the subject as shown below.

być – past tense			
I m/f	was	*byłem/am*	bi·wem/wam
you m/f sg	were	*byłeś/aś*	bi·wesh/wash
he/she/it	were	*był/była/było*	biw/bi·wa/bi·wo
we m/f	were	*byliśmy/ byłyśmy*	bi·leesh·mi/ bi·wish·mi
you m/f pl	were	*byliście/ byłyście*	bi·leesh·chye/ bi·wish·chye
they m/f	were	*byli/były*	bi·lee/bi·wi

I was homesick.

Byłem/am stęskniony/a   *bi·*wem/wam stensk·*nyo·*ni/na
za domem. m/f   za *do·*mem
(lit: I-was-m/f longing-m/f for home)

Below are the future tense forms of *być*:

byc – future tense			
I	will be	*będę*	ben·de
you sg	will be	*będziesz*	ben·jyesh
he/she/it	will be	*będzie*	ben·jye
we	will be	*będziemy*	ben·jye·mi
you pl	will be	*będziecie*	ben·jye·chye
they	will be	*będą*	ben·dom

How long will you be here for?

Jak długo tutaj będziesz? inf   yak *dwoo·*go *too·*tai ben·jyesh
(lit: how long here you-will-be)

The future tense forms of *być* are also used before imperfective
infinitive verbs to form the continuous future tense (see the
future heading in the **verbs** section for more on this).

See also **negatives**.

case

doing things • giving instructions •
indicating location • making statements •
naming people/things • possessing

Polish has a system of seven case endings, shown in the table
on the next page, which are used to indicate the grammatical
role of nouns, adjectives, pronouns and demonstratives in a
sentence and their relationship to other words. The word lists
and **dictionaries** in this book provide nouns in the nominative
case. If you use the nominative case in any context, even when
it's not grammatically correct, you'll still be understood.

nominative nom – shows the subject of a sentence

The guide will pay.
Przewodnik zapłaci.   pshe·*vod*·neek za·*pwa*·chee
(lit: guide-nom will-pay)

accusative acc – shows the direct object in affirmative sentences

I'd like to reserve a table.
Chciałam   khchow·am
zarezerwować stolik.   za·re·zer·*vo*·vach *sto*·leek
(lit: like-I reserve table-acc)

genitive gen – primarily shows possession ('of') but also indicates the direct object in negative sentences

That's my friend's seat.
To jest miejsce   to yest *myeys*·tse
mojego kolegi.   mo·*ye*·go ko·*le*·gee
(lit: this is place my-gen friend-gen)

dative dat – shows the indirect object of a sentence

I gave my son a present.
Dałem prezent   *da*·wem *pre*·zent
mojemu synowi.   mo·*ye*·moo si·*no*·vi
(lit: gave-I present to-my-dat son-dat)

instrumental inst – shows how something is done

Can we go there by car?
Czy możemy tam   chi mo·*zhe*·mi tam
dojechać samochodem?   do·*ye*·khach sa·mo·*kho*·dem
(lit: question-particle can-we there go car-inst)

locative loc – used with prepositions to show location

What should I visit in the old town?
Co powinienem zobaczyć   tso po·vee·*nye*·nem zo·*ba*·chich
na Starym Mieście?   na *sta*·rim *myesh*·chye
(lit: what should-I visit in old-loc town-loc)

vocative voc – used to address someone directly

My friend, I love it here!
Podoba mi się tu,   po·*do*·ba mee shye too
mój przyjacielu.   mooy pshi·ya·*chye*·loo
(lit: like me-dat myself here my-voc friend-voc)

demonstratives

**giving instructions · indicating location ·
naming people/things · pointing things out**

The Polish words for 'this' and 'that' agree in case, gender and
number with the noun they refer to and come before the noun
they refer to, eg *ta droga* ta dro·ga (lit: this-**f-nom** road-**f-nom**).
The different forms (in the nominative case) are shown in the
table below.

| | singular | | | plural | |
	m	f	n	m personal *	general *
this	*ten* ten	*ta* ta	*to* to	*ci* chee	*te* te
that	*tamten* tam·ten	*tamta* tam·ta	*tamto* tam·to	*tamci* tam·chee	*tamte* tam·te

* see **gender** below for more on these categories

gender

describing people/things · naming people/things

All Polish nouns have gender – masculine m, feminine f or
neuter n. The distinction is purely grammatical and not related
to a noun's meaning. You need to learn the grammatical gender for each noun as you go, but you can often recognise it by
the noun's ending.

• Masculine nouns generally end in a consonant:

stół m   stoow   **table**

• Feminine nouns generally end in *-a*:

gazeta f   ga·ze·ta   **newspaper**

• Neuter nouns generally end in *-e* or *-o*:

słońce n   swon'·tse   **sun**
lato n   la·to   **summer**

In the plural, nouns, adjectives, demonstratives and possessive pronouns have only two types of ending – masculine personal (for men only and mixed groups of both men and women), and general (for women, children, animals, objects and abstract nouns). These categories are marked as **m pers** and **general pl**.

The nouns in this book's word lists, **dictionaries** and **menu decoder** have their gender marked unless they belong to the general plural category. Alternative gender endings on adjectives and verbs are separated with a slash and marked **m/f/n**, eg *czerwony/a/e* cher·vo·ni/na/ne (red).

have

possessing

An easy way of expressing possession in Polish is by using the verb *mieć* myech (have).

I have a tourist visa.
   Mam wizę turystyczną.   mam *vee·*ze too·ris·*tich·*nom
   (lit: have-I visa-**f-acc** tourist-**f-acc**)

The present tense forms of *mieć* are shown below. To form past and future tense forms, see **verbs**.

mieć – present tense			
I	have	*mam*	mam
you sg	have	*masz*	mash
he/she/it	has	*ma*	ma
we	have	*mamy*	*ma·*mi
you pl	have	*macie*	*ma·*chye
they	have	*mają*	*ma·*yom

See also **negatives** and **possessive pronouns**.

negatives

negating

In Polish, negative statements are made simply by adding the word *nie* nye (not) before the verb:

I (don't) understand.
   (Nie) Rozumiem.   (nye) ro·*zoo*·myem
   (lit: (not) understand-I)

See also **be**, **have** and **verbs**.

personal pronouns

doing things • making statements • naming people/things

Personal pronouns ('I', 'you', etc) are mostly omitted in Polish, as the subject of the sentence is indicated by the verb's ending (see **verbs**). However, they can be used for emphasis:

I will carry the bags.
   Ja poniosę bagaże.   ya po·*nyo*·se ba·*ga*·zhe
   (lit: I carry-will-I bags)

The pronoun 'they' has two forms. One form, *oni* o·nee, is used for men and mixed groups of both men and women and is known as the masculine personal form. The other form, *one* o·ne, is known as the general form and is used for women, children, animals, objects and abstract nouns. The nominative case forms of personal pronouns are given in the table below.

subject pronouns (nominative case)					
I	*ja*	ya	we	*my*	mi
you sg	*ty*	ti	you pl	*wy*	vi
he	*on*	on	they m personal	*oni*	o·nee
she	*ona*	o·na	they general	*one*	o·ne
it m/f/n	*on/ona/ono*	on/o·na/o·no			

The singular and plural forms of 'you' (*ty* ti and *wy* vi) are only used in informal situations, such as with friends, family and younger people. In more formal situations, the titles shown below are used, along with the third-person form of the verb in the singular or plural (see also **verbs**). These words mean literally 'Mr' and 'Mrs' etc but translate as 'you' in most contexts.

you – polite forms				
	masculine		feminine	
singular	*pan*	pan	*pani*	pa·nee
plural	*panowie*	pa·no·vye	*panie*	pa·nye
	państwo		pan'·stfo	

We've used the abbreviations **pol** and **inf** to indicate where you have a choice between polite and informal language. In all other cases we've chosen the appropriate form for the context.

plurals

describing people/things • naming people/things

Plurals of Polish nouns can take different forms, depending on the noun's gender and its final letter. You don't need to worry much about this, as the nouns in all phrases in this book are in the correct form, and even if you use the singular form given in the dictionaries, you'll be understood.

possessive pronouns

naming people/things • possessing

In Polish, possessive pronouns change to match the case, number and gender of the noun they describe.

That child is mine.
  To jest moje dziecko.   to yest mo·ye jyets·ko
  (lit: that-n-nom-sg child-n-nom-sg is mine-n-nom-sg)

The forms in the nominative case are on the opposite page.

	singular			**plural**	
	m	**f**	**n**	**m personal**	**general**
my	*mój* mooy	*moja* mo·ya	*moje* mo·ye	*moi* mo·ee	*moje* mo·ye
your sg	*twój* tfooy	*twoja* tfo·ya	*twoje* tfo·ye	*twoi* tfo·ee	*twoje* tfo·ye
his/its	*jego* ye·go				
her	*jej* yey				
our	*nasz* nash	*nasza* na·sha	*nasze* na·she	*nasi* na·shee	*nasze* na·she
your pl	*wasz* vash	*wasza* va·sha	*wasze* va·she	*wasi* va·shee	*wasze* va·she
their	*ich* eekh				

prepositions

indicating location • pointing things out

Prepositions are used to show relationships between words and come before the nouns they modify. Here are some useful ones, with the cases (see **case**) that are commonly used with them:

english	polish	transliteration	case
about	*o*	o	locative
at (place)	*na*	na	locative
at (time)	*o*	o	locative
for	*dla*	dla	genitive
from (place)	*z*	z	genitive
from (time)	*od*	od	genitive
in	*w/we*	v/ve	locative
of	*o*	o	locative
on	*na*	na	locative
to (place)	*do*	do	genitive

questions

To form a yes/no question, start the sentence with the question particle *czy* chi.

Is this seat free?
> *Czy to miejsce jest wolne?*   chi to *myeys*·tse yest *vol*·ne
> (lit: question-particle this seat is free)

Questions may also begin with a question word such as 'what', 'when' or 'where' and these come at the beginning of the sentence.

What do you recommend?
> *Co polecasz?*   tso po·*le*·tsash
> (lit: what recommend-you-inf)

question words		
How?	*Jak?*	yak
How much?	*Ile?*	ee·le
What?	*Co?*	tso
When?	*Kiedy?*	kye·di
Where?	*Gdzie?*	gjye
Which? m/f/n	*Który/a/e?*	ktoo·ri/ra/re
Who?	*Kto?*	kto
Why?	*Dlaczego?*	dla·che·go

verbs

The infinitive (or the 'dictionary form') of Polish verbs usually ends in *-ać*, *-eć*, *-ieć* or *-ować*. There are three main tenses: past, present and future.

Most Polish verbs have two infinitive forms. For example, dictionaries often have two entries for 'to read', *czytać* chi·tach and *przeczytać* pshe·chi·tach. The first is the 'imperfective aspect', used for unfinished, habitual or continuing actions.

I often read in Polish.
   Często czytam po polsku.   chen·sto chi·tam po pol·skoo
   (lit: often read-I-imp-pres in Polish)

The second form is the 'perfective aspect', and is used to refer to actions that have already been completed, or that are intended to be completed in the future.

I finished reading the book.
   Przeczytałam ksiażkę.   pshe·chi·tow·am ksyonzh·ke
   (lit: read-I-perf-past book)

present

You use only the imperfective aspect in the present tense. The following table shows the present-tense endings for the four main verb groups. You drop *-ać*, *-eć*, *-ieć* and *-ować* and add the endings indicated.

present tense verb endings			
	czytać chi·tach **to read**	*umieć* oo·myech **to know**	*widzieć* vee·jyech **to see**	*pracować* pra·tso·vach **to work**
I	*-am* am	*-em* em	*-ę* e	*-uję* oo·ye
you sg	*-asz* ash	*-esz* esh	*-isz* eesh	*-ujesz* oo·yesh
he/she/it	*-a* a	*-e* e	*-i* ee	*-uje* oo·ye
we	*-amy* a·mi	*-emy* e·mi	*-imy* ee·mi	*-ujemy* oo·ye·mi
you pl	*-acie* a·chye	*-ecie* e·chye	*-icie* ee·chye	*-ujecie* oo·ye·chye
they	*-ają* a·yom	*-eją* e·yom	*-ą* om	*-ują* oo·yom

past

Both imperfective and perfective verb forms are used in the past tense. To form the past tense of both aspects remove the infinitive -ć ending and replace it with the endings in the table below:

past tense verb forms	m		f		n	
I	-łem	wem	-łam	wam		
you sg	-łeś	wesh	-łaś	wash		
he/she/it	-ł	w	-ła	wa	-ło	wo
we	-liśmy	leesh·mi	-łyśmy	wish·mi		
you pl	-liście	leesh·chye	-łyście	wish·chye		
they	-li	lee	-ły	wi		

future

A continuous action in the future is expressed by the verb *być* bich (see **be**) in the future tense followed by the imperfective infinitive of the main verb.

I will read on the plane.
Będę czytać w samolocie.   ben·de chi·tach v sa·mo·lo·chye
(lit: be-I-**fut** read-**imp** in aeroplane-**loc**)

An action that will be completed in the future is indicated by a perfective verb with endings indentical to the present tense endings shown in the table on page 27.

I will read the guidebook before I go there.
Przeczytam przewodnik   pshe·chi·tam pshe·vod·neek
zanim tam pojadę.   za·neem tam po·ya·de
(lit: read-I-**fut-perf** guidebook before there go-I-**fut-perf**)

glossary

accusative (case)	type of *case marking* (usually) used to show the *direct object* of the sentence – 'she poured **the vodka**'
adjective	a word that describes something – 'the **alcoholic** content'
adverb	word that explains how an action was done – 'he drank **quickly**'
affirmative sentence	a sentence that doesn't express negation – 'I **saw** the bottle', as opposed to 'I **didn't see** the bottle'
article	the words 'a', 'an' and 'the'
aspect	Polish verbs have two aspects – *perfective* and *imperfective*
case (marking)	word ending which tells us the role of a thing or person in the sentence
dative (case)	type of *case marking* which shows the *indirect object* – 'I gave the glasses **to the pourer**'
demonstrative	a word that means 'this' or 'that'
direct object	the thing or person in the sentence that has the action directed to it – 'I read **the label**'
gender	classification of *nouns* into classes (like masculine and feminine), requiring other words (eg *adjectives*) to belong to the same class
genitive (case)	type of *case marking* which shows ownership or possession – 'the **barman's** shout'
imperfective (aspect)	*verb aspect* showing a continuous, habitual or incomplete action – 'he **was drinking** vodka all day'
indirect object	the person or thing in the sentence that is the recipient of the action – 'I gave **him** ice'
infinitive	dictionary form of a *verb* – 'we started **to drink** to his health'

instrumental (case)	type of *case marking* which shows how something is done – 'she drank it down **with one gulp**'
locative (case)	type of *case marking* which shows where the *subject* is – 'the vodka is **in the freezer**'
nominative (case)	type of *case marking* used for the *subject* of the sentence – 'the **drinking session** ended'
noun	a thing, person or idea – 'the **bottle**'
number	whether a word is singular or plural – 'our **hangovers** were terrible'
perfective (aspect)	*verb aspect* showing a complete action – 'they **cleared away** the party debris'
personal pronoun	a word that means 'I', 'you', etc
possessive pronoun	a word that means 'mine', 'yours', etc
preposition	a word like 'in' or 'at' in English
question particle	a word that signals a question
subject	the thing or person in the sentence that does the action – '**the inebriated people** started dancing'
tense	form of a *verb* that tells you whether the action is in the present, past or future – eg 'eat' (present), 'ate' (past), 'will eat' (future)
verb	a word that tells you what action happened – 'I **refused** another drink'
vocative (case)	type of *case marking* used to address someone directly – 'leave me alone, **you drunkard**'

language difficulties

Do you speak (English)?
Czy pan/pani mówi
po (angielsku)? m/f pol
Czy mówisz
po (angielsku)? inf

chi pan/*pa*·nee moo·vee
po (an·*gyel*·skoo)
chi moo·veesh
po (an·*gyel*·skoo)

Does anyone speak (English)?
Czy ktoś mówi
po (angielsku)?

chi ktosh moo·vee
po (an·*gyel*·skoo)

Do you understand (me)?
Czy pan/pani (mnie)
rozumie? m/f pol
Czy (mnie) rozumiesz? inf

chi pan/*pa*·nee (mnye)
ro·*zoo*·mye
chi (mnye) ro·*zoo*·myesh

Yes, I understand.
Tak, rozumiem.

tak ro·*zoo*·myem

No, I don't understand.
Nie, nie rozumiem.

nye nye ro·*zoo*·myem

I (don't) understand.
(Nie) Rozumiem.

(nye) ro·*zoo*·myem

Pardon?
Proszę?

pro·she

I speak (English).
Mówię po (angielsku).

moo·vyem po (an·*gyel*·skoo)

I don't speak (Polish).
Nie mówię po (polsku).

nye moo·vyem po (*pol*·skoo)

I speak a little.
Mówię trochę.

moo·vyem *tro*·khe

Let's speak (Polish).
Rozmawiajmy po (polsku).

roz·mav·*yai*·mi po (*pol*·skoo)

What does (nieczynne) mean?
Co to znaczy (nieczynne)?

tso to *zna*·chi (nye·*chi*·ne)

How do you ...?	*Jak się ...?*	yak shye ...
pronounce this	*to wymawia*	to vi·*mav*·ya
write *(pierogi)*	*pisze (pierogi)*	*pee*·she (pye·*ro*·gee)
Could you please ...?	*Proszę ...*	*pro*·she ...
repeat that	*to powtórzyć*	to pov·*too*·zhich
speak more slowly	*mówić trochę wolniej*	*moo*·veech *tro*·khe *vol*·nyey
write it down	*to napisać*	to na·*pee*·sach

cardinal numbers

The numbers 'one' and 'two' are the only ones that take different forms for masculine, feminine and neuter words. Numbers also change form to reflect their case (see **case** in the **a–z phrasebuilder** for an explanation of this term). When counting, use *raz* ras instead of *jeden* etc for 'one'.

0	zero	ze·ro
1	jeden/jedna/ jedno m/f/n	ye·den/yed·na/ yed·no
2	dwa/dwie/ dwoje m/f/n	dva/dvye/ dvo·ye
3	trzy	tshi
4	cztery	chte·ri
5	pięć	pyench
6	sześć	sheshch
7	siedem	shye·dem
8	osiem	o·shyem
9	dziewięć	jye·vyench
10	dziesięć	jye·shench
11	jedenaście	ye·de·nash·chye
12	dwanaście	dva·nash·chye
13	trzynaście	tshi·nash·chye
14	czternaście	chter·nash·chye
15	piętnaście	pyent·nash·chye
16	szesnaście	shes·nash·chye
17	siedemnaście	shye·dem·nash·chye
18	osiemnaście	o·shem·nash·chye
19	dziewiętnaście	jye·vyet·nash·chye
20	dwadzieścia	dva·jyesh·chya
21	dwadzieścia jeden	dva·jyesh·chya ye·den
30	trzydzieści	tshi·jyesh·chee

40	*czterdzieści*	chter·*jyesh*·chee
50	*pięćdziesiąt*	pyen·*jye*·shont
60	*sześćdziesiąt*	shesh·*jye*·shont
70	*siedemdziesiąt*	shye·dem·*jye*·shont
80	*osiemdziesiąt*	o·shem·*jye*·shont
90	*dziewięćdziesiąt*	jye·vyen·*jye*·shont
100	*sto*	sto
200	*dwieście*	dvyesh·chye
300	*trzysta*	*tshi*·sta
400	*czterysta*	chte·*ri*·sta
500	*pięćset*	pyench·set
600	*sześćset*	sheshch·set
700	*siedemset*	shye·dem·set
800	*osiemset*	o·shyem·set
900	*dziewięćset*	jye·vyench·set
1000	*tysiąc*	ti·shonts
1,000,000	*milion*	mee·lyon

in the numbers

In this phrasebook you might notice that when numbers are used in combination with nouns, the form of the noun changes. So you might see, for instance, that 'a piece' is *jeden kawałek* ye·den ka·*vow*·ek, 'three pieces' is *trzy kawałki* tshi ka·*vow*·kee and 'five pieces' is *pięć kawałków* pyench ka·*vo*·w·koof. This morphing of noun endings happens because numbers in Polish also determine the case of the nouns that follow them (for an explanation of the term 'case', see the **a–z phrasebuilder**, page 19).

The rules for which numbers take which case and the various endings for the different cases are a little complex. You needn't worry about them because if you say the number and use the nominative (dictionary) form of the noun, people will still understand what you mean, even if it's not grammatically correct. Keep in mind that Poles are warmly appreciative of any attempt to communicate with them in their native tongue. They're also well aware of the complexities of Polish and will make allowances for less-than-perfect speech by foreigners.

ordinal numbers

The correct format of ordinal numbers is to write the number followed by a dot, eg *2. piętro* droo·gye pyen·tro (2nd floor). Ordinal numbers agree in gender and case with the noun they refer to, in much the same way as adjectives do. (See the **a–z phrasebuilder**, pages 15–30, for an explanation of these grammatical terms.)

1st	*pierwszy/a/e* m/f/n	pyerf·shi/sha/she
2nd	*drugi/a/ie* m/f/n	droo·gee/ga/gye
3rd	*trzeci/a/ie* m/f/n	tshe·chee/cha/chye
4th	*czwarty/a/e* m/f/n	chfar·ti/ta/te
5th	*piąty/a/e* m/f/n	pyon·ti/ta/te
6th	*szósty/a/e* m/f/n	shoos·ti/ta/te
7th	*siódmy/a/e* m/f/n	shyood·mi/ma/me
8th	*ósmy/a/e* m/f/n	oos·mi/ma/me
9th	*dziewiąty/a/e* m/f/n	jyev·yon·ti/ta/te
10th	*dziesiąty/a/e* m/f/n	jye·shon·ti/ta/te
11th	*jedenasty/a/e* m/f/n	ye·de·nas·ti/ta/te
12th	*dwunasty/a/e* m/f/n	dvoo·nas·ti/ta/te

decimals & fractions

liczby dziesiętne i ułamki

Polish decimals use a *przecinek* pshe·chee·nek (comma) rather than a dot, eg *2,5*. In large numbers the digits are grouped by thousands with spaces between rather than commas, eg one million is written as 1 000 000 (as opposed to 1,000,000).

3.14	*trzy przecinek*	tshi pshe·chee·nek
	czternaście	chter·nash·chye
4.2	*cztery przecinek*	chte·ri pshe·chee·nek
	dwa	dva
5.1	*pięć przecinek*	pyench pshe·chee·nek
	jeden	ye·den

a quarter	jedna czwarta	yed·na chfar·ta
a third	jedna trzecia	yed·na tshe·chya
a half	pół	poow
three-quarters	trzy czwarte	tshi chfar·te
all	całość	tsa·woshch
none	nic	neets

useful amounts

Weights smaller than a kilogram are given in *dekagramy* de·ka·*gra*·mi (decagrams), commonly abbreviated to *deko* de·ko, unless you want to be very precise about a given weight. You'd use decagrams, for instance, if you were ordering ham at a delicatessen. One *deko* is equal to 10 grams and there are 100 *deko* (decagrams) in a kilogram.

How much/many?	Ile?	ee·le
Please give me …	*Proszę …*	pro·she …
(100) grams	(sto) gram	(sto) gram
(10) decagrams	(10) deko	(jye·shench) de·ko
half a kilo	pół kilo	poow kee·lo
a kilo	kilo	kee·lo
a bottle	butelkę	boo·tel·ke
a jar	słoik	swo·eek
a packet	paczkę	pach·ke
a slice	plasterek	plas·te·rek
a tin	puszkę	poosh·ke
a few	kilka	keel·ka
less	mniej	mnyey
(just) a little	(tylko) trochę	(til·ko) tro·khe
a lot/many	dużo	doo·zho
more	więcej	vyen·tsey
some	trochę	tro·khe

For more amounts, see **self-catering**, page 174.

telling the time

Official times are given according to the 24-hour clock, but in everyday life people use the 12-hour clock. Rather than using cardinal numbers when referring to time, the feminine forms of ordinal numbers are used so that 'four o'clock' is *czwarta godzina* chfar·ta go·jee·na (lit: fourth hour). The word *godzina* is often left out so that four o'clock can be just *czwarta* chfar·ta (lit: fourth). Refer to **ordinal numbers** in **numbers & amounts**, page 35, for ordinal numbers to help you form time expressions.

What time is it?	*Która jest godzina?*	ktoo·ra yest go·jee·na
It's one o'clock.	*Pierwsza.*	pyerf·sha

Times 'half past' the hour refer to the coming hour rather than the current one, so that 'half past ten' is literally 'half to eleven'. The equivalents of 'past' and 'to' are the words *po* po and *za* za.

Five past (ten).	*Pięć po (dziesiątej).*	pyench po (jye·shon·tey)
Quarter past (ten).	*Piętnaście po (dziesiątej).*	pyent·nash·chye po (jye·shon·tey)
Half past (ten).	*Wpół do (jedenastej).*	fpoow do (ye·de·nas·tey)
Twenty to (eleven).	*Za dwadzieścia (jedenasta).*	za dva·jyesh·chya (ye·de·nas·ta)
Quarter to (eleven).	*Za piętnaście (jedenasta).*	za pyent·nash·chye (ye·de·nas·ta)

In conversation, to prevent any misunderstandings about whether you mean 'am' or 'pm', add the part of the day, eg 'in the morning', 'in the afternoon' or 'at night' using the expressions below. You can also use the Polish for 'am' and 'pm' (which mean literally 'morning' and 'in the afternoon'), but bear in mind that hours from 11pm to 3am or 4am are usually described as 'at night', whereas hours from roughly 6pm till 9pm or 10pm are referred to as 'in the evening'.

am	rano	ra·no
pm	po południu	po po·wood·nyoo
in the morning	rano	ra·no
in the afternooon	po południu	po po·wood·nyoo
in the evening	wieczorem	vye·cho·rem
at night	w nocy	v no·tsi

At what time?	O której godzinie?	o ktoo·rey go·jee·nye
At (five).	O (piątej).	o (pyon·tey)
At (7.57pm).	O (19.57).	o (jye·vyet·nas·tey pyen·jye·shont shye·dem)

the calendar

kalendarz

days

You will see the days of the week abbbreviated to Pn., Wt., Śr., Cz., Pt., So. and Nd. on timetables and signs etc.

Monday	poniedziałek m	po·nye·jya·wek
Tuesday	wtorek m	fto·rek
Wednesday	środa f	shro·da
Thursday	czwartek m	chfar·tek
Friday	piątek m	pyon·tek
Saturday	sobota f	so·bo·ta
Sunday	niedziela f	nye·jye·la

BASICS

38

months

The names of the months are often abbreviated as follows: *Sty., Lut., Mar., Kwi., Maj., Cze., Lip., Sie., Wrz., Paź., Lis.* and *Gru.* The forms following the slashes are the forms of the months that you'll need to use when saying dates (see below for more on this).

January	*styczeń/stycznia* m	sti·chen´/stich·nya
February	*luty/lutego* m	loo·ti/loo·te·go
March	*marzec/marca* m	ma·zhets/mar·tsa
April	*kwiecień/ kwietnia* m	kfye·chyen´/ kfyet·nya
May	*maj/maja* m	mai/ma·ya
June	*czerwiec/czerwca* m	cher·vyets/cherf·tsa
July	*lipiec/lipca* m	lee·pyets/leep·tsa
August	*sierpień/ sierpnia* m	shyer·pyen´/ shyerp·nya
September	*wrzesień/ września* m	vzhe·shyen´/ vzhesh·nya
October	*październik/ października* m	pazh·jyer·neek/ pazh·jyer·nee·ka
November	*listopad/ listopada* m	lees·to·pat/ lees·to·pa·da
December	*grudzień/ grudnia* m	groo·jyen´/ grood·nya

dates

Ordinal numbers are used when saying dates, just as in English. The ordinal number takes an *-ego* e·go ending, so that 13 September is *trzynastego września* tshi·nas·te·go vzhesh·nya (lit: thirteenth of-September). The form of the month changes from the nominative to the genitive case. Genitive case forms are given above for each month following the slashes. See **case** in the **a–z phrasebuilder** for an explanation of these terms.

Dates may be written in one of three ways: using Arabic numerals (in day–month–year order) separated by dots (eg *13.09.2007*), using Roman numerals for the month and no dots (eg *13 IX 2007*), or you can write the month out longhand (eg *13 września 2007*).

time & dates

What date is it today?
> *Którego jest dzisiaj?*   ktoo·*re*·go yest *jee*·shai

It's (18 October).
> *Jest (osiemnastego*   yest (o·shem·nas·*te*·go
> *października).*   pazh·jyer·*nee*·ka)

seasons

spring	*wiosna* f	*vyos*·na
summer	*lato* n	*la*·to
autumn/fall	*jesień* f	ye·shyen'
winter	*zima* f	*zhee*·ma

---

times past

It might be useful to know the time expressions below (some of which are followed by their abbreviated forms) when you're reading timetables or checking out museums, artworks and monuments.

bieżącego roku (br.)	bye·zhon·*tse*·go *ro*·koo	this year
epoka	e·*po*·ka	era/age
godzina (godz.)	go·*jee*·na	time/hour/ o'clock
koniec	*ko*·nyets	end
okres	*o*·kres	period
początek	po·*chon*·tek	beginning
przed naszą erą (p.n.e)	pshed *na*·shom e·rom	BC
rok (r.)	rok	year
roku Pańskiego	*ro*·koo pan'·*skye*·go	AD
stulecie	stoo·*le*·chye	century
tysiąclecie	ti·shyonts·*le*·chye	millennium

present

'Today' is both *dziś* jeesh and *dzisiaj* jee·shai – there's no difference in meaning between the two.

now	*teraz*	te·ras
today	*dziś/dzisiaj*	jeesh/jee·shai
tonight	*dziś wieczorem*	jeesh vye·cho·rem
this ...		
morning	*dziś rano*	jeesh ra·no
afternoon	*dziś po*	jeesh po
	południu	po·wood·nyoo
evening	*dziś wieczorem*	jeesh vye·cho·rem
week	*w tym tygodniu*	f tim ti·god·nyoo
month	*w tym miesiącu*	f tim mye·shon·tsoo
year	*w tym roku*	f tim ro·koo

past

day before yesterday	*przedwczoraj*	pshet·fcho·rai
(three days) ago	*(trzy dni) temu*	(tshi dnee) te·moo
since (May)	*od (maja)*	od (ma·ya)
last night	*wczoraj*	fcho·rai
	wieczorem	vye·cho·rem
last ...	*w zeszłym ...*	v zesh·wim ...
week	*tygodniu*	ti·god·nyoo
month	*miesiącu*	mye·shon·tsoo
year	*roku*	ro·koo
yesterday ...	*wczoraj ...*	fcho·rai ...
morning	*rano*	ra·no
afternoon	*po południu*	po po·wood·nyoo
evening	*wieczorem*	vye·cho·rem

time & dates

41

future

day after tomorrow	*pojutrze*	po·yoo·tshe
in (six days)	*za (sześć dni)*	za (sheshch dnee)
until (June)	*do (czerwca)*	do (*cherf*·tsa)
next ...	*w przyszłym ...*	v *pshish*·wim ...
week	*tygodniu*	ti·*god*·nyoo
month	*miesiącu*	mye·*shon*·tsoo
year	*roku*	*ro*·koo
tomorrow ...	*jutro ...*	*yoo*·tro ...
morning	*rano*	*ra*·no
afternoon	*po południu*	po po·*wood*·nyoo
evening	*wieczorem*	vye·*cho*·rem

during the day

afternoon	*popołudnie* n	po·po·*wood*·nye
dawn	*świt* m	shveet
day	*dzień* m	jyen'
evening	*wieczór* m	vye·choor
midday/noon	*południe* n	po·*wood*·nye
midnight	*północ* f	*poow*·nots
morning	*rano* n	*ra*·no
night	*noc* f	nots
sunrise	*wschód słońca* m	fskhoot *swon'*·tsa
sunset	*zachód słońca* m	za·khoot *swon'*·tsa

How much is it?
Ile to kosztuje? — ee·le to kosh·*too*·ye

It's free.
Jest bezpłatny/a/e. m/f/n — yest bes·*pwat*·ni/na/ne

It's (12) złotys.
To kosztuje — to kosh·*too*·ye
(12) złotych. — (dva·*nash*·chye) *zwo*·tikh

Can you write down the price?
Proszę napisać cenę. — *pro*·she na·*pee*·sach *tse*·ne

Do I have to pay?
Czy muszę płacić? — chi *moo*·she *pwa*·cheech

There's a mistake in the bill/check.
Na czeku jest pomyłka. — na *che*·koo yest po·*miw*·ka

Do you accept ...?	Czy mogę zapłacić ...?	chi *mo*·ge za·*pwa*·cheech ...
credit cards	kartą kredytową	*kar*·tom kre·di·*to*·vom
debit cards	kartą debetową	*kar*·tom de·be·*to*·vom
travellers cheques	czekami podróżnymi	che·*ka*·mee pod·roozh·*ni*·mee

I'd like ..., please.	Proszę o ...	*pro*·she o ...
a receipt	rachunek	ra·*khoo*·nek
a refund	zwrot pieniędzy	zvrot pye·*nyen*·dzi
my change	moją resztę	*mo*·yom *resh*·te

Where's ...?	Gdzie jest ...?	gjye yest ...
an ATM	bankomat	ban·*ko*·mat
a foreign exchange office	kantor walut	*kan*·tor va·loot

I'd like to ...	Chciałem/am ... m/f	khchow·em/am ...
cash a cheque	wymienić czek	vi·mye·neech chek
	na gotówkę	na go·toof·ke
change a	wymienić czek	vi·mye·neech chek
travellers	podróżny	po·droozh·ni
cheque		
change money	wymienić	vi·mye·neech
	pieniądze	pye·nyon·dze
get a cash	dostać zaliczkę	dos·tach za·leech·ke
advance	na moją kartę	na mo·yom kar·te
	kredytową	kre·di·to·vom
get change	rozmienić	roz·mye·neech
for this note	pieniądze	pye·nyon·dze
withdraw	wypłacić	vi·pwa·tseech
money	pieniądze	pye·nyon·dze

What's the ...?	Jaki/a jest ...? m/f	ya·kee/ka yest ...
charge	prowizja f	pro·veez·ya
exchange rate	kurs wymiany m	koors vi·mya·ni

How much is	Ile kosztuje	ee·le kosh·too·ye
it per ...?	za ...?	za ...
caravan	przyczepę	pshi·che·pe
	kampingową	kam·peen·go·vom
day	dzień	jyen'
game	grę	gre
hour	godzinę	go·jee·ne
(five) minutes	(pięć) minut	(pyench) mee·noot
night	noc	nots
page	stronę	stro·ne
person	osobę	o·so·be
tent	namiot	na·myot
week	tydzień	ti·jyen'
vehicle	samochód	sa·mo·khood
visit	wizytę	vee·zi·te

For more money-related phrases, see **banking**, page 91.

getting around

komunikacja

Which ... goes to (Zakopane)?	*Który ... jedzie do (Zakopanego)?*	ktoo·ri ... ye·jye do (za·ko·pa·ne·go)
bus	*autobus*	ow·to·boos
minibus	*minibus*	mee·nee·boos
train	*pociąg*	po·chonk
Which ... goes to (Sopot)?	*Który ... jedzie do (Sopotu)?*	ktoo·ri ... ye·jye do (so·po·too)
tram	*tramwaj*	tram·vai
trolleybus	*trolejbus*	tro·ley·boos

Is this the ... to (Wrocław)?	*Czy to jest ... do (Wrocławia)?*	chi to yest ... do (vrots·wa·vya)
bus	*autobus*	ow·to·boos
minibus	*minibus*	mee·nee·boo
train	*pociąg*	po·chonk
Is this the ... to (Orłowo)?	*Czy to jest ... do (Orłowa)?*	chi to yest ... do (or·wo·va)
tram	*tramwaj*	tram·vai
trolleybus	*trolejbus*	tro·ley·boos
When's the ... (bus)?	*Kiedy jest ... (autobus)?*	kye·di yest ... (ow·to·boos)
first	*pierwszy*	pyerf·shi
last	*ostatni*	os·tat·nee
next	*następny*	nas·temp·ni

Which ferry goes to (Ystad)?
Który prom płynie — ktoo·ri prom pwi·nye
do (Ystad)? — do (ees·tad)

Is this the ferry to (Copenhagen)?
Czy to jest prom — chi to yest prom
do (Kopenhagi)? — do (ko·pen·kha·gee)

What time does it leave?
O której godzinie — o ktoo·rey go·jee·nye
odjeżdża? — ot·yezh·ja

What time does it get to (Toruń)?
O której godzinie — o ktoo·rey go·jee·nye
przyjeżdża do (Torunia)? — pshi·yezh·ja do (to·roo·nya)

How long will it be delayed?
Jakie będzie — ya·kye ben·jye
opóźnienie? — o·poozh·nye·nye

Is this seat free?
Czy to miejsce jest wolne? — chi to myeys·tse yest vol·ne

That's my seat.
To jest moje miejsce. — to yest mo·ye myeys·tse

Please tell me when we get to (Krynica).
Proszę mi powiedzieć — pro·she mee po·vye·jyech
gdy dojedziemy — gdi do·ye·jye·mi
do (Krynicy). — do (kri·nee·tsi)

Please stop here.
Proszę się tu zatrzymać. — pro·she shye too za·tshi·mach

How long do we stop here?
Na jak długo się — na yak dwoo·go shye
tu zatrzymamy? — too za·tshi·ma·mi

---

move over!

When using public transport in Poland, always offer up your seat to the elderly, pregnant women or people with a disability if there are no other seats free by saying *proszę usiąść* pro·she oo·shyonshch (please take a seat). Failure to cede your seat might just precipitate a storm of invective from the injured party.

46

tickets

Excuse me, where's the ticket office?
Przepraszam, gdzie jest   pshe·*pra*·sham gjye yest
kasa biletowa?   *ka*·sa bee·le·*to*·va

Where do I buy a ticket?
Gdzie mogę kupić bilet?   gjye *mo*·ge *koo*·peech *bee*·let

Do I need to book (well in advance)?
Czy muszę rezerwować   chi *moo*·she re·zer·*vo*·vach
(z dużym wyprzedzeniem)?   (z *doo*·zhim vi·pshe·*dze*·nyem)

A ... ticket	*Proszę bilet ...*	*pro*·she *bee*·let ...
(to Katowice).	*(do Katowic).*	(do ka·*to*·veets)
1st-class	*pierwszej klasy*	*pyerf*·shey *kla*·si
2nd-class	*drugiej klasy*	*droo*·gyey *kla*·si
child's	*dla dziecka*	dla *jyets*·ka
one-way	*w jedną stronę*	v *yed*·nom *stro*·ne
reserved seat	*miejscówkę*	*myeys*·*tsoof*·ke
return	*powrotny*	po·*vro*·tni
student	*studencki*	stoo·*den*·tskee

I'd like	*Proszę miejsce ...*	*pro*·she *myeys*·tse ...
a/an ... seat.		
aisle	*przy*	pshi
	przejściu	*pshey*·shchyoo
window	*przy oknie*	pshi *ok*·nye

Is there (a) ...?	*Czy jest tam ...?*	chi yest tam ...
air conditioning	*klimatyzacja*	klee·ma·ti·*za*·tsya
blanket	*koc*	kots
sick bag	*torebka na*	to·*rep*·ka na
	wymioty	vi·*myo*·ti
toilet	*toaleta*	to·a·*le*·ta

How much is it?
Ille kosztuje?   *ee·le kosh·too·ye*

How long does the trip take?
Ille trwa podróż?   *ee·le trfa po·droosh*

Is it a direct route?
*Czy to jest bezpośrednie
połączenie?*   chi to yest bes·po·*shred*·nye
po·won·*che*·nye

Can I get a stand-by ticket?
*Czy mogę dostać
bilet z listy rezerwowej?*   chi *mo·*ge *do·*stach
*bee·*let z *lees·*ti re·zer·*vo·*vey

Can I get a sleeping berth?
*Czy mogę dostać
miejsce sypialne?*   chi *mo·*ge *do·*stach
*myeys·*tse si·*pyal·*ne

Can I get a couchette?
*Czy mogę dostać
kuszetkę?*   chi *mo·*ge *do·*stach
koo·*shet·*ke

What time should I check in?
*O której godzinie
muszę się zgłosić?*   o *ktoo·*rey go·*jee·*nye
*moo·*she shye *zgwo·*sheech

I'd like to … **my ticket, please.**	*Chcę … mój bilet.*	khtse … mooy *bee·*let
cancel	*odwołać*	od·*vo·*wach
change	*zmienić*	*zmye·*neech
collect	*odebrać*	o·*de·*brach
confirm	*potwierdzić*	po·*tvyer·*jyeech

PRACTICAL

48

luggage

bagaż

Where can I find (a/the) ...?	Gdzie jest ...?	gjye yest ...
baggage claim	odbiór bagażu	*od*·byoor ba·*ga*·zhoo
left-luggage office	przechowalnia bagażu	pshe·kho·*val*·nya ba·*ga*·zhoo
luggage locker	schowek na bagaż	*skho*·vek na ba·gazh
trolley	wózek na bagaż	*voo*·zek na ba·gazh
My luggage has been ...	Mój bagaż został ...	mooy ba·gazh zos·tow ...
damaged	uszkodzony	oosh·ko·*dzo*·ni
lost	zagubiony	za·goo·*byo*·ni
stolen	skradziony	skra·*jyo*·ni

That's (not) mine.
To (nie) jest moje.   to (nye) yest *mo*·ye

Can I have some coins?
Czy mogę prosić o drobne monety?   chi *mo*·ge *pro*·sheech o *dro*·bne mo·*ne*·ti

Can I have some tokens?
Czy mogę prosić o żetony?   chi *mo*·ge *pro*·sheech o zhe·*to*·ni

transport

49

plane

samolot

Where's (the) …?	Gdzie jest …?	gjye yest …
airport shuttle	autobus lotniskowy	ow·to·boos lot·nees·ko·vi
arrivals hall	hala przylotów	kha·la pshi·lo·toof
departures hall	hala odlotów	kha·la od·lo·toof
duty-free shop	sklep wolnocłowy	sklep vol·no·tswo·vi
gate (5)	wejście (numer pięć)	veysh·chye (noo·mer pyench)

Where does flight (LO125) arrive/depart?

Skąd przylatuje/ odlatuje lot (LO125)?

skont pshi·la·too·ye/ od·la·too·ye lot (el o sto dva·jyesh·chya pyench)

listen for …		
karta pokładowa f	kar·ta po·kwa·do·va	boarding pass
paszport m	pash·port	passport
przesiadka f	pshe·shyat·ka	transfer
tranzyt m	tran·zit	transit

bus, coach, tram & trolleybus

autobus, autokar, tramwaj i trolejbus

Most of Poland's bus transport is operated by the former state bus company *PKS* pe ka es. There are two types of *PKS* bus service: *autobusy zwykłe* ow·to·boo·si zvi·kwe (local buses) and *autobusy pospieszne* ow·to·boo·si pos·pyesh·ne (fast buses) which are marked in red and cover long-distance routes.

Is this a bus stop?

Czy to jest przystanek autobusowy?

chi to yest pshi·sta·nek ow·to·boo·so·vi

How often do buses come?
Jak często przyjeżdżają autobusy?
yak chen·sto pshi·yezh·ja·yom ow·to·boo·si

Does it stop at (Bielsko)?
Czy się zatrzymuje w (Bielsku)?
chi shye za·tshi·moo·ye v (byel·skoo)

What's the next stop?
Jaki jest następny przystanek?
ya·kee yest nas·tem·pni pshi·sta·nek

I'd like to get off at (Gliwice).
Chcę wysiąść w (Gliwicach).
khtse vi·shyonshch v (glee·vee·tsakh)

How much is it to (Olsztyn)?
Ile kosztuje żeby dojechać do (Olsztyna)?
ee·le kosh·too·ye zhe·bi do·ye·khach do (ol·shti·na)

intercity	*międzymiastowy* m	myen·dzi·myas·to·vi
local bus	*lokalny autobus* m	lo·kal·ni ow·to·boos
hotel bus	*autobus hotelowy* m	ow·to·boos kho·te·lo·vi

For bus numbers, see **numbers & amounts**, page 33.

train

pociąg

What's the next station?
Jaka jest następna stacja?
ya·ka yest nas·temp·na sta·tsya

Does it stop at (Kalisz)?
Czy on się zatrzymuje w (Kaliszu)?
chi on shye za·tshi·moo·ye f (ka·lee·shoo)

Do I need to change?
Czy trzeba się przesiadać?
chi tshe·ba shye pshe·shya·dach

Is it …?	*Czy to jest pociąg …?*	chi to yest *po*·chonk …
express	*ekspresowy*	eks·pre·*se*·vi
a fast train	*pospieszny*	pos·*pyesh*·ni
an InterCity train	*InterCity*	een·ter·*see*·tee
a suburban train	*podmiejski*	pod·*myey*·skee
Which carriage is (for) …?	*Który wagon jest …?*	*ktoo*·ri *va*·gon yest …
1st class	*z pierwszą klasą*	z *pyer*·fshom *kla*·som
dining	*restauracyjny*	res·tow·ra·*tsiy*·ni
(Kołobrzeg)	*(do Kołobrzegu)*	(do ko·wo·*bzhe*·goo)

train timetable reader

EC. (EuroCity)	ew·ro·*see*·tee	EuroCity service
IC. (InterCity)	een·ter·*see*·tee	InterCity service
EX. (Expres)	eks·pres	express service
TLK. (Tanie Linie Kolejowe)	*ta*·nye *lee*·nye ko·le·*yo*·ve	discounted intercity service
p. (pospieszny)	pos·*pyesh*·ni	fast train
os. (osobowy)	o·so·*bo*·vi	local train
codziennie	tso·*jye*·nye	daily
do	do	till
od	od	from
oprócz	o·*prooch*	except
także	*tak*·zhe	also

For abbreviations of the names of months and days of the week, see **time & dates**, pages 38–39.

ferry

What's the sea like today?
Jaki jest dzisiaj   ya·kee yest jee·shai
stan morza?   stan mo·zha

Are there life jackets?
Czy są tam kamizelki   chi som tam ka·mee·zel·kee
ratunkowe?   ra·toon·ko·ve

I feel seasick.
Mam chorobę morską.   mam kho·ro·be mor·skom

boat	*statek* m	*sta*·tek
cabin	*kabina* f	ka·*bee*·na
captain	*kapitan* m	ka·*pee*·tan
(car) deck	*pokład*	*pok*·wad
	(samochodowy) m	(sa·mo·kho·*do*·vi)
ferry	*prom* m	prom
lifeboat	*szalupa*	sha·*loo*·pa
	ratunkowa f	ra·toon·*ko*·va
life jacket	*kamizelka*	ka·mee·*zel*·ka
	ratunkowa f	ra·toon·*ko*·va

taxi

I'd like a	*Chcę zamówić*	khtse za·*moo*·veech
taxi …	*taksówę na …*	tak·*soof*·ke na …
now	*teraz*	*te*·ras
tomorrow	*jutro*	*yoo*·tro
at (9am)	*na (dziewiątą*	na (jye·*vyon*·tom
	rano)	*ra*·no)

Where's the taxi rank?
Gdzie jest postój taksówek?   gjye yest pos·tooy tak·*soo*·vek

Is this taxi available?
Czy ta taksówka jest wolna?   chi ta tak·*soof*·ka yest *vol*·na

Please take me to (this address).
Proszę mnie zawieźć   pro·she mnye za·vyeshch
pod (ten adres).   pod (ten ad·res)

Please put the meter on.
Proszę włączyć taksometr.   pro·she vwon·chich tak·so·metr

Please put the day-time rate on.
Proszę ustawić   pro·she oo·sta·veech
dzienną taryfę.   jyen·nom ta·ri·fe

How much is ...?	*Ile kosztuje ...?*	ee·le kosh·too·ye ...
it to (Szczecin)	*do (Szczecina)*	(do shche·chee·na)
the flag fall/	*złamanie*	zwa·ma·nye
hiring charge	*chorągiewki*	kho·ron·gyef·kee

Please ...	*Proszę ...*	pro·she ...
come back at	*wrócić o*	vroo·cheech o
(10 o'clock)	*(dziesiątej)*	(jye·shon·tey)
slow down	*zwolnić*	zvol·neech
stop here	*się tu*	shye too
	zatrzymać	za·tshi·mach

car & motorbike

car & motorbike hire

I'd like to hire	*Chcę*	khtse
a/an ...	*wypożyczyć*	vi·po·zhi·chich
	samochód ...	sa·mo·khoot ...
4WD	*terenowy*	te·re·no·vi
automatic	*z automa-*	z ow·to·ma·
	tyczną	tich·nom
	skrzynią biegów	skshi·nyom bye·goof
manual	*z ręczną*	z rench·nom
	skrzynią biegów	skshi·nyom bye·goof

I'd like to hire a motorbike.
Chcę wypożyczyć motocykl.   khtse vi·po·zhi·chich mo·to·tsikl

with ...	z ...	z ...
air conditioning	klimatyzacją	klee·ma·ti·za·tsyom
a driver	kierowcą	kye·rof·tsom
How much for ... hire?	Ile kosztuje wypożyczenie na ...?	ee·le kosh·too·ye vi·po·zhi·che·nye na ...
daily	dzień	jyen′
weekly	tydzień	ti·jyen′

Does that include insurance?
Czy ubezpieczenie jest wliczone? — chi oo·bes·pye·che·nye yest vlee·cho·ne

Does that include mileage?
Czy kilometry są wliczone? — chi kee·lo·me·tri som vlee·cho·ne

Do you have a guide to the road rules (in English)?
Czy jest objaśnienie kodeksu drogowego (po angielsku)? — chi yest ob·yash·nye·nye ko·de·ksoo dro·go·ve·go (po an·gyel·skoo)

Do you have a road map?
Czy jest mapa drogowa? — chi yest ma·pa dro·go·va

on the road

What's the speed limit?
Jakie jest ograniczenie prędkości? — ya·kye yest o·gra·nee·che·nye prent·kosh·chee

Is this the road to (Malbork)?
Czy to jest droga do (Malborka)? — chi to yest dro·ga do (mal·bor·ka)

Where's a petrol/gas station?
Gdzie jest stacja benzynowa? — gjye yest sta·tsya ben·zi·no·va

Can you check the ...?	Czy może pan sprawdzić ...?	chi mo·zhe pan sprav·jeech ...
oil	olej	o·ley
tyre pressure	ciśnienie w oponach	cheesh·nye·nye v o·po·nakh
water	wodę	vo·de

diesel	diesel m	dee-zel
leaded petrol	benzyna	ben-zi-na
	ołowiowa f	o-wo-vyo-va
LPG	gaz m	gaz
98-octane	dziewięćdziesię-	jye-vyen-jye-shen-
unleaded	cioośmio	cho-osh-myo
petrol	oktanowa f	ok-ta-no-va
unleaded	bezołowiowa f	bes-o-wo-vyo-va

Can I park here?
Czy można tu parkować?   chi *mozh*-na too par-*ko*-vach

How long can I park here?
Jak długo można   yak *dwoo*-go *mozh*-na
tu parkować?   too par-*ko*-vach

Do I have to pay?
Czy muszę płacić?   chi *moo*-she *pwa*-cheech

problems

I need a mechanic.
Potrzebuję mechanika.   po-tshe-*boo*-ye me-kha-*nee*-ka

I've had an accident.
Miałem/am wypadek. m/f   *myow*-em/am vi-*pa*-dek

The car/motorbike has broken down at (Kozia Wólka).
Samochód/Motocykl   sa-*mo*-khoot/mo-*to*-tsikl
się zepsuł w   shye zep-*soow* v
(Koziej Wólce).   (ko-zhyey *vool*-tse)

road signs		
Opłata	o-*pwa*-ta	Toll
Stop	stop	Stop
Uwaga	oo-*va*-ga	Danger
Wjazd	vyazd	Entrance
Wyjazd	vi-yazd	Exit

The car/motorbike won't start.
 Samochód/Motocykl   sa·mo·khoot/mo·to·tsikl
 nie chce zapalić.   nye khtse za·pa·leech

I have a flat tyre.
 Złapałem/am gumę. m/f zwa·pa·wem/wam *goo*·me

I've lost my car keys.
 Zgubiłem/am   zgoo·bee·wem/wam
 kluczyki do samochodu. m/f kloo·chi·kee do sa·mo·kho·doo

I've locked the keys inside.
 Zatrzasnąłem/   za·tsha·sno·wem/
 Zatrzasnęłam   za·tsha·sne·wam
 kluczyki w środku. m/f kloo·chi·kee v *shrot*·koo

I've run out of petrol.
 Zabrakło mi benzyny. za·bra·kwo mee ben·zi·ni

Can you fix it (today)?
 Czy może pan to   chi *mo*·zhe pan to
 (dzisiaj) naprawić? (jee·shai) na·pra·veech

How long will it take?
 Ile czasu to zajmie? ee·le cha·soo to *zai*·mye

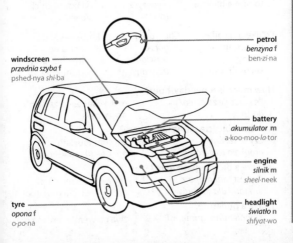

petrol
benzyna f
ben·zi·na

windscreen
przednia szyba f
pshed·nya *shi*·ba

battery
akumulator m
a·koo·moo·la·tor

engine
silnik m
sheel·neek

tyre
opona f
o·po·na

headlight
światło n
shfyat·wo

transport

listen for ...

bilet na autostradę m	*bee*·let na ow·to·*stra*·de	**motorway pass**
kilometry m pl	ki·lo·*me*·tri	**kilometres**
parkometr m	par·*ko*·metr	**parking meter**
prawo jazdy n	*pra*·vo *yaz*·di	**driving licence**

bicycle

rower

The Polish word for 'bicycle' is *rower* ro·ver. The first bicycles were imported into Poland by the British car manufacturer Rover and the name stuck.

I'd like ...	Chcę ...	khtse ...
my bicycle repaired	oddać rower do naprawy	ot·dach ro·ver do na·*pra*·vi
to buy a bicycle	kupić rower	*koo*·peech ro·ver
to hire a bicycle	wypożyczyć rower	vi·po·*zhi*·chich ro·ver

I'd like a ... bike.	Chcę rower ...	khtse ro·ver ...
mountain	górski	*goor*·skee
racing	wyścigowy	vish·chee·*go*·vi
secondhand	używany	oo·zhi·*va*·ni

How much is it per day/hour?
Ile kosztuje za dzień/ godzinę?
ee·le kosh·*too*·ye za jyen'/ go·*jee*·ne

Are there bicycle paths here/there?
Czy są tu/tam drogi dla rowerów?
chi som too/tam *dro*·gee dla ro·*ve*·roof

Is there a bicycle-path map?
Czy jest tam mapa z drogami dla rowerów?
chi yest tam *ma*·pa z dro·*ga*·mee dla ro·*ve*·roof

I have a puncture.
Złapałem/am gumę. m/f
zwa·*pa*·wem/wam *goo*·me

border crossing

przekraczanie granicy

I'm ...	Jestem ...	yes·tem ...
in transit	w tranzycie	v tran·zi·chye
on business	służbowo	swoozh·bo·vo
on holiday	na wakacjach	na va·kats·yakh

I'm here for ...	Będę tu przez ...	ben·de too pshes ...
(10) days	(dziesięć) dni	(jye·shench) dnee
(three) weeks	(trzy) tygodnie	(tshi) ti·god·nye
a month	jeden miesiąc	ye·den mye·shonts
(two) months	(dwa) miesiące	(dva) mye·shon·tse
(five) months	(pięć) miesięcy	(pyench) mye·shyen·tsi

I'm going to (Kraków).
Jadę do (Krakowa).   ya·de do (kra·ko·va)

I'm staying at the (Pod Różą Hotel).
Zatrzymuję się w   za·tshi·moo·ye shye v
(hotelu 'pod Różą').   (ho·te·loo pód roo·zhom)

The children are on this passport.
Dzieci są wpisane   jye·chee som fpee·sa·ne
do paszportu.   do pash·por·too

listen for ...

grupa f	groo·pa	group
indywidualny	een·di·vee·doo·al·ni	alone
paszport m	pash·port	passport
rodzina f	ro·jee·na	family
wiza f	vee·za	visa

59

at customs

I have nothing to declare.
Nie mam nic do   nye mam neets do
zgłoszenia.   zgwo·*she*·nya

I have something to declare.
Mam coś do zgłoszenia.   mam tsosh do zgwo·*she*·nya

Do I have to declare this?
Czy muszę to zgłosić?   chi *moo*·she to *zgwo*·sheech

That's (not) mine.
To (nie) jest moje.   to (nye) yest *mo*·ye

I didn't know I had to declare it.
Nie wiedziałem/am,   nye vye·*ja*·wem/wam
że muszę to zgłosić. **m/f**   zhe *moo*·she to *zgwo*·sheech

Could I please have a/an (English) interpreter?
Proszę o tłumacza   *pro*·she o twoo·*ma*·cha
(angielskiego).   (an·gyel·*skye*·go)

For phrases on payments and receipts, see **money**, page 43.

signs

Kontrola	kon·*tro*·la	**Passport Control**
paszportowa	pash·por·*to*·va	
Kwarantanna	kfa·ran·*ta*·na	**Quarantine**
Odprawa celna	ot·*pra*·va *tsel*·na	**Customs**
Odprawa	ot·*pra*·va	**Immigration**
imigracyjna	ee·mee·gra·*tsiy*·na	
Wolny od opłaty	*vol*·ni od o·*pwa*·ti	**Duty-Free**
celnej	*tsel*·ney	

Where's a/the ...?	Gdzie jest ...?	gjye yest ...
bank	bank	bank
market	targ	tark
tourist office	biuro	byoo·ro
	turystyczne	too·ris·tich·ne

How do I get there?
Jak tam mogę się dostać?
yak tam mo·ge
shye dos·tach

Do you know the way?
Czy znasz drogę?
chi znash dro·ge

How far is it?
Jak daleko to jest?
yak da·le·ko to yest

Can you show me (on the map)?
Czy może pan/pani mi pokazać (na mapie)? m/f
chi mo·zhe pan/pa·nee
mee po·ka·zach (na ma·pye)

What's the address?
Jaki jest adres?
ya·kee yest ad·res

---

typical addresses

You'll probably see the words *mieszkanie, aleja, ulica, plac* and *osiedle* (see below) abbreviated to *m., al., ul., pl* and *os.* respectively. A *województwo* vo·ye·voots·tfo (which is commonly abbreviated to *woj.*) is an administrative region of which there are 16 in Poland. In English it's translated as 'voivode'.

apartment	mieszkanie n	myesh·ka·nye
avenue	aleja f	a·le·ya
road/street	ulica f	oo·lee·tsa
square	plac n	plats
suburb	osiedle n	o·shyed·le
voivode	województwo n	vo·ye·voots·tfo

listen for ...		
kilometry	kee·lo·*me*·tri	**kilometres**
metry	*me*·tri	**metres**
minuty	mee·*noo*·ti	**minutes**
przecznice	pshech·*nee*·tse	**blocks**

It's ...	*Jest ...*	yest ...
behind ...	*za ...*	za ...
close	*blisko*	*blees*·ko
here	*tu*	too
in front of ...	*przed ...*	pshet ...
near ...	*koło ...*	*ko*·wo ...
next to ...	*obok ...*	*o*·bok ...
on the corner	*na rogu*	na *ro*·goo
opposite ...	*naprzeciwko ...*	nap·she·*cheef*·ko ...
straight ahead	*na wprost*	na fprost
there	*tam*	tam

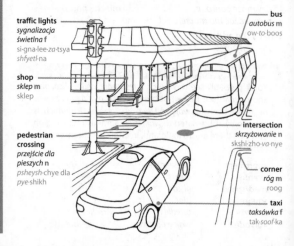

traffic lights
sygnalizacja świetlna f
si·gna·lee·*za*·tsya *shfyetl*·na

shop
sklep m
sklep

pedestrian crossing
przejście dla pieszych n
psheysh·chye dla *pye*·shikh

bus
autobus m
ow·to·boos

intersection
skrzyżowanie n
skshi·zho·*va*·nye

corner
róg m
roog

taxi
taksówka f
tak·*soof*·ka

PRACTICAL

62

Turn ...	*Proszę*	pro·she
	skręcić ...	skren·cheech ...
at the corner	*na rogu*	na ro·goo
at the traffic lights	*na światłach*	na shfyat·wakh
left	*w lewo*	v le·vo
right	*w prawo*	v pra·vo
What ... is this?	*Jak się nazywa ...?*	yak shye na·zi·va ...
square	*ten plac*	ten plats
street	*ta ulica*	ta oo·lee·tsa
village	*ta miejscowość*	ta myeys·tso·voshch
north	*północ*	poow·nots
south	*południe*	po·wood·nye
east	*wschód*	fskhoot
west	*zachód*	za·khoot

writing home

When addressing a letter in Polish you use the titles *Pan* pan (Mr) or *Pani* pa·nee (Mrs) before the first name and then the surname, or simply the abbreviation *Sz. P.* This stands for either *Szanowny Pan* sha·nov·ni pan or *Szanowna Pani* sha·nov·na pa·nee – the *Szanowny/a* element means 'respected'.

If you're writing to more than one person, you just put *Sz. P* before the surname. This is an abbreviation of *Szanowni Państwo* sha·nov·ni pan'·stfo, *państwo* being the plural form of *pan* and the correct way of addressing a couple or family.

For the address itself, you follow the order below. The box on page 61 will give you the correct abbreviations to use.

Pan Stanisław Załęski	**Mr Stanisław Załęski**
ul. Tokarska 57 m. 1	**St. Tokarska 57 Apartment 1**
32–100 Kraków	**32–100 Kraków**

directions

The symbol for male toilets is an inverted triangle and for female toilets a circle.

Wstęp	fstemp	**Entrance**
Wyjście	viysh·chye	**Exit**
Otwarte	ot·var·te	**Open**
Zamknięte	zamk·nyen·te	**Closed**
Zakaz …	za·kas …	**… Prohibited**
Palenie wzbronione	pa·le·nye vzbro·nyo·ne	**No Smoking**
Toalety	to·a·le·ti	**Toilets**
Dla mężczyzn	dla menzh·chizn	**Men**
Dla kobiet	dla ko·byet	**Women**

by …

bicycle	*rowerem*	ro·ve·rem
bus	*autobusem*	ow·to·boo·sem
foot	*pieszo*	pye·sho
minibus	*minibusem*	mee·nee·boo·sem
taxi	*taksówką*	tak·soof·kom
train	*pociągiem*	po·chon·gyem
tram	*tramwajem*	tram·va·yem

finding accommodation

Where's a/an ...?	Gdzie jest ...?	gjye yest ...
agritourist farm	gospodarstwo	gos·po·darst·fo
	agroturystyczne	a·gro·too·ris·tich·ne
bed and breakfast	pensjonat	pen·syo·nat
camping ground	kamping	kam·peeng
guesthouse	pokoje	po·ko·ye
	gościnne	gosh·chee·ne
hotel	hotel	ho·tel
mountain lodge	schronisko	skhro·nees·ko
	górskie	goors·kye
youth hostel	schronisko	skhro·nees·ko
	młodzieżowe	mwo·jye·zho·ve
I want something	Chcę coś	khtse tsosh
near the ...	blisko ...	blees·ko ...
beach	plaży	pla·zhi
city centre	centrum	tsen·troom
train station	dworca	dvor·tsa
	kolejowego	ko·le·yo·ve·go

accommodation

Can you recommend somewhere ...?	*Czy może pan/ pani polecić coś ...?* m/f	chi *mo*·zhe pan/ *pa*·nee po·*le*·cheech tsosh ...
cheap	*taniego*	ta·*nye*·go
clean	*schludnego*	skhlood·*ne*·go
good	*dobrego*	do·*bre*·go
luxurious	*ekskluzywnego*	eks·kloo·ziv·*ne*·go
nearby	*coś w pobliżu*	tsosh f po·*blee*·zhoo
romantic	*romantycznego*	ro·man·tich·*ne*·go

Where can I find a room in a private flat?
Gdzie mogę wynająć pokój?

gjye *mo*·ge vi·*na*·yonch *po*·kooy

What's the address?
Gdzie jest ten adres?

gjye yest ten *ad*·res

For phrases on how to get there, see **directions**, page 61.

booking ahead & checking in

I'd like to book a room, please.
Chcę zarezerwować pokój.

khtse za·re·zer·*vo*·vach *po*·kooy

I have a reservation.
Mam rezerwację.

mam re·zer·*va*·tsye

My name's ...
Nazywam się ...

na·*zi*·vam shye ...

For (three) nights/weeks.
Na (trzy) noce/tygodnie.

na (tshi) *no*·tse/ti·*god*·nye

From (2 July) to (6 July).
Od (drugiego lipca) do (szóstego lipca).

od (droo·*gye*·go *leep*·tsa) do (shoos·*te*·go *leep*·tsa)

Do I need to pay upfront?
Czy muszę płacić z góry?

chi *moo*·she *pwa*·cheech z *goo*·ri

Do you have a ... room?	Czy jest pokój ...?	chi yest *po*·kooy ...
single	jednoosobowy	yed·no·o·so·*bo*·vi
double	z podwójnym łóżkiem	z pod·*vooy*·nim *woozh*·kyem
twin	z dwoma łożkami	z *dvo*·ma wozh·*ka*·mee

How much is it per ...?	Ile kosztuje za ...?	*ee*·le kosh·*too*·ye za ...
person	osobę	o·*so*·be
night	noc	nots
week	tydzień	*ti*·jyen'

Can I see it?	Czy mogę go zobaczyć?	chi *mo*·ge go zo·*ba*·chich
I'll take it.	Wezmę go.	*vez*·me go

Can I pay by ...?	Czy mogę zapłacić ...?	chi *mo*·ge za·*pwa*·cheech ...
credit card	kartą kredytową	*kar*·tom kre·di·*to*·vom
travellers cheque	czekami podróżnymi	che·*ka*·mee po·droozh·*ni*·mee

For other methods of payment, see **money**, page 43, and **banking**, page 91.

local talk		
comfortable	wygodny	vi·*god*·ni
dive	speluna f	spe·*loo*·na
rat-infested	nora f	*no*·ra
top spot	pierwsza klasa f	*pyerf*·sha *kla*·sa

Łazienka	wa·*zhyen*·ka	**Bathroom**
Pralnia	*pral*·nya	**Laundry**
Brak wolnych miejsc	brak *vol*·nih myeysts	**No Vacancy**
Wolne pokoje	*vol*·ne po·ko·ye	**Vacancy**

requests & queries

prośby i pytania

When is breakfast served?
O której jest śniadanie?   o *ktoo*·rey yest shnya·*da*·nye

Where is breakfast served?
Gdzie jest śniadanie?   gjye yest shnya·*da*·nye

Is there hot water all day?
Czy jest ciepła woda   chi yest *chyep*·wa *vo*·da
przez cały dzień?   pshes *tsa*·wi jyen´

Please wake me at (seven).
Proszę obudzić mnie   *pro*·she o·*boo*·jeech mnye
o (siódmej).   o (*shyood*·mey)

Do you have a laundry service?
Czy są tu usługi   chi som too oos·*woo*·gee
pralnicze?   pral·*nee*·che

Can I use the ...?	*Czy mogę*	chi *mo*·ge
	używać ...?	oo·*zhi*·vach ...
kitchen	*kuchnię*	*kookh*·nye
laundry	*pralnię*	*pral*·nye
telephone	*telefon*	te·*le*·fon

Do you have a/an ...?	*Czy jest ...?*	chi yest ...
lift/elevator	*winda*	*veen*·da
message board	*tablica*	ta·*blee*·tsa
	ogłoszeń	o·*gwo*·shen'
safe	*sejf*	seyf
swimming pool	*basen*	*ba*·sen

Do you ... here?	*Czy tu ...?*	chi too ...
arrange tours	*organizujecie*	or·ga·nee·zoo·*ye*·chye
	wycieczki	vi·*chyech*·kee
change money	*wymieniacie*	vi·mye·*nya*·chye
	pieniądze	pye·*nyon*·dze

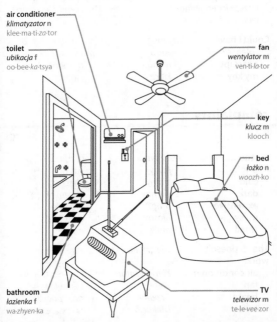

air conditioner
klimatyzator n
klee·ma·ti·*za*·tor

toilet
ubikacja f
oo·bee·*ka*·tsya

fan
wentylator m
ven·ti·*la*·tor

key
klucz m
klooch

bed
łóżko n
woozh·ko

bathroom
łazienka f
wa·*zhyen*·ka

TV
telewizor m
te·le·*vee*·zor

accommodation

69

Is there a message for me?
Czy jest dla mnie   chi yest dla mnye
jakaś wiadomość?   ya·kash vya·*do*·moshch

Can I leave a message for someone?
Czy mogę zostawić   chi *mo*·ge zos·*ta*·veech
wiadomość dla   vya·*do*·moshch dla
kogoś?   *ko*·gosh

I'm locked out of my room.
Nie mogę się dostać   nye *mo*·ge shye *dos*·tach
do mojego pokoju.   do mo·*ye*·go po·*ko*·yoo

Can I get another ...?
Czy mogę prosić o   chi *mo*·ge *pro*·sheech o
jeszcze jeden/jedną/   *yesh*·che *ye*·den/*yed*·nom/
jedno ...? m/f/n   *yed*·no ...

Could I have ...,	*Czy mogę*	chi *mo*·ge
please?	*prosić o ...?*	*pro*·sheech o ...
a receipt	*rachunek*	ra·*khoo*·nek
my key	*klucz*	klooch

complaints

skargi

It's too ...	*Jest zbyt ...*	yest zbit ...
bright	*jasny*	*yas*·ni
cold	*zimny*	*zheem*·ni
dark	*ciemny*	*chyem*·ni
expensive	*drogi*	*dro*·gee
noisy	*głośny*	*gwosh*·ni
small	*mały*	*ma*·wi

The ... doesn't work.	*... nie działa.*	... nye *jya*·wa
air conditioner	*Klimatyzator*	klee·ma·ti·*za*·tor
fan	*Wentylator*	ven·ti·*la*·tor
heater	*Grzejnik*	*gzhey*·neek
toilet	*Ubikacja*	oo·bee·*kats*·ya

This ... isn't clean.
Ten/Ta/To ... nie jest czysty/a/e. m/f/n
ten/ta/to ... nye yest *chis*·ti/ta/te

There's no hot water.
Nie ma ciepłej wody.
nye ma *chyep*·wey *vo*·di

checking out

What time is checkout?
O której godzinie muszę się wymeldować?
o *ktoo*·rey go·*jye*·nye *moo*·she shye vi·mel·*do*·vach

Can you call a taxi for me (for 11 o'clock)?
Proszę zamówić mi taksówkę (na jedenastą).
pro·she za·*moo*·veech mee tak·*soof*·ke (na ye·de·*nas*·tom)

I'm leaving now.
Wyjeżdżam teraz.
vi·*yezh*·jam *te*·ras

Can I leave my bags here?
Czy mogę tu zostawić moje bagaże?
chi *mo*·ge too zo·*sta*·veech *mo*·ye ba·*ga*·zhe

There's a mistake in the bill/check.
Na czeku jest pomyłka.
na *che*·koo yest po·*miw*·ka

Could I have my ... please?	Czy mogę prosić o mój/moje ...? sg/pl	chi *mo*·ge *pro*·sheech o mooy/*mo*·ye ...
deposit	depozyt sg	de·*po*·zit
passport	paszport sg	*pash*·port
valuables	kosztowności pl	kosh·tov·*nosh*·chee

I'll be back ...	Wrócę ...	*vroo*·tse ...
in (three) days	za (trzy) dni	za (tshi) dnee
on (Thursday)	w (czwartek)	v (*chfar*·tek)

I had a great stay, thanks.
Miałem/am przyjemny pobyt. Dziękuję. m/f
myow·em/am pshi·*yem*·ni *po*·bit jyen·*koo*·ye

I'll recommend it to my friends.
Polecę to moim znajomym.
po·*le*·tse to *mo*·yeem zna·*yo*·mim

camping

kamping

How much is it per ...?	Ile kosztuje od ...?	*ee*·le kosh·*too*·ye od ...
caravan	przyczepy kampingowej	pshi·*che*·pi kam·peen·*go*·vey
person	osoby	o·*so*·bi
tent	namiotu	na·*myo*·too
vehicle	samochodu	sa·mo·*kho*·doo

Do you have (a) ...?	Czy jest tu ...?	chi yest too ...
laundry	pralnia	*pral*·nya
site	miejsce pod namiot	*myeys*·tse pod *na*·myot
electricity	elektryczność	e·lek·*trich*·noshch

Do you have ...?	Czy są tu ...?	chi som too ...
shower facilities	prysznice	prish·*nee*·tse
tents for hire	namioty do wynajęcia	na·*myo*·ti do vi·na·*yen*·chya

PRACTICAL

72

Can I ...?	*Czy mogę ...?*	chi *mo*·ge ...
camp here	*się tutaj*	shye *too*·tai
	rozbić	*roz*·beech
park next	*zaparkować*	za·par·*ko*·vach
to my tent	*obok mojego*	o·bok mo·*ye*·go
	namiotu	na·*myo*·too

Who do I ask to stay here?
Kogo muszę zapytać — ko·go *moo*·she za·*pi*·tach
o pozwolenie na nocleg? — o poz·vo·*le*·nye na *nots*·leg

Is it coin-operated?
Czy to jest na monety? — chi to yest na mo·*ne*·ti

Is the water drinkable?
Czy woda jest — chi *vo*·da yest
zdatna do picia? — *zdat*·na do *pee*·chya

Could I borrow ...?
Czy mogę pożyczyć ...? — chi *mo*·ge po·*zhi*·chich ...

renting

wynajmowanie

Do you have	*Czy jest ...*	chi yest ...
a/an ... for rent?	*do wynajęcia?*	do vi·na·*yen*·chya
apartment	*mieszkanie*	myesh·*ka*·nye
cabin	*domek*	*do*·mek
	kampingowy	kam·peen·*go*·vi
house	*dom*	dom
room	*pokój*	*po*·kooy
villa	*dom letniskowy*	dom let·nees·*ko*·vi
(partly) furnished	*(częściowo)*	(chensh·*chyo*·vo)
	umeblowany	oo·me·blo·*va*·ni
unfurnished	*nieumeblowany*	nye·oo·me·blo·*va*·ni

accommodation

73

staying with locals

There's no need to bring gifts when staying with locals but a *butelka wina* boo·*tel*·ka *vee*·na (bottle of wine) or *bombonierka* bom·bo·*nyer*·ka (box of chocolates) would be appreciated.

Can I stay at your place?	*Czy mogę u was zostać?*	chi *mo*·ge oo vas *zos*·tach
I have my own ...	*Ja mam swój ...*	ya mam sfooy ...
mattress	*materac*	ma·*te*·rats
sleeping bag	*śpiwór*	shpee·voor
Can I ...?	*Czy mogę ...?*	chi *mo*·ge ...
bring anything for the meal	*coś przynieść do jedzenia*	tsosh *pshi*·nyeshch do ye·*dze*·nya
clear the table	*posprzątać ze stołu*	pos·*pshon*·tach ze *sto*·woo
do the dishes	*umyć naczynia*	oo·mich na·*chi*·nya
set the table	*nakryć stół*	na·*krich* stoow

Thanks for your hospitality.
Dziękuję za gościnność.
jyen·*koo*·ye za gosh·*cheen*·noshch

---

the host with the most

Poles are nothing if not hospitable. There's a saying, *Gość w dom – Bóg w dom* gosh v dom boog v dom, which translates as 'a guest in the house is like God in the house'. If you're lucky enough to be invited to someone's house, your hosts will revel in plying you with home-cooked delicacies and *wódka vood*·ka (no prizes for guessing what that is). To signal that it's time to tuck in, your hosts will probably exclaim *Smacznego!* smach·*ne*·go (Enjoy your meal!).

You'll definitely win a few hearts if you declare your appreciation of the meal in the following terms:

To było bardzo dobre!
to *bi*·wo *bar*·dzo *do*·bre   That was really tasty!

looking for ...

Are shops open on (the Corpus Christi holiday)?

Czy sklepy są otwarte	chi *skle*·pi som ot·*far*·te
w (Boże Ciało)?	v (*bo*·zhe *chya*·wo)

What hours are shops open?

W jakich godzinach	v *ya*·keekh go·*jee*·nakh
otwarte są sklepy?	ot·*far*·te som *skle*·pi

Where can I buy (a padlock)?

Gdzie mogę kupić	gjye *mo*·ge *koo*·peech
(kłódkę)?	(*kwoot*·ke)

Where's a/the ...?	*Gdzie jest ...?*	gjye yest ...
department store	*dom towarowy*	dom to·va·*ro*·vi
supermarket	*supermarket*	soo·per·*mar*·ket
24-hour shop	*sklep nocny*	sklep *nots*·ni
newsstand	*kiosk*	kyosk

For more items and shopping locations, see the **dictionary**.

---

service please!

Although service in shops has been improving slowly since Poland's accession to the EU, it's not always up to the standards that people from the West expect. You might need to verbally indicate that you require assistance by saying *Proszę Pana/Pani* m/f *pro*·she *pa*·na/*pa*·nee (Excuse me).

If the service happens to be slow and grumpy, don't take it personally. It's a hangover from the Communist past and a reflection of the low wages still paid in the service industry. Your most effective ally in these circumstances is a smile and an attempt at friendliness.

making a purchase

I'm just looking.
Tylko oglądam. — til·ko o·*glon*·dam

I'd like to buy (an adaptor plug).
Chcę kupić (adapter — khtse *koo*·peech (a·*da*·pter
do wtyczki). — do *ftich*·kee)

Can I look at it?
Czy mogę to zobaczyć? — chi *mo*·ge to zo·*ba*·chich

How much is it?
Ile to kosztuje? — ee·le to kosh·*too*·ye

Can you write down the price?
Proszę napisać cenę. — pro·she na·*pee*·sach *tse*·ne

Do you have any others?
Czy są jakieś inne? — chi som *ya*·kyesh ee·ne

The quality isn't good.
To nie jest dobrej — to nye yest *do*·brey
jakości. — ya·*kosh*·chee

Is this (240) volts?
Czy to działa na — chi to *jya*·wa na
(dwieście czterdzieści) — (*dvyesh*·chye chter·*jyesh*·chee)
woltów? — *vol*·toof

Do you accept …?	*Czy mogę zapłacić …?*	chi *mo*·ge za·*pwa*·cheech …
credit cards	*kartą kredytową*	*kar*·tom kre·di·*to*·vom
debit cards	*kartą debetową*	*kar*·tom de·be·*to*·vom
travellers cheques	*czekami podróżnymi*	che·*ka*·mee pod·roozh·*ni*·mee

Could I have a ..., please?	Czy moge prosić o ...?	chi *mo*·ge pro·sheech o ...
bag	torbę	*tor*·be
receipt	rachunek	ra·*khoo*·nek
I'd like ..., please.	Proszę o ...	*pro*·she o ...
a refund	zwrot pieniędzy	zvrot pye·*nyen*·dzi
my change	moją resztę	*mo*·yom *resh*·te

I don't need a bag, thanks.
Dziękuję, nie
potrzebuję torby.
jyen·*koo*·ye nye
po·tshe·*boo*·ye *tor*·bi

Could I have it wrapped?
Proszę zapakować.
pro·she za·pa·*ko*·vach

Does it have a guarantee?
Czy to ma gwarancję?
chi to ma gva·*ran*·tsye

Can I have it sent abroad?
Czy mogę to wysłać
za granicę?
chi *mo*·ge to *vi*·swach
za gra·*nee*·tse

Can you order it for me?
Czy może pan/pani
to dla mnie zamówić? m/f
chi *mo*·zhe pan/*pa*·nee
to dla mnye za·*moo*·veech

Can I pick it up later?
Czy mogę odebrać
to później?
chi *mo*·ge o·*de*·brach
to *poozh*·nyey

It's faulty.
To jest wadliwe.
to yest vad·*lee*·ve

I'd like to return this.
Chciałem/am to
zwrócić. m/f
khchow·em/am to
zvroo·cheech

local talk		
bargain	okazja f	o·*kaz*·ya
rip-off	zdzierstwo n	zjyerst·fo
specials	promocja f	pro·*mo*·tsya
sale	wyprzedaż m	vip·*she*·dash

shopping

77

bargaining

That's too expensive.
To jest za drogie.   to yest za *dro*·gye

Can you lower the price?
Czy może pan/pani   chi *mo*·zhe pan/*pa*·nee
obniżyć cenę? m/f   ob·*nee*·zhich *tse*·ne

Do you have something cheaper?
Czy jest coś tańszego?   chi yest tsosh tan'·*she*·go

What's your final price?
Jaka jest pana/pani   *ya*·ka yest *pa*·na/*pa*·nee
ostateczna cena? m/f   os·ta·*tech*·na *tse*·na

I'll give you (10 złotys).
Dam panu/pani   dam *pa*·noo/*pa*·nee
(dziesięć złotych). m/f   (*jye*·shench *zwo*·tikh)

books & reading

Do you have …?	*Czy jest …?*	chi yest …
a book by	*książka*	*kshyonsh*·ka
(Ryszard	*(Ryszarda*	(ri·*shar*·da
Kapuscinski)	*Kapuściń-*	ka·poosh·cheen'·
	skiego)	*skye*·go)
an entertainment	*informator*	een·for·*ma*·tor
guide	*rozrywkowy*	roz·rif·*ko*·vi

mysterious mickiewicz

If you want to immerse yourself in the very essence of Polish culture, there's no better way than delving into the works of the romantic poet and patriot Adam Mickiewicz (1798–1855). Mickiewicz (pronounced meets·*kye*·veech) is to the Poles what Shakespeare is to the British, which is to say he's a cultural icon of the first order. His best-known work is the epic book-length poem *Pan Tadeusz* pan ta·*de*·oosh, written in 1834, which you should be able to find in English translation.

Your Polish acquaintances will be impressed no end should they discover that you're reading Mickiewicz. Much to the chagrin of Poles, the works of Mickiewicz (who's considered the greatest Slavic poet after Pushkin) are little known beyond Polish borders.

Is there an English-language …?	*Czy jest tu …* *angielski/a?* m/f	chi yest too … an·*gyel*·skee/ska
bookshop	*księgarnia* f	kshyen·*gar*·nya
section	*dział* m	jyow
I'd like a …	*Chciałem/am …* m/f	khchow·em/am …
dictionary	*słownik*	*swov*·neek
newspaper (in English)	*gazetę* *(w języku angielskim)*	ga·*ze*·te (v yen·*zi*·koo an·*gyel*·skeem)
notepad	*notatnik*	no·*tat*·neek

Can you recommend a good book?
Czy może mi pan/pani   chi *mo*·zhe mee pan/*pa*·nee
coś polecić?   tsosh po·*le*·cheech

Do you have Lonely Planet guidebooks?
Czy są przewodniki   chi som pshe·vod·*nee*·kee
wydawnictwa Lonely Planet?   vi·dav·*neets*·tfa *lon*·li *pla*·net

Do you have Lonely Planet phrasebooks?
Czy są rozmówki   chi som roz·*moof*·kee
wydawnictwa Lonely Planet?   vi·dav·*neets*·tfa *lon*·li *pla*·net

shopping

79

clothes

My size is ...	Noszę rozmiar ...	no·she roz·myar ...
(40)	(czterdzieści)	(chter·jyesh·chee)
large	L	el·ke
medium	M	em·ke
small	S	es·ke

Can I try it on?
Czy mogę przymierzyć?   chi mo·ge pshi·mye·zhich

It doesn't fit.
Nie pasuje.   nye pa·soo·ye

For different types of clothing see the **dictionary**, and for sizes see **numbers & amounts**, page 33.

hairdressing

I'd like (a) ...	Chciałem/am ... m/f	khchow·em/am ...
colour	zafarbować	za·far·bo·vach
	włosy	vwo·si
foils/streaks	folie/pasemka	fol·ye/pa·sem·ka
haircut	strzyżenie	stshi·zhe·nye
my beard	podciąć	pod·chyonch
trimmed	brodę	bro·de
my hair	umyć/	oo·mich/
washed/dried	wysuszyć włosy	vi·soo·shich vwo·si
shave	golenie	go·le·nye
trim	podciąć	pod·chyonch
	włosy	vwo·si

Don't cut it too short.
 Proszę nie podcinać   pro·she nye pod·*chee*·nach
 za krótko.   za *kroot*·ko

Please use a new blade.
 Proszę użyć nowe ostrza.   pro·she oo·zhich *no*·ve ost·sha

Shave it all off!
 Proszę ogolić „na zero".   pro·she o·go·leech na ze·ro

I (don't) like it!
 (Nie) Podoba mi się!   (nye) po·*do*·ba mee shye

I should never have come here!
 Żałuję że tu   zha·*woo*·ye zhe too
 przyszedłem/przyszłam! m/f   pshi·*shed*·wem/*pshi*·shwam

music & DVDs

I'd like a ...	*Chciałem/am ... m/f*	khchow·em/am ...
blank tape	*czystą taśmę*	chis·tom tash·me
CD	*płytę CD*	pwi·te tse de
DVD	*płytę DVD*	pwi·te dee vee dee
video tape	*taśmę wideo*	tash·me vee·de·o

I'm looking for something by (Henryk Górecki).
 Szukam czegoś   shoo·kam *che*·gosh
 (Henryka Góreckiego).   (hen·*ri*·ka goo·rets·*kye*·go)

What's their best recording?
 Jakie jest ich   *ya*·kye yest eekh
 najlepsze nagranie?   nai·*lep*·she na·*gra*·nye

Can I listen to this?
 Czy mogę tego posłuchać?   chi *mo*·ge *te*·go po·*swoo*·khach

Will this work on any DVD player?
 Czy to będzie grało na   chi to *ben*·jye *gra*·wo na
 każdym odtwarzaczu?   *kazh*·dim odt·fa·*zha*·choo

Is this for a (PAL/NTSC) system?
 Czy to jest na system   chi to yest na *sis*·tem
 (PAL/NTSC)?   (pal/en te es tse)

... camera	aparat ... m	a·pa·rat ...
digital	cyfrowy	tsi·fro·vi
disposable	jednorazowy	yed·no·ra·zo·vi
underwater	wodoszczelny	vo·dosh·chel·ni
video camera	kamera wideo f	ka·me·ra vee·de·o
Can you ...?	Czy może pan/ pani ...? m/f	chi mo·zhe pan/ pa·nee ...
develop this film	wywołać ten film	vi·vo·wach ten film
enlarge this photo	powiększyć to zdjęcie	po·vyenk·shich to zdyen·chye
load my film	założyć film	za·wo·zhich film
print digital photos	zrobić odbitki zdjęcia cyfrowe	zro·beech od·beet·kee zdyen·cha tsif·ro·ve
recharge the battery for my digital camera	naładować baterię do mojego aparatu cyfrowego	na·wa·do·vach ba·te·rye do mo·ye·go a·pa·ra·too tsif·ro·ve·go
transfer photos from my camera to CD	skopiować zdjęcia z mojego aparatu na płytę kompaktową	sko·pyo·vach zdyen·chya z mo·ye·go a·pa·ra·too na pwi·te kom·pak·to·vom
Do you have ... for this camera?	Czy są ... do tego aparatu?	chi som ... do te·go a·pa·ra·too
batteries	baterie	ba·ter·ye
flashbulbs	żarówki	zha·roof·kee
(zoom) lenses	soczewki	so·chef·kee
light meters	światłomierze	shfyat·wo·mye·zhe
memory cards	karty pamięci	kar·ti pa·myen·chee

I need ... film for this camera.	Potrzebuję film ... do tego aparatu.	po·tshe·*boo*·ye film ... do *te*·go a·pa·*ra*·too
APS	APS	a pe es
B&W	panchromatyczny	pan·khro·ma·*tich*·ni
colour	kolorowy	ko·lo·*ro*·vi
slide	do slajdów	do *slai*·doof
(200) ASA	(200) ASA	(*dvyesh*·chye) *a*·sa

I need a cable to connect my camera to a computer.
Potrzebuję kabel do podłączenia aparatu do komputera.
po·tshe·*boo*·ye *ka*·bel do pod·won·*che*·nya a·pa·*ra*·too do kom·poo·*te*·ra

I need a cable to recharge this battery.
Potrzebuję kabel do ładowania tej baterii.
po·tshe·*boo*·ye *ka*·bel do wa·do·*va*·nya tey ba·*ter*·yee

I need a video cassette for this camera.
Potrzebuję taśmę wideo do tej kamery.
po·tshe·*boo*·ye *tash*·me vee·*de*·o do tey ka·*me*·ri

When will it be ready?
Na kiedy będzie gotowe?
na *kye*·di *ben*·jye go·*to*·ve

How much is it?
Ile to kosztuje?
ee·le to kosh·*too*·ye

I need a passport photo taken.
Chciałem/am zrobić zdjęcie paszportowe. m/f
khchow·em/am *zro*·beech *zdyen*·chye pash·por·*to*·ve

I'm not happy with these photos.
Nie jestem zadowolony/a z tych zdjęć. m/f
nye *ye*·stem za·do·vo·*lo*·ni/na z tikh zdyench

I don't want to pay the full price.
Nie chcę płacić pełnej ceny.
nye khtse *pwa*·cheech *pew*·ney *tse*·ni

repairs

Can I have my … repaired here?
Czy mogę tu oddać …   chi mo·ge too ot·dach …
do naprawy?   do na·pra·vi

When will my … be ready?	*Na kiedy będzie gotowy/a …? m/f*	na kye·di ben·jye go·to·vi/va …
backpack	*mój plecak* m	mooy ple·tsak
bag	*moja torba* f	mo·ya tor·ba
(video) camera	*moja kamera (wideo)* f	mo·ya ka·me·ra (vee·de·o)

When will my … be ready?	*Na kiedy będą gotowe …?*	na kye·di ben·dom go·to·ve …
(sun)glasses	*moje okulary (przeciwsłoneczne)*	mo·ye o·koo·la·ri (pshe·cheef·swo·nech·ne)
shoes	*moje buty*	mo·ye boo·ti

---

souvenirs

If it's Polish crafts you're after, seek out the network of shops that sell the artefacts made by local artisans which are known as *Cepelia* tse·pe·lya.

amber jewellery	*biżuteria z bursztynu* f	bee·zhoo·ter·ya z boorsh·ti·noo
Ćmielów porcelain	*porcelana ćmielowska* f	por·tse·la·na chmye·lof·ska
folk art	*sztuka ludowa* f	shtoo·ka loo·do·va
painted glass	*kolorowe szkło* n	ko·lo·ro·ve shkwo
posters	*plakaty* pl	pla·ka·ti
Silesian cut glass	*kryształy śląskie* pl	krish·ta·wi shlons·kye
Toruń gingerbread	*pierniki toruńskie* pl	pyer·nee·kee to·roon´·skye

the internet

internet

Where's the local internet café?
Gdzie jest kawiarnia   gjye yest ka·*vyar*·nya
internetowa?   een·ter·ne·*to*·va

I'd like to ...	*Chciałem/am ...* m/f	khchow·em/am ...
check my	*sprawdzić*	sprav·jeech
email	*mój email*	mooy ee·mayl
burn a CD	*wypalić*	vi·pa·leech
	kompakt	kom·pakt
download my	*pobrać moje*	po·brach mo·ye
photos	*zdjęcia*	zdyen·chya
get internet	*podłączyć się*	pod·won·chich shye
access	*do internetu*	do een·ter·ne·too
use a printer	*użyć*	oo·zhich
	drukarki	droo·kar·kee
use a scanner	*użyć skaner*	oo·zhich ska·ner
Do you have ...?	*Czy ma pan/*	chi ma pan/
	pani ...? m/f	pa·nee ...
Macs	*Mcintosha*	ma·keen·to·sha
PCs	*peceta*	pe·tse·ta
a Zip drive	*napęd Zip*	na·pend zeep
Can I connect	*Czy mogę*	chi mo·ge
my ... to this	*podłączyć ... do*	pod·won·chich ... do
computer?	*tego komputera?*	te·go kom·poo·te·ra
camera	*aparat*	a·pa·rat
media player	*odtwarzacz*	odt·fa·zhach
	multimedialny	mool·tee·me·dyal·ni
portable hard	*zewnętrzny*	zev·nentsh·ni
drive	*dysk twardy*	disk tfar·di
USB drive	*dysk USB*	disk oo es be

How much per ...?	Ile kosztuje za ...?	ee·le kosh·too·ye za ...
hour	godzinę	go·jee·ne
(five) minutes	(pięć) minut	(pyench) mee·noot
page	stronę	stro·ne

How do I log on?	Jak się mam zalogować?	yak shye mam za·lo·go·vach
Bloody internet!	Cholerny internet!	kho·ler·ni een·ter·net
It's crashed.	Zawiesił się.	za·vye·sheew shye
I've finished.	Skończyłem/ am. m/f	skon·chi·wem/ wam

mobile/cell phone

telefon komórkowy

What are the call rates?
Jakie są stawki
za rozmowy?
ya·kye som staf·kee
za roz·mo·vi

(Two złotys) per (30) seconds.
(Dwa złote) za
(trzydzieści) sekund.
(dva zwo·te) za
(tshi·jyesh·chee) se·koond

I'd like a ...	Chciałem/am ... m/f	khchow·em/am ...
charger for my phone	ładowarkę do mojego telefonu	wa·do·var·ke do mo·ye·go te·le·fo·noo
mobile/cell phone for hire	wypożyczyć telefon komórkowy	vi·po·zhi·chich te·le·fon ko·moor·ko·vi
prepaid mobile/ cell phone	telefon komórkowy na konto z przedpłatą	te·le·fon ko·moor·ko·vi na kon·to z pshet·pwa·tom
SIM card for your network	kartę SIM na waszą sieć	kar·te seem na va·shom shyech
(flat) battery	(wyczerpana) bateria f	(vi·cher·pa·na) ba·ter·ya
(send an) SMS	(wysłać) SMS m	(vi·swach) es em es

phone

What's your phone number?

Jaki jest pana/pani	ya·kee yest *pa*·na/*pa*·nee
numer telefonu? m/f pol	noo·mer te·le·*fo*·noo
Jaki jest twój numer	ya·kee yest tfooy *noo*·mer
telefonu? inf	te·le·*fo*·noo

Where's the nearest public phone?

Gdzie jest najbliższy	gjye yest nai·*bleezh*·shi
telefon?	te·*le*·fon

Can I look at a phone book?

Czy mogę zobaczyć	chi *mo*·ge zo·*ba*·chich
książkę telefoniczną?	kshyonzh·ke te·le·fo·*neech*·nom

Can I have some coins/tokens?

Czy mogę prosić o	chi *mo*·ge *pro*·sheech o
kilka monet/żetonów?	*keel*·ka *mo*·net/zhe·*to*·noof

I want to ...	*Chciałem/am ...* m/f	khchow·em/am ...
buy a chip	*kupić*	*koo*·peech
phonecard	*czipową kartę*	chee·*po*·vom *kar*·te
	telefoniczną	te·le·fo·*neech*·nom
call (Singapore)	*zadzwonić do*	zad·*zvo*·neech do
	(Singapuru)	(seen·ga·*poo*·roo)
make a (local)	*zadzwonić (pod*	zad·*zvo*·neech (pod
call	*lokalny numer)*	lo·*kal*·ni *noo*·mer)
reverse the	*zamówić*	za·*moo*·veech
charges	*rozmowę*	roz·*mo*·ve
	na koszt odbiorcy	na kosht od·*byor*·tsi
send an email/	*wysłać email/*	*vi*·swach e·*mayl*/
SMS	*SMS*	es em es
speak for	*rozmawiać przez*	roz·*ma*·vyach pshes
(five) minutes	*(pięć) minut*	(pyench) *mee*·noot

Here are a few useful informal words and phrases for telephone conversations, some of which you might see in SMS messages:

Cze/Cz.	che	Hi.
Dam znać.	dam znach	I'll let you know.
Dozo.	*do*·zo	See you later.
Hej/Witam.	hey/*vee*·tam	Hi.
Hello.	*he*·lo	Hello.
Nara.	*na*·ra	See you later.
Nawzajem.	nav·*za*·yem	Same to you.
Odezwę się.	o·*dez*·ve shye	I'll be in touch.
Oki.	o·kee	OK.
Spoko.	*spo*·ko	No worries.

How much does ... cost?	*Ile kosztuje ...?*	*ee*·le kosh·*too*·ye ...
a (three)-minute call	*rozmowa (trzy) minutowa*	roz·*mo*·va (tshi) mee·noo·*to*·va
each extra minute	*każda dodatkowa minuta*	*kazh*·da do·dat·*ko*·va mee·*noo*·ta

What's the country code for (New Zealand)?
Jaki jest numer kierunkowy do (Nowej Zelandii)?
ya·kee yest *noo*·mer kye·roon·*ko*·vi do (*no*·vey ze·*lan*·dyee)

It's engaged.
Jest zajęty.
yest za·*yen*·ti

The connection's bad.
Jakość połączenia jest zła.
ya·koshch po·won·*che*·nya yest zwa

I've been cut off.
Zostałem/łam rozłączony/na. m/f
zo·*sta*·wem/wam roz·won·*cho*·ni/na

Hello.
Halo.
ha·lo

Can I speak to (Wojtek)?
 Czy mogę rozmawiać   chi *mo*·ge roz·*ma*·vyach
 z (Wojtkiem)?   z (*voyt*·kyem)

It's …
 Tu …   too …

Please tell him/her I called.
 Proszę mu/jej powiedzieć,   *pro*·she moo/yey po·*vye*·jyech
 że dzwoniłem/am. m/f   zhe dzvo·*nee*·wem/wam

Can I leave a message?
 Czy mogę zostawić   chi *mo*·ge zos·*ta*·veech
 wiadomość?   vya·*do*·moshch

My number is …
 Mój numer telefonu jest …   mooy *noo*·mer te·le·*fo*·noo yest …

I don't have a contact number.
 Nie mam numeru   nye mam noo·*me*·roo
 telefonicznego.   te·le·fo·neech·*ne*·go

I'll call back later.
 Zadzwonię później.   zad·*zvo*·nye *poozh*·nyey

---

listen for …

Chwileczkę.	khfee·*lech*·ke	**One moment.**
Kto mówi?	kto *moo*·vee	**Who's calling?**
Nie ma (go/jej).	nye ma (go/yey)	**(He/She) isn't here.**
Pomyłka.	po·*miw*·ka	**Wrong number.**

---

post office

                              poczta

I want to send a …	*Chciałem/am wysłać …* m/f	*khchow*·em/am *vis*·wach …
fax	*faks*	faks
letter	*list*	leest
parcel	*paczkę*	*pach*·ke
postcard	*pocztówkę*	poch·*toof*·ke

I want to buy	Chciałem/am	khchow·em/am
a/an ...	kupić ... m/f	koo·peech ...
(padded)	kopertę	ko·per·te
envelope	(bąbelkową)	(bom·bel·ko·vom)
stamp	znaczek	zna·chek

customs	deklaracja	de·kla·ra·tsya
declaration	celna f	tsel·na
domestic	krajowy	kra·yo·vi
fragile	kruchy	kroo·khi
international	zagraniczny	za·gra·neech·ni
mail	przesyłka f	pshe·siw·ka
postcode	kod pocztowy m	kod poch·to·vi
PO box	skrytka pocztowa f	skrit·ka poch·to·va

Please send it by air/surface mail to (Australia).

Proszę wysłać to pocztą	pro·she vis·wach to poch·tom
lotniczą/lądową do	lot·nee·chom/lon·do·vom do
(Australii).	(aus·tra·lyee)

It contains (souvenirs).

| Zawiera (upominki). | za·vye·ra (oo·po·meen·kee) |

Where's the poste restante section?

| Gdzie jest dział z | gjye yest jyow z |
| poste restante? | pos·te res·tant |

Is there any mail for me?

| Czy jest dla mnie jakaś | chi yest dla mnye ya·kash |
| korespondencja? | ko·res·pon·den·tsya |

snail mail		
by ... mail	pocztą ...	poch·tom ...
express	ekspresową	eks·pre·so·vom
registered	poleconą	po·le·tso·nom
sea	morską	mor·skom
surface	lądową	lon·do·vom
by airmail	pocztą	poch·tom
	lotniczą	lot·nee·chom

Popular places to change money are the *kantor walut* kan·tor va·loot (small foreign exchange offices), as they usually offer a better rate than banks. Unlike a bank, a *kantor* (as they're commonly called) doesn't charge a commission or require any paperwork.

What times/days is the bank open?

W jakich godzinach/ dniach jest bank otwarty?	v ya·keekh go·jee·nakh/ dnyakh yest bank ot·far·ti

Where can I ...?	*Gdzie mogę ...?*	gjye mo·ge ...
I'd like to ...	*Chciałem/am ...* **m/f**	khchow·em/am ...
cash a cheque	*wymienić czek na gotówkę*	vi·mye·neech chek na go·toof·ke
change a travellers cheque	*wymienić czeki podróżne*	vi·mye·neech che·kee po·droozh·ne
change money	*wymienić pieniądze*	vi·mye·neech pye·nyon·dze
get a cash advance	*dostać zaliczkę na moją kartę kredytową*	dos·tach za·leech·ke na mo·yom kar·te kre·di·to·vom
get change for this note	*rozmienić pieniądze*	roz·mye·neech pye·nyon·dze
withdraw money	*wypłacić pieniądze*	vi·pwa·cheech pye·nyon·dze
Where's ...?	*Gdzie jest ...?*	gjye yest ...
an ATM	*bankomat*	ban·ko·mat
a foreign exchange office	*kantor walut*	kan·tor va·loot

The ATM took my card.
Bankomat połknął
moją kartę.

ban·*ko*·mat *powk*·now
mo·yom *kar*·te

I've forgotten my PIN.
Zapomniałem/am
mój numer PIN. m/f

za·pom·*nyow*·em/am
mooy *noo*·mer peen

Can I use my credit card to withdraw money?
Czy mogę użyć
kartę kredytową do
wypłacenia pieniędzy?

chi *mo*·ge oo·zhich
kar·te kre·di·*to*·vom do
vi·pwa·*tse*·nya pye·*nyen*·dzi

Has my money arrived yet?
Czy doszły już moje
pieniądze?

chi *dosh*·wi yoosh *mo*·ye
pye·*nyon*·dze

How long will it take to arrive?
Ile czasu zajmie
przesyłka?

ee·le *cha*·soo *zai*·mye
pshe·*siw*·ka

What's the ...? | *Jaki/a jest ...?* m/f | *ya*·kee/ka yest ...
exchange rate | *kurs wymiany* m | koors vi·*mya*·ni
charge for that | *prowizja* f | pro·*veez*·ya

For other useful phrases, see **money**, page 43.

For other useful phrases, see **money**, page 43.

listen for ...		
dokument *tożsamości* m	do·*koo*·ment tozh·sa·*mosh*·chee	**identification**
paszport m	*pash*·port	**passport**

Jest pewien problem.
yest *pe*·vyen *prob*·lem — **There's a problem.**

Nie ma pan/pani pieniędzy na koncie. m/f
nye ma pan/*pa*·nee
pye·*nyen*·dzi na *kon*·chye — **You have no funds left.**

Nie możemy tego zrobić.
nye *mo*·zhe·mi *te*·go *zro*·beech — **We can't do that.**

Proszę tu podpisać.
pro·she too pod·*pee*·sach — **Sign here.**

PRACTICAL

92

I'd like a/an …	Chciałem/am … m/f	khchow·em/am …
audio set	zestaw audio	zes·taf ow·dyo
catalogue	broszurę	bro·shoo·re
guidebook	przewodnik	pshe·vod·neek
(in English)	(po angielsku)	(po an·gyel·skoo)
(local) map	mapę (okolic)	ma·pe (o·ko·leets)

Do you have information on … sights?	Czy jest informcja o miejscach o szczególnych walorach …?	chi yest een·for·ma·tsya o myeys·tsakh o shche·gool·nikh va·lo·rakh …
cultural	kulturowych	kool·too·ro·vikh
historical	historycznych	khees·to·rich·nikh
religious	religijnych	re·lee·geey·nikh

I'd like to see …
Chciałem/am obejrzeć … m/f   khchow·em/am o·bey·zhech …

What's that?
Co to jest?   tso to yest

Who built/made it?
Kto to zbudował/zrobił?   kto to zboo·do·vow/zro·beew

How old is it?
Ile to ma lat?   ee·le to ma lat

Could you take a photo of me?
Czy może pan/pani zrobić mi zdjęcie? m/f   chi mo·zhe pan/pa·nee zro·beech mee zdyen·che

Could you take a photo of us?
  Czy może pan/pani zrobić   chi *mo*·zhe pan/*pa*·ni
  nam zdjęcie. m/f   zro·beech nam *zdyen*·chye

Can I take a photo (of you)?
  Czy mogę (panu/pani)   chi *mo*·ge (*pa*·noo/*pa*·nee)
  zrobić zdjęcie? m/f   zro·beech *zdyen*·chye

I'll send you the photo.
  Przyślę panu/pani   pshi·shle pa·noo/*pa*·nee
  zdjęcie. m/f   *zdyen*·chye

---

skansen hopping

High on any sightseeing agenda in Poland is a visit to a *skansen* skan·sen. *Skansen* is a word of Scandinavian origin referring to an open-air ethnographic museum. Aimed at preserving traditional folk culture and architecture, a *skansen* gathers together a selection of typical, mostly wooden rural buildings, collected from a region and reassembled to look like a village. The buildings are furnished and decorated in their traditional style. Visiting one is a little like a time-capsule travel experience, giving visitors insights into the life, work and customs of bygone days.

The term *skansen* is a collective term and museums of this kind may be given one of the following three specific designations as well: *muzeum budownictwa ludowego* moo·ze·oom boo·dov·neets·tva loo·do·ve·go (museum of folk architecture), *muzeum wsi* moo·ze·oom fshee (museum of the village) or *park etnograficzny* park et·no·gra·*feech*·ni (ethnographic park).

---

getting in

What time does it open?
  O której godzinie jest   o *ktoo*·rey go·*jee*·nye yest
  otwarte?   ot·*far*·te

What time does it close?
  O której godzinie jest   o *ktoo*·rey go·*jee*·nye yest
  zamknięte?   zam·*knyen*·te

What's the admission charge?
Ile kosztuje wstęp?   ee·le kosh·*too*·ye fstemp

Is there a discount for …?	*Czy jest zniżka dla…?*	chi yest *zneezh*·ka dla …
children	*dzieci*	*jye*·chee
families	*rodzin*	*ro*·jeen
groups	*grup*	groop
older people	*osób starszych*	*o*·soob *star*·shikh
pensioners	*emerytów*	e·me·*ri*·toof
students	*studentów*	stoo·*den*·toof

tours

wycieczki

When's the next …?	*Kiedy jest następna wycieczka …?*	*kye*·di yest nas·*temp*·na vi·*chyech*·ka …
boat trip	*statkiem*	*stat*·kyem
day trip	*jednodniowa*	yed·no·*dnyo*·va
(sightseeing) tour	*krajoznawcza*	kra·yo·*znaf*·cha

Is ... included?	Czy ... wliczone?	chi ... vlee·*cho*·ne
accommodation	noclegi są	nots·*le*·gee som
food	wyżywienie jest	vi·zhi·*vye*·nye yest

Is transport included?
| Czy transport jest | chi *trans*·port yest |
| wliczony ? | vlee·*cho*·ni |

Can you recommend (a tour)?
Czy może pan/pani	chi *mo*·zhe pan/*pa*·nee
polecić (jakąś	po·*le*·cheech (*ya*·komsh
wycieczkę)? m/f	vi·*chyech*·ke)

How long is the tour?
| Jak długo trwa wycieczka? | yak *dwoo*·go trfa vi·*chyech*·ka |

The guide will pay.
| Przewodnik zapłaci. | pshe·*vod*·neek zap·*wa*·chee |

What time should we be back?
| O której godzinie | o *ktoo*·rey go·*jee*·nye |
| powinniśmy wrócić? | po·vee·*neesh*·mi *vroo*·cheech |

I've lost my group.
| Zgubiłem/am | zgoo·*bee*·wem/wam |
| moją grupę. m/f | *mo*·yom *groo*·pe |

---

money talks

The Polish currency is the *złoty* zwo·ti, which is also a masculine adjective meaning 'golden'. *Złoty* is often abbreviated to *zł.* but in official documents and banks the abbreviations *PLZ* or *PLN* are used. The final letter in the latter acronym stands for nowy *no*·vi (new) because the currency was revalued after rampant inflation in the '80s.

One *złoty* is the equivalent of 100 *groszy* gro·shi (abbreviated to *gr.*). The word *grosz*, adopted in the 14th century, is said to have entered Polish via Czech from the Middle High German word *grosse* (thick), which was in turn an adaption of the Latin word *grossus* with the same meaning. There's a Polish proverb encouraging thrift that goes:

Grosz do grosza, a będzie kokosza.
grosh do *gro*·sha a *ben*·jye ko·*ko*·sha
(Save your pennies and you'll buy a hen.)

I'm attending a …	Jestem na …	yes·tem na …
conference	konferencji	kon·fe·ren·tsyee
course	kursie	koor·shye
meeting	spotkaniu	spot·ka·nyoo
trade fair	targach	tar·gakh

I'm with …	Jestem …	yes·tem …
(LOT)	zatrudniony/a	za·trood·nyo·ni/na
	w (Locie) m/f	v (lo·chye)
my colleague	z kolegą/	z ko·le·gom/
	koleżanką m/f	ko·le·zhan·kom
my colleagues	z kolegami	z ko·le·ga·mee
(two) others	z (dwoma)	z (dvo·ma)
	innymi	ee·ni·mee
	osobami	o·so·ba·mee

I'm alone.
Podróżuję samotnie.   po·droo·zhoo·ye sa·mot·nye

I have an appointment with (Mr Mossakowski).
Mam umówione   mam oo·moo·vyo·ne
spotkanie z (panem   spot·ka·nye z (pa·nem
Mossakowskim).   mo·sa·kof·skeem)

I'm here for (two) days/weeks.
Będę tu przez (dwa)   ben·de too pshes (dva)
dni/tygodnie.   dnee/ti·god·nye

oiling the wheels

A verb in common usage in Polish and that might come in handy in business circles is *kombinować* kom·bee·no·vach. It's a product of a complicated history and is virtually untranslatable into English but means something along the lines of: 'to achieve your aim by a mixture of subterfuge, cunning and knowing people in the right places or being able to charm them into acquiescence'.

Here's my ...	Tu jest mój ...	too yest mooy ...
What's your ...?	Jaki jest pana/ pani ...? m/f	ya·kee yest pa·na/ pa·nee ...
address	adres	a·dres
mobile/cell number	numer telefonu komórkowego	noo·mer te·le·fo·noo ko·moor·ko·ve·go
email address	adres emailowy	a·dres e·mai·lo·vi
fax number	numer faksu	noo·mer fak·soo
pager number	numer pagera	noo·mer pey·je·ra
work number	numer telefonu do pracy	noo·mer te·le·fo·noo do pra·tsi

Where's the ...?	Gdzie jest ...?	gjye yest ...
business centre	centrum handlowe	tsen·troom hand·lo·ve
conference	konferencja	kon·fe·ren·tsya
meeting	spotkanie	spot·ka·nye

I need (a/an) ...	Potrzebuję ...	po·tshe·boo·yem ...
computer	komputer	kom·poo·ter
internet connection	połączenie do internetu	po·won·che·nye do een·ter·ne·too
interpreter	tłumacza	twoo·ma·cha
to send a fax	wysłać faks	vis·wach faks

Can I please have your business card?
Czy mogę prosić o pana/ pani wizytówkę? m/f
chi mo·ge pro·sheech o pa·na/ pa·nee vee·zi·toof·ke

That went very well.
Dobrze poszło.
dob·zhe posh·wo

Thank you for your time.
Dziękuję za poświęcony mi czas.
jyen·koo·ye za posh·vyen·tso·ni mee chas

Shall we go for a drink?
Pójdziemy na drinka?
pooy·jye·mi na dreen·ka

Shall we go for a meal?
Pójdziemy coś zjeść?
pooy·jye·mi tsosh zyeshch

It's on me.
Ja funduję.
ya foon·doo·ye

senior & disabled travellers
osoby starsze i niepełnosprawne

I have a disability.
*Jestem
niepełnosprawny/a.* m/f
yes·tem
nye·pew·no·*sprav*·ni/na

I need assistance.
Potrzebuję pomocy.
po·tshe·*boo*·ye po·*mo*·tsi

Are there disabled toilets?
*Czy są toalety dla osób
niepełnosprawnych?*
chi som to·a·*le*·ti dla o·soob
nye·pew·no·*sprav*·nikh

Is there wheelchair access?
*Czy da się wjechać
wózkiem inwalidzkim?*
chi da shye *vye*·khach
vooz·kyem een·va·*leets*·keem

How wide is the entrance?
Jak szerokie jest wejście?
yak she·*ro*·kye yest *veysh*·chye

I'm deaf.
Jestem głuchy/a. m/f
yes·tem *gwoo*·khi/kha

I have a hearing aid.
Mam aparat słuchowy.
mam a·*pa*·rat swoo·*kho*·vi

My companion's blind.
*Moja osoba
towarzysząca jest
niewidoma.*
mo·ya o·*so*·ba
to·va·zhi·*shon*·tsa yest
nye·vee·*do*·ma

Are guide dogs permitted?
*Czy psy przewodniki
są dozwolone?*
chi psi pshe·vod·*nee*·kee
som doz·vo·*lo*·ne

How many steps are there?
Ile tam jest schodów?
ee·le tam yest *skho*·doof

Is there an lift/elevator?
Czy jest winda?
chi yest *veen*·da

Are there rails in the bathroom?
*Czy są poręcze
w łazience?*
chi som po·*ren*·che
v wa·*zhyen*·tse

99

Could you call me a disabled taxi?

Proszę zamówić dla — pro·she za·*moo*·veech dla
mnie taksówkę dla osób — mnye tak·*soof*·ke dla o·soob
niepełnosprawnych. — nye·pew·no·*sprav*·nikh

Could you help me cross the street safely?

Proszę mnie przeprowadzić — pro·she mnye pshe·pro·*va*·jeech
przez ulicę. — pshes oo·*lee*·tse

Is there somewhere I can sit down?

Czy mogę gdzieś usiąść? — chi mo·ge gjyesh oo·shyonshch

older person	*osoba starsza* f	o·*so*·ba *star*·sha
person with	*osoba*	o·*so*·ba
a disability	*niepełnosprawna* f	nye·pew·no·*sprav*·na
ramp	*rampa* f	*ram*·pa
walking frame	*rama do chodzenia* f	*ra*·ma do kho·*dze*·nya
walking stick	*laska* f	*las*·ka
wheelchair	*wózek*	*voo*·zek
	inwalidzki m	een·va·*leets*·kee

it's all about you

When speaking Polish you need to use either polite or informal language (indicated in this book by the abbreviations pol and inf). Informal forms use the *ty* ti form of 'you' in the singular and the *wy* vi form in the plural and the corresponding second-person verb forms. As pronouns are often left out, you might just see these verb forms.

Polite language uses the words *pan* pan and *pani* pa·nee for men and women respectively (lit: 'Mr' and 'Mrs') and *państwo* pan'·stfo in the plural. These all translate as 'you' so you'll get very used to hearing them. You use third-person singular verb forms (the same forms as for 'he' and 'she') with *pan* and *pani* and third-person plural forms with *państwo*. For more information, see the **a–z phrasebuilder**, page 23.

In this book we've chosen the appropriate form for the situations that the phrase is used in. For phrases where either form might be suitable, we've given both forms.

travelling with children

podróżowanie z dziećmi

Is there a …?	Czy jest …?	chi yest …
baby change room	przebieralnia dla dzieci	pshe·bye·ral·nya dla jye·chee
child's portion	porcja dla dziecka	por·tsya dla jye·tska
crèche	przedszkole	pshet·shko·le
discount for children	zniżka dla dziecka	zneezh·ka dla jye·tska
family ticket	bilet rodzinny	bee·let ro·jee·ni
I need a/an …	Potrzebuję …	po·tshe·boo·ye …
baby seat	fotelik dla dziecka	fo·te·leek dla jye·tska
(English-speaking) babysitter	opiekunkę do dziecka (mówiącą po angielsku)	o·pye·koon·ke do jye·tska (moo·vyon·tsom po an·gyel·skoo)
booster seat	podstawkę podwyższającą dla dziecka	pod·staf·ke pod·vizh·sha·yon·tsom dla jye·tska
cot	łóżeczko	woo·zhech·ko
highchair	wysokie krzesełko dla dziecka	vi·so·kye kshe·sew·ko dla jye·tska
plastic bag	torbę plastykową	tor·be plas·ti·ko·vom
potty	nocnik	nots·neek
pram	wózek głęboki	voo·zek gwem·bo·kee
pushchair/stroller	wózek spacerowy	voo·zek spa·tse·ro·vi
sick bag	torbę na wymioty	tor·be na vi·myo·ti

Do you sell …?	Czy sprzedajecie …?	chi spshe·da·ye·chye …
baby wipes	chusteczki pielęgnacyjne	khoos·tech·kee pye·leng·na·tsiy·ne
disposable nappies	pieluszki jednorazowe	pye·loosh·kee yed·no·ra·zo·ve
painkillers for infants	środki przeciw-bólowe dla niemowląt	shrod·kee pshe·cheev·boo·lo·ve dla nye·mov·lont
tissues	chusteczki higieniczne	khoos·tech·kee khee·gye·neech·ne

Where's the nearest …?	Gdzie jest najbliższy/e …? m/n	gjye yest nai·bleezh·shi/she …
park	park m	park
playground	plac zabaw m	plats za·baf
swimming pool	basen m	ba·sen
tap	kran m	kran
theme park	wesołe miasteczko n	ve·so·we myas·tech·ko
toyshop	sklep zabawkowy m	sklep za·baf·ko·vi

Is there a child-minding service?
Czy są usługi pilnowania dzieci?　　chi som oos·woo·gee peel·no·va·nya jye·chee

Are there any good places to take children around here?
Czy są niedaleko jakieś ciekawe miejsca dla dzieci?　　chi som nye·da·le·ko ya·kyesh chye·ka·ve myeys·tsa dla jye·chee

Is there space for a pram?
Czy jest miejsce na wózek?　　chi yest myeys·tse na voo·zek

Are children allowed?
Czy dzieci mogą wchodzić?　　chi jye·chee mo·gom fkho·jeech

Where can I change a nappy/diaper?
Gdzie mogę zmienić pieluchę?　　gjye mo·ge zmye·neech pye·loo·khe

Do you mind if I breast-feed here?
   Czy będzie panu/pani/   chi *ben*·jye pa·noo/*pa*·nee/
   państwu przeszkadzało   panst·foo pshesh·ka·*dza*·wo
   jeśli będę karmiła   yesh·lee ben·de kar·*mee*·wa
   piersią? m/f/pl   pyer·shom

Could I have some paper and pencils, please?
   Czy mogę prosić o   chi *mo*·ge *pro*·sheech o
   papier i kredki?   pa·pyer ee *kred*·kee

Is this suitable for (six)-year-old children?
   Czy jest to odpowiednie   chi yest to od·pov·*yed*·nye
   dla dziecka które ma   dla *jye*·tska *ktoo*·re ma
   (sześć) lat?   (sheshch) lat

Do you know a dentist/doctor who is good with children?
   Czy pan/pani zna dobrego   chi pan/*pa*·nee zna do·*bre*·go
   dentystę/lekarza   den·*tis*·te/le·*ka*·zha
   dla dzieci? m/f   dla *jye*·chee

If your child is sick, see **health**, page 193.

talking with children

                              rozmawianie z dziećmi

What's your name?
   Jak masz na imię?   yak mash na *ee*·mye

How old are you?
   Ile masz lat?   *ee*·le mash lat

When's your birthday?
   Kiedy masz urodziny?   *kye*·di mash oo·ro·*jee*·ni

Do you go to school/kindergarten?
   Czy chodzisz do szkoły/   chi *kho*·jeesh do *shko*·wi/
   przedszkola?   pshet·*shko*·la

children

Do you like …?	Czy lubisz …?	chi *loo*·beesh …
school	szkołę	*shko*·we
sport	sport	sport
your teacher	swojego	svo·*ye*·go
	nauczyciela	na·oo·chi·*chye*·la

talking about children

When's the baby due?
Kiedy urodzi się dziecko?   *kye*·di oo·*ro*·jee shye *jyet*·sko

What are you going to call the baby?
Jak dziecko będzie   yak *jyet*·sko *ben*·jye
miało na imię?   *myow*·o na *ee*·mye

How many children do you have?
Ile pan/pani ma   *ee*·le pan/*pa*·nee ma
dzieci? m/f   *jye*·chee

What a beautiful child!
Ależ piękne dziecko!   *a*·lesh *pyenk*·ne *jyet*·sko

Is it a boy or a girl?
Czy to jest chłopiec czy   chi to yest *khwo*·pyets chi
dziewczynka?   jev·*chin*·ka

How old is he/she?
Ile ma lat?   *ee*·le ma lat

How many months is he/she?
Ile ma miesięcy?   *ee*·le ma mye·*shyen*·tsi

Does he/she go to school?
Czy on/ona chodzi   chi on/*o*·na *kho*·jee
do szkoły?   do *shko*·wi

What's his/her name?
Jak ma na imię?   yak ma na *ee*·mye

He/She …	On/Ona …	on/*o*·na …
has your eyes	ma pana/pani	ma *pa*·na/*pa*·nee
	oczy m/f	*o*·chi
looks like you	jest podobny/a	yest po·*dob*·ni/na
	do pana/pani m/f	do *pa*·na/*pa*·nee

basics

podstawy

Yes.	*Tak.*	tak
No.	*Nie.*	nye
Please.	*Proszę.*	*pro*·she
Thank you (very much).	*Dziękuję (bardzo).*	jyen·*koo*·ye (*bar*·dzo)
You're welcome.	*Proszę.*	*pro*·she
Excuse me/Sorry.	*Przepraszam.*	pshe·*pra*·sham

greetings & goodbyes

powitania i pożegnania

Be prepared to shake hands often in Poland as it's the usual manner of greeting. Etiquette dictates that a handshake be initiated by a woman (if one is present), the older party or a superior at work. Family members or close friends also kiss each other three times on the cheeks in the French manner on special occasions such as parties, welcomes or farewells.

Hello/Hi.	*Cześć.*	cheshch
Good afternoon/ day/morning.	*Dzień dobry.*	jyen´ *do*·bri
Good evening.	*Dobry wieczór.*	*do*·bri *vye*·choor
How are you?	*Jak pan/pani się miewa?* m/f pol	yak pan/*pa*·nee shye *mye*·va
	Jak się masz? inf	yak shye mash
Fine. And you?	*Dobrze.*	*dob*·zhe
	A pan/pani? m/f pol	a pan/*pa*·nee
	Dobrze. A ty? inf	*dob*·zhe a ti

What's your first name?

Jak pan/pani ma na imię? m/f pol	yak pan/*pa*·nee ma na *ee*·mye
Jak masz na imię? inf	yak mash na *ee*·mye

My first name is …

Mam na imię …	mam na *ee*·mye …

What's your (full) name?

Jak się pan/pani nazywa? m/f pol	yak shye *pa*·na/*pa*·nee na·*zi*·va
Jakie się nazywasz? inf	yak shye na·*zi*·vash

My (full) name is …

Nazywam się …	na·*zi*·vam shye …

I'd like to introduce you to …

Chciałem/am pana/ panią przedstawić … m/f pol	khchow·em/am *pa*·na/ *pa*·nyom pshet·*sta*·veech …
Chciałem/am cię przedstawić … inf	khchow·em/am chye pshet·*sta*·veech …

I'm pleased to meet you.

Miło mi pana/ panią poznać. m/f pol	*mee*·wo mee *pa*·na/ *pa*·nyom *po*·znach
Miło mi ciebie poznać. inf	*mee*·wo mee *chye*·bye *po*·znach

hi there!

It's best not to use the informal *cześć!* cheshch (hi) with people who are older than you as it could be construed as impolite. Use *dzień dobry* jyen´ *do*·bri (lit: good day) as the all-purpose greeting in the morning, daytime and early evening. In the late evening use *dobry wieczór* *do*·bri *vye*·choor (lit: good evening).

This is my ...	*To jest mój/moja/*	to yest mooy/*mo*·ya/
	moje ... m/f/n	*mo*·ye ...
child	*dziecko* n	*jye*·tsko
colleague	*kolega/*	ko·*le*·ga/
	koleżanka m/f	ko·le·*zhan*·ka
friend	*przyjaciel/*	pzhi·*ya*·chyel/
	przyjaciółka m/f	pzhi·*ya*·chyoow·ka
husband	*mąż* m	monzh
partner	*partner/*	*part*·ner/
(intimate)	*partnerka* m/f	part·*ner*·ka
wife	*żona* f	*zho*·na
See you later.	*Do zobaczenia.*	do zo·ba·*che*·nya
Bye.	*Pa.*	pa
Goodbye.	*Do widzenia.*	do vee·*dze*·nya
Good night.	*Dobranoc.*	do·*bra*·nots

knights ahoy!

Sisters, don't panic if an older man kisses you on the hand. This rather antiquated custom, known as *całowanie w rękę* tsa·wo·*va*·nye v *ren*·ke, was once the usual cross-gender greeting and is still practised by chivalrous members of the older generation.

addressing people

zwracanie się do ludzi

Polish society tends to be quite conservative and formal. One manifestation of this is the rules for addressing people. Never address a person who's older than you or senior to you by their first name unless you're invited to. An invitation to do so is called *bruderszaft* broo·der·shaft and is often quite a formal occasion officially completed with a toast of vodka. If you're the older party it's OK to use a person's first name, as it is with your peers. In all other cases, address people by their professional title, a selection of which are given on the next page.

chairperson	*Panie Prezesie/*	*pa*·nye pre·*ze*·shye/
	Pani Prezes m/f	*pa*·nee *pre*·zes
director	*Panie Dyrektorze/*	*pa*·nye di·rek·*to*·zhe/
	Pani Dyrektor m/f	*pa*·nee di·*rek*·tor
doctor/dentist	*Panie Doktorze/*	*pa*·nye dok·*to*·zhe/
	Pani Doktor m/f	*pa*·nee *dok*·tor
engineer	*Panie*	*pa*·nye
	Inżynierze/	een·zhi·*nye*·zhe/
	Pani Inżynier m/f	*pa*·nee een·*zhi*·nyer
professor/high-	*Panie Profesorze/*	*pa*·nye pro·fe·*so*·zhe/
school teacher	*Pani Profesor* m/f	*pa*·nee pro·*fe*·sor

In everyday situations such as in the street or in shops, address people by using the forms below. While they translate literally as 'Mr', 'Mrs' etc, they're used just as you'd use 'you' in English.

Mr/Sir	*Pan*	pan
Ms/Mrs/Madam	*Pani*	*pa*·nee
Miss	*Panna*	*pa*·na

making conversation

You can converse freely on most topics with Poles but tread lightly when it comes to the holy-of-holies – the Catholic Church.

What's new?
Co tam nowego?   tso tam no·*ve*·go

What a beautiful day!
Co za piękny dzień!   tso za *pyenk*·ni jyen'

Nice/Awful weather, isn't it?
Piękna/Okropna   *pyenk*·na/o·*kro*·pna
pogoda, prawda?   po·*go*·da *prav*·da

Do you live here?
Czy pan/pani tu   chi pan/*pa*·nee too
mieszka? m/f pol   *myesh*·ka
Czy tu mieszkasz? inf   chi too *myesh*·kash

Where are you going?

Dokąd pan/pani idzie? m/f pol	*do*·kond pan/*pa*·nee *ee*·jye
Dokąd idziesz? inf	*do*·kond *ee*·jyesh

What are you doing?

Co pan/pani robi? m/f pol	tso pan/*pa*·nee *ro*·bee
Co robisz? inf	tso *ro*·beesh

Do you like it here?

Czy się panu/pani tu podoba? m/f pol	chi shye *pa*·noo/*pa*·nee too po·*do*·ba
Czy ci się tu podoba? inf	chi chee shye too po·*do*·ba

I love it here.

Bardzo mi się tu podoba.	*bar*·dzo mee shye too po·*do*·ba

What's this called?

Jak się to nazywa?	yak shye to na·*zi*·va

That's (beautiful), isn't it?

To jest (piękne), prawda?	to yest (*pyenk*·ne) *prav*·da

How long are you here for?

Jak długo pan/pani tutaj będzie? m/f pol	yak *dwoo*·go pan/*pa*·nee *too*·tai *ben*·jye
Jak długo tutaj będziesz? inf	yak *dwoo*·go *too*·tai *ben*·jyesh

I'm here for (four) weeks/days.

Będę tutaj przez (cztery) tygodnie/dni.	*ben*·de *too*·tai pshes (*chte*·ri) ti·*go*·dnye/dnee

I'm here ...	*Jestem tutaj ...*	*yes*·tem *too*·tai ...
for a holiday	*na wakacjach*	na va·*kats*·yakh
on business	*służbowo*	swoozh·*bo*·vo
to study	*na studiach*	na *stood*·yakh

Hey!	*Cześć!*	cheshch
Great!	*Świetnie!*	shvyet·nye
Just a minute.	*Chwileczkę.*	khfee·lech·ke
Just joking.	*Żartuję.*	zhar·too·ye
It's OK.	*W porządku.*	v po·zhont·koo
Maybe.	*Może.*	mo·zhe
No problem.	*Nie ma sprawy.*	nye ma spra·vi
No way!	*W żadnym*	v zhad·nim
	bądź razie.	bonj ra·zhye
Sure.	*Pewnie.*	pev·nye

nationalities

narodowości

Where are you from?

Skąd pan/pani jest? m/f pol	skont pan/*pa*·nee yest
Skąd jesteś? inf	skont *yes*·tesh

I'm from …	*Jestem z …*	*yes*·tem z …
Australia	*Australii*	ow·*stra*·lyee
Canada	*Kanady*	ka·*na*·di
Singapore	*Singapuru*	seen·ga·*poo*·roo

For more nationalities, see the **dictionary**.

age

wiek

How old is …?	*Ile lat ma …?*	*ee*·le lat ma …
your son	*pana/i*	*pa*·na/nee
	syn m/f pol	sin
	twój syn inf	tfooy sin
your daughter	*pana/i córka* pol	*pa*·na/nee *tsoor*·ka
	twoja córka inf	*tfo*·ya *tsoor*·ka

How old are you?

Ile pan/pani ma lat? m/f pol		*ee*·le pan/*pa*·nee ma lat
Ile masz lat?		*ee*·le mash lat

I'm … years old.

Mam … lat.		mam … lat

He/She is … years old.

On/Ona ma … lat.		on/*o*·na ma … lat

I'm younger than I look.

Jestem młodszy/a		*yes*·tem *mwod*·shi/sha
niż wyglądam. m/f		neesh vi·*glon*·dam

For your age, see **numbers & amounts**, page 33.

occupations & studies

zawody i studia

What's your occupation?

Jaki jest pana/pani		*ya*·kee yest *pa*·na/*pa*·nee
zawód? m/f pol		*za*·vood
Jaki jest twój zawód? inf		*ya*·kee yest tfooy *za*·vood

I'm a/an …	*Jestem …*	*yes*·tem …
architect	*architektem* m&f	ar·khee·*tek*·tem
chef	*kucharzem/*	koo·*kha*·zhem/
	kucharką m/f	koo·*khar*·kom
dentist	*dentystą/*	den·*tis*·tom/
	dentystką m/f	den·*tist*·kom
doctor	*lekarzem* m&f	le·*ka*·zhem
engineer	*inżynierem* m&f	een·zhi·*nye*·rem
farmer	*rolnikiem* m&f	rol·*nee*·kyem
journalist	*dziennikarzem/*	jyen·nee·*ka*·zhem/
	dziennikarką m/f	jyen·nee·*kar*·kom
lawyer	*prawnikiem* m&f	prav·*nee*·kyem
miner	*górnikiem* m&f	goor·*nee*·kyem
nurse	*pielęgniarzem/*	pye·leng·*nya*·zhem/
	pielęgniarką m/f	pye·leng·*nyar*·kom
teacher	*nauczycielem/*	na·oo·chi·*chye*·lem/
	nauczycielką m/f	na·oo·chi·*chyel*·kom

meeting people

I work in …	*Pracuję w …*	pra·*tsoo*·ye v …
administration	*admini-stracji*	ad·mee·nee·*stra*·tsyee
health	*służbie zdrowia*	*swoozh*·bye *zdro*·vya
sales & marketing	*marketingu*	mar·ke·*teen*·goo

I'm …	*Jestem …*	*yes*·tem …
retired	*emerytem/ emerytką* m/f	e·me·*ri*·tem/ e·me·*rit*·kom
self-employed	*samozatrud-niony/ą* m/f	sa·mo·za·*trood*·nyo·ni/nom
unemployed	*bezrobotny/ą* m/f	bez·ro·*bot*·ni/nom

I'm studying …	*Studiuję …*	stood·*yoo*·ye …
humanities	*humanistykę*	khoo·ma·nees·*ti*·ke
Polish	*polonistykę*	po·lo·nees·*ti*·ke
science	*nauki ścisłe*	na·*oo*·kee *shchee*·swe

What are you studying?

Co pan/pani studiuje? m/f pol	tso pan/*pa*·nee stoo·*dyoo*·ye
Co studiujesz? inf	tso stoo·*dyoo*·yesh

SOCIAL

112

family

Do you have a ...?	Czy pan/pani ma ...? m/f pol	chi pan/pa·nee ma ...
	Czy masz ...? inf	chi mash ...
I have a ...	Mam ...	mam ...
brother	brata	bra·ta
daughter	córkę	tsoor·ke
family	rodzinę	ro·jee·ne
father	ojca	oy·tsa
granddaughter	wnuczkę	vnooch·ke
grandfather	dziadka	jyad·ka
grandmother	babcię	bab·chye
grandson	wnuczka	vnooch·ka
husband	męża	men·zha
mother	matkę	mat·ke
partner	partnera/	part·ne·ra/
(intimate)	partnerkę m/f	part·ner·ke
sister	siostrę	shyos·tre
son	syna	si·na
wife	żonę	zho·ne
I don't have a ...	Nie mam ...	nye mam ...
brother	brata	bra·ta
daughter	córki	tsoor·kee
family	rodziny	ro·jee·ni
father	ojca	oy·tsa
granddaughter	wnuczki	vnooch·kee
grandfather	dziadka	jyad·ka
grandmother	babci	bab·chee
grandson	wnuczka	vnooch·ka
husband	męża	men·zha
mother	matki	mat·kee
partner	partnera/	part·ne·ra/
(intimate)	partnerki m/f	part·ner·kee
sister	siostry	shyos·tri
son	syna	si·na
wife	żony	zho·ni

Are you married? (addressed to a man)
Czy jest pan żonaty? pol — chi yest pan zho·*na*·ti
Czy jesteś żonaty? inf — chi *yes*·tesh zho·*na*·ti

Are you married? (addressed to a woman)
Czy jest pani zamężna? pol — chi yest *pa*·nee za·*menzh*·na
Czy jesteś zamężna? inf — chi *yes*·tesh za·*menzh*·na

I live with someone.
Mieszkam z kimś. — *myesh*·kam z keemsh

I'm ...	Jestem ...	*yes*·tem ...
married	*żonaty/*	zho·*na*·ti/
	zamężna m/f	za·*menzh*·na
separated	*w separacji*	f se·pa·*ra*·tsyee
single	*nieżonaty/*	nye·zho·*na*·ti/
	niezamężna m/f	nye·za·*menzh*·na

farewells

Tomorrow is my last day here.
Jutro jest tu mój — *yoo*·tro yest too mooy
ostatni dzień. — os·*ta*·tnee jyen´

Keep in touch!
Bądźmy w kontakcie! — *bonj*·mi v kon·*tak*·chye

It's been great meeting you.
Miło było pana/ — *mee*·wo *bi*·wo *pa*·na/
pania poznać. m/f pol — *pa*·nyom *poz*·nach
Miło było cię poznać. inf — *mee*·wo *bi*·wo chye *poz*·nach

Here's my ...	Tu jest mój ...	too yest mooy ...
What's your ...?	*Jaki jest pan/*	*ya*·kee yest pan/
	pani ...? m/f pol	*pa*·nee ...
	Jaki jest	*ya*·kee yest
	twój ...? inf	tfooy ...
address	*adres*	*ad*·res
email address	*adres emailowy*	*ad*·res e·mai·*lo*·vi
phone number	*numer*	*noo*·mer
	telefonu	te·le·*fo*·noo

In this chapter we've given informal verb forms. If you're not sure what this means, see the **a-z phrasebuilder**, page 24.

common interests

wspólne zainteresowania

What do you do in your spare time?

Co robisz w wolnym czasie?		tso *ro*·beesh v *vol*·nim *cha*·shye

Do you like ...?	*Czy lubisz ...?*	chi *loo*·beesh ...
I (don't) like ...	*(Nie) Lubię ...*	(nye) *loo*·bye ...
computer games	*grać na komputerze*	grach na kom·poo·*te*·zhe
cooking	*gotować*	go·*to*·vach
dancing	*tańczyć*	*tan'*·chich
drawing	*rysować*	ri·*so*·vach
gardening	*zajmować się ogródkiem*	zai·*mo*·vach shye o·*grood*·kyem
ice skating	*jeździć na łyżwach*	*yezh*·jeech na *wizh*·vakh
painting	*malować*	ma·*lo*·vach
photography	*fotografować*	fo·to·gra·*fo*·vach
reading	*czytać*	*chi*·tach
surfing the Internet	*żeglować po internecie*	zhe·*glo*·vach po een·ter·*ne*·chye
travelling	*podróżować*	po·droo·*zho*·vach

Do you like …?	*Czy lubisz …?*	chi *loo*·beesh …
I like …	*Lubię …*	*loo*·bye …
films	*oglądać filmy*	o·*glon*·dach *feel*·mi
hiking	*piesze*	*pye*·she
	wycieczki	vi·*chyech*·kee
music	*muzykę*	moo·*zi*·ke
playing cards	*grać w karty*	grach f *kar*·ti
shopping	*chodzić po*	*kho*·jeech po
	sklepach	*skle*·pakh
socialising	*spędzać czas z*	*spend*·zach chas z
	przyjaciółmi	pshi·ya·*chyoow*·mee
sport	*sport*	sport
watching TV	*oglądać*	o·*glon*·dach
	telewizję	te·le·*veez*·ye
I don't like …	*Nie lubię …*	nye *loo*·bye …
films	*oglądać*	o·*glon*·dach
	filmów	*feel*·moof
hiking	*pieszych*	*pye*·shikh
	wycieczek	vi·*chye*·chek
music	*muzyki*	moo·*zi*·kee
playing cards	*grać w karty*	grach f *kar*·ti
shopping	*chodzić po*	*kho*·jeech po
	sklepach	*skle*·pakh
socialising	*spędzać czasu z*	*spend*·zach *cha*·soo z
	przyjaciółmi	pshi·ya·*chyoow*·mee
sport	*sportu*	*spor*·too
watching TV	*oglądać*	o·*glon*·dach
	telewizji	te·le·*veez*·yee

going solo

In our pronunciation guides you'll notice the single consonants f, v, s and z. They might look like mistakes but in fact f and v represent the preposition *w* (meaning 'in') and s and z represent *z* (meaning 'with'), which are words in their own right. Don't get tongue-tied over these single-consonant syllables – as you're pronouncing them try linking them with the word that comes after them.

SOCIAL

music

Do you …?	Czy …?	chi …
dance	tańczysz	tan'·chish
go to concerts	chodzisz na	kho·jeesh na
	koncerty	kon·tser·ti
listen to music	słuchasz	swoo·khash
	muzyki	moo·zi·kee
play an	grasz na	grash na
instrument	jakimś	ya·keemsh
	instrumencie	een·stroo·men·chye
sing	śpiewasz	shpye·vash
What … do	… lubisz?	… loo·beesh
you like?		
bands	Jakie zespoły	ya·kye zes·po·wi
music	Jaką muzykę	ya·kom moo·zi·ke
performers	Jakich	ya·keekh
	wykonawców	vi·ko·naf·tsoof
singers	Jakich	ya·keekh
	piosenkarzy	pyo·sen·ka·zhi
classical music	muzyka	moo·zi·ka
	klasyczna f	kla·sich·na
blues	blues m	bloos
electronic music	muzyka	moo·zi·ka
	elektroniczna f	e·lek·tro·nee·chna
folk music	muzyka ludowa f	moo·zi·ka loo·do·va
jazz	jazz m	jez
pop	muzyka	moo·zi·ka
	popularna f	po·poo·lar·na
rock	rock m	rok
traditional music	muzyka	moo·zi·ka
	tradycyjna f	tra·di·tsiy·na
world music	muzyka świata f	moo·zi·ka shvya·ta

Planning to go to a concert? See **tickets**, page 47, and **going out**, page 127.

cinema & theatre

Did you like the …?	Czy ci się podobał/ podobała …? m/f	chi chee shye … po·do·bow/ po·do·bow·a …
ballet	balet m	ba·let
film	film m	feelm
opera	opera f	o·pe·ra
play	sztuka f	shtoo·ka

I feel like going to (a ballet).
Mam ochotę pójść
na (balet).
mam o·kho·te pooyshch
na (ba·let)

What's showing at the cinema/theatre tonight?
Co grają dzisiaj
wieczorem w kinie/
teatrze?
tso gra·yom jee·shai
vye·cho·rem v kee·nye/
te·a·tshe

Is it in (English)?
Czy to jest po (angielsku)?   chi to yest po (an·gyel·skoo)

Does it have (English) subtitles?
Czy ma (angielskie) napisy?   chi ma (an·gyel·skye) na·pee·si

Do you have tickets for …?
Czy są bilety na …?   chi som bee·le·ti na …

Are there any extra tickets?
Czy są dodatkowe bilety?   chi som do·dat·ko·ve bee·le·ti

I'd like the cheapest tickets.
Chciałem/am najtańsze
miejsca. m/f
khchow·em/am nai·tan'·she
myeys·tsa

I'd like the best tickets.
Chciałem/am
najlepsze miejsca. m/f
khchow·em/am
nai·lep·she myeys·tsa

Is there a matinée show?
Czy jest seans
popołudniowy?
chi yest se·ans
po·po·wood·nyo·vi

Is this seat taken?
Czy to miejsce jest zajęte?   chi to myeys·tse yest za·yen·te

In all the phrases in this book the gender markers **m** and **f** signal who the subject of the sentence is. For instance, when you see the English phrase 'I'd like …' you'll see it translated in Polish as *Chciałbym/Chciałabym* … m/f *khcho-w·bim/khchow·a·bim* … The gender markers indicate that if you're a man you select the first option and if you're a woman you select the second one.

Have you seen (Man of Marble)?
Czy widziałeś/aś — chi vee·*jya*·wesh/wash
(Człowieka z marmuru)? m/f — (chwo·*vye*·ka z mar·*moo*·roo)

Who's in it?
Kto tam występuje? — kto tam vis·tem·*poo*·ye

It stars (Piotr Adamczyk).
Występuje — vis·tem·*poo*·ye
(Piotr Adamczyk). — (pyotr a·*dam*·chik)

I thought it was … *Myślę, że to było …* — *mish*·le zhe to *bi*·wo …
  excellent *wspaniałe* — fspa·*nya*·we
  long *za długie* — za *dwoo*·gye
  OK *niezłe* — *nye*·zwe

interests

119

I like …	Lubię …	loo·bye …
action movies	filmy akcji	feel·mi ak·tsyee
animated films	filmy animowane	feel·mi a·nee·mo·va·ne
comedies	komedie	ko·me·dye
documentaries	filmy dokumentalne	feel·mi do·koo·men·tal·ne
drama	dramaty	dra·ma·ti
(Polish) cinema	(polskie) kino	(pol·skye) kee·no
horror movies	horrory	ho·ro·ri
sci-fi	fantastykę naukową	fan·tas·ti·ke now·ko·vom
short films	filmy krótkometrażowe	feel·mi kroot·ko·me·tra·zho·ve
thrillers	thrillery	tree·le·ri
war movies	filmy wojenne	feel·mi vo·ye·ne

I don't like …	Nie lubię …	nye loo·bye …
action movies	filmów akcji	feel·moof ak·tsyee
animated films	filmów animowanych	feel·moof a·nee·mo·va·nikh
comedies	komedii	ko·me·dyee
documentaries	filmów dokumentalnych	feel·moof do·koo·men·tal·nikh
drama	dramatów	dra·ma·toof
(Polish) cinema	(polskiego) kina	(pol·skye·go) kee·na
horror movies	horrorów	ho·ro·roof
sci-fi	fantastyki naukowej	fan·tas·ti·kee now·ko·vey
short films	filmów krótkometrażowych	feel·moof kroot·ko·me·tra·zho·vikh
thrillers	thrillerów	tree·le·roof
war movies	filmów wojennych	feel·moof vo·ye·nikh

feelings

uczucia

Are you ...?	*Czy jest pan/*	chi yest pan/
	pani ...? m/f pol	*pa*·nee ...
	Czy jesteś ...? inf	chi *yes*·tesh ...
I'm (not) ...	*(Nie) Jestem ...*	(nye) *yes*·tem ...
annoyed	*zły/zła* m/f	zwi/zwa
cold	*zmarznięty/a* m/f	zmar·*znyen*·ti/ta
disappointed	*rozczarowany/a* m/f	roz·cha·ro·*va*·ni/na
embarrassed	*zakłopotany/a* m/f	zak·wo·po·*ta*·ni/na
happy	*szczęśliwy/a* m/f	shchen·*shlee*·vi/va
homesick	*stęskniony/a*	stensk·*nyo*·ni/na
	za domem m/f	za *do*·mem
hungry	*głodny/a* m/f	*gwod*·ni/na
sad	*smutny/a* m/f	*smoot*·ni/na
surprised	*zaskoczony/a* m/f	za·sko·*cho*·ni/na
thirsty	*spragniony/a* m/f	sprag·*nyo*·ni/na
tired	*zmęczony/a* m/f	zmen·*cho*·ni/na
worried	*zmartwiony/a* m/f	zmart·*fyo*·ni/na

I'm (not) hot.	*(Nie) Jest mi*	(nye) yest mee
	gorąco.	go·*ron*·tso
I'm (not)	*(Nie)*	(nye)
in a hurry.	*Śpieszę się.*	*shpye*·she shye
I'm (not) well.	*(Nie) Czuję się*	(nye) *choo*·ye shye
	dobrze.	*dob*·zhe

If you're not feeling well, see **health**, page 193.

not at all	wcale	ftsa·le
I don't care at all.	Wcale mnie to nie obchodzi.	ftsa·le mnye to nye ob·kho·jee
a little	trochę	tro·khe
I'm a little sad.	Trochę mi smutno.	tro·khe mee smoot·no
very	bardzo	bar·dzo
I feel very lucky.	Czuję się bardzo szczęśliwy/a. m/f	choo·ye shye bar·dzo shchen·shlee·vi/va

opinions

opinie

Did you like it?

Czy się to panu/pani podobało? m/f pol — chi shye to pa·noo/pa·nee po·do·bow·o

Czy ci się to podobało? inf — chi chee shye to po·do·bow·o

What do you think of it?

Co pan/pani o tym myśli? m/f pol — tso pan/pa·nee o tim mish·lee

Co o tym myślisz? inf — tso o tim mish·leesh

I thought it was ...	Myślę, że to było ...	mish·le zhe to bi·wo ...
It's ...	To jest ...	to yest ...
awful	okropne	o·krop·ne
beautiful	piękne	pyenk·ne
boring	nudne	nood·ne
great	wspaniałe	fspa·nya·we
interesting	interes- ujące	een·te·re- soo·yon·tse
OK	dobre	dob·re
original	oryginalne	o·ri·gee·nal·ne
strange	dziwne	jeev·ne
too expensive	za drogie	za dro·gye

politics & social issues

The major political preoccupations of Poles these days are
bezrobocie bez·ro·bo·chye (unemployment) and *korupcja*
ko·roo·ptsya (corruption) in government – both problems
symptomatic of the difficult transition the country has made
from communist rule to a market economy. Another hot social
issue in ultra-Catholic Poland is *aborcja* a·bor·tsya (abortion),
which is illegal in most cases.

Who do you vote for?

Na kogo pan/pani	na ko·go pan/pa·nee
głosuje? m/f pol	gwo·soo·ye
Na kogo głosujesz? inf	na ko·go gwo·soo·yesh

I support the … party.

Popieram partię …	po·pye·ram par·tye …

I'm a member of the … party.

	Jestem członkiem partii …	yes·tem chwon·kyem par·tyee …
communist	*komunistycznej*	ko·moo·nees·tich·ney
conservative	*konserwatywnej*	kon·ser·va·tiv·ney
democratic	*demokratycznej*	de·mo·kra·tich·ney
green	*zielonych*	zhye·lo·nikh
liberal	*liberalnej*	lee·be·ral·ney
social	*socjal-*	so·tsyal·
democratic	*demokratycznej*	de·mo·kra·tich·ney
socialist	*socjalistycznej*	so·tsya·lee·sti·chney

---

the eyes have it

Pulling the lower eyelid down with the index finger indicates ironic disbelief in what someone else is saying. You
can also simultaneously say *Czy jedzie mi tu czołg?* chi ye·jye
mee too chowg (Do you see a tank driving here?) – a
colourful equivalent of the English expression 'pull the
other leg'.

123

Gdzie dwóch Polaków, tam trzy opinie.
gje dvookh po·*la*·koov tam tzhi o·*pee*·nye
(Where there are two Poles there are three opinions.)

Mądry Polak po szkodzie.
mon·dri *po*·lak po *shko*·jye
(A Pole is wise after the damage has been done.)

Włażąc między wrony, krakaj jak i one.
vwa·zhach *myen*·dzi *vro*·ni *kra*·kai yak ee *o*·ne
(If you hang out with crows, then squawk like them –
ie when in Rome …)

Did you hear about …?

Czy słyszał pan o …? m pol	chi *swi*·show pan o …
Czy słyszała pani o …? f pol	chi swi·*sha*·wa *pa*·nee o …
Czy słyszałeś/aś o …? m/f inf	chi swi·*sha*·wesh/wash o …

Do you agree with it?

Czy pan/pani zgadza	chi pan/*pa*·nee *zga*·dza
się z tym? m/f pol	shye z tim
Czy zgadzasz się z tym? inf	chi *zga*·dzash shye z tim

I (don't) agree with …

(Nie) Zgadzam się z …	(nye) *zga*·dzam shye z …

How do people feel about …?

Co ludzie myślą o …?	tso *loo*·jye *mish*·lom o …

How can we protest against …?

Jak możemy	yak mo·*zhe*·mi
zaprotestować	za·pro·tes·*to*·vach
przeciwko …?	pshe·*cheef*·ko …

How can we support …?

Jak możemy wspomóc …?	yak mo·*zhe*·mi *fspo*·moots …

abortion	*aborcja* f	a·*bor*·tsya
animal rights	*prawa*	*pra*·va
	zwierząt pl	*zvye*·zhont
corruption	*korupcja* f	ko·*roo*·ptsya
crime	*przestępstwo* n	pshe·*stemp*·stfo
discrimination	*dyskryminacja* f	dis·kri·mee·*na*·tsya
drugs	*narkotyki* pl	nar·ko·*ti*·kee
the economy	*gospodarka* f	gos·po·*dar*·ka
education	*edukacja* f	e·doo·*ka*·tsya
the environment	*środowisko* n	shro·do·*vees*·ko
equal opportunity	*równo-*	roov·no·
	uprawnienie n	oo·prav·*nye*·nye
euthanasia	*eutanazja* f	ew·ta·*na*·zya
globalisation	*globalizacja* f	glo·ba·lee·*za*·tsya
human rights	*prawa*	*pra*·va
	człowieka pl	chwo·*vye*·ka
immigration	*imigracja* f	ee·mee·*gra*·tsya
inequality	*nierówność* f	nye·*roov*·noshch
poverty	*ubóstwo* n	oo·*boos*·tfo
privatisation	*prywatyzacja* f	pri·va·ti·*za*·tsya
racism	*rasizm* m	*ra*·sheezm
religious	*fundamentalizm*	foon·da·men·*ta*·leezm
fundamentalism	*religijny*	re·lee·*geey*·ni
sexism	*seksizm* m	*sek*·sheezm
terrorism	*terroryzm* m	te·ro·*ri*·zm
social welfare	*świadczenia*	shvyad·*che*·nya
	socjalne pl	so·*tsyal*·ne
unemployment	*bezrobocie* n	bez·ro·*bo*·chye
war (in Iraq)	*wojna*	*voy*·na
	(w Iraku) f	(v ee·*ra*·koo)
Is there help	*Czy jest pomoc*	chi yest *po*·mots
for (the) …?	*dla …?*	dla …
aged	*osób starszych*	o·soob *star*·shikh
beggars	*żebrzących*	zheb·*zhon*·tsikh
disabled	*niepełno-*	nye·pew·no·
	sprawnych	*sprav*·nikh
homeless	*bezdomnych*	bez·*dom*·nikh
street kids	*uliczników*	oo·leech·*nee*·koof

feelings & opinions

125

the environment

Is there a ... problem here?
   Czy jest tam problem ...?   chi yest tam *pro*·blem ...

What should be done about ...?
   Co powinno się   tso po·*vi*·no shye
   zrobić aby ...?   *zro*·beech *a*·bi ...

acid rain	*kwaśny deszcz* m	*kvash*·ni deshch
deforestation	*ogołacenie z*	o·go·wa·*tse*·nye z
	lasów n	*la*·soof
drought	*susza* f	*soo*·sha
endangered	*zagrożone*	za·gro·*zho*·ne
species	*gatunki* pl	ga·*toon*·kee
genetically	*żywność*	*zhiv*·noshch
modified food	*zmodyfikowana*	zmo·di·fee·ko·*va*·na
	genetycznie f	ge·ne·*tich*·nye
hunting	*polowanie* n	po·lo·*va*·nye
hydroelectricity	*hydroelektryczność* f	hi·dro·e·lek·*trich*·noshch
irrigation	*nawadnianie* n	na·vad·*nya*·nye
nuclear energy	*energia*	e·*ner*·gya
	jądrowa f	yon·*dro*·va
ozone layer	*warstwa*	*vars*·tfa
	ozonowa f	o·zo·*no*·va
pesticides	*pestycydy* pl	pes·ti·*tsi*·di
pollution	*zanieczyszczenie* n	za·nye·chish·*che*·nye
recycling	*program*	*pro*·gram
programme	*recyklingowy* m	re·tsi·kleen·*go*·vi
toxic waste	*odpady*	od·*pa*·di
	toksyczne pl	tok·*sich*·ne
water supply	*zapasy wody* pl	za·*pa*·si *vo*·di
Is this a	*Czy ten ...*	chi ten ...
protected ...?	*jest chroniony?*	yest khro·*nyo*·ni
forest	*las*	las
park	*park*	park
species	*gatunek*	ga·*too*·nek

In this chapter we've given informal forms. If you're not sure what this means, see the **a-z phrasebuilder**, page 24.

where to go

dokąd iść

What's there to do in the evenings?

Co można tu robić wieczorami?	tso *mozh*·na too ro·beech vye·cho·*ra*·mee

What's on …?	*Co jest ciekawego …?*	tso yest chye·ka·*ve*·go …
locally	*tu na miejscu*	too na *myeys*·tsoo
today	*dzisiaj*	jee·shai
tonight	*dzisiaj wieczorem*	jee·shai vye·*cho*·rem
this weekend	*podczas weekendu*	*pod*·chas wee·*ken*·doo

Where can I find …?	*Gdzie mogę znaleźć …?*	gjye *mo*·ge zna·*lezhch* …
clubs	*kluby nocne*	*kloo*·bi *nots*·ne
gay/lesbian venues	*kluby dla gejów/lesbijek*	*kloo*·bi dla ge·*yoof*/les·*bee*·yek
places to eat	*miejsce gdzie można coś zjeść*	*myeys*·tse gjye *mozh*·na tsosh zyeshch
pubs	*puby*	*pa*·bi

Is there a local … guide?	Czy jest lokalny informator …?	chi yest lo·*kal*·ni een·for·*ma*·tor …
entertainment	rozrywkowy	roz·riv·*ko*·vi
film	filmowy	feel·*mo*·vi
gay/lesbian	dla gejów/ lesbijek	dla ge·yoof/ les·*bee*·yek
music	muzyczny	moo·*zi*·chni

I feel like going to a …	Mam ochotę pójść …	mam o·*kho*·te pooyshch …
ballet	na balet	na *ba*·let
bar	do baru	do *ba*·roo
café	do kawiarnii	do ka·*vyar*·nee
concert	na koncert	na *kon*·tsert
film	na film	na feelm
karaoke bar	do baru karaoke	do *ba*·roo ka·ra·o·ke
nightclub	do klubu nocnego	do *kloo*·boo nots·*ne*·go
party	na imprezę	na eem·*pre*·ze
performance	na przedstawienie	na pshet·sta·*vye*·nye
play	na sztukę	na *shtoo*·ke
pub	do pubu	do *pa*·boo
restaurant	do restauracji	do res·tow·*ra*·tsyee

bottoms up!

Wherever there's a social gathering in Poland it's a fairly safe bet that the *wódka* vood·ka (vodka) will be flowing freely. Before you make an idiot of yourself, remember that the national beverage is *not* sipped but downed in a single gulp, or *do dna* do dna (to the bottom) as the Poles say. A sip of water, juice or coke is the usual chaser and there'll often be some kind of snack on hand to help line your stomach, such as *śledź* shlej (pickled herring) or a plate of *grzyby marynowane* gzhi·bi ma·ri·no·va·ne (marinated wild mushrooms), a much-prized local delicacy.

Remember to say *Na zdrowie!* na zdro·vye (To your health!) or *Sto lat!* sto lat (lit: 100 years) as you down your firewater.

invitations

What are you doing now?
Co teraz robisz? — tso *te*·ras *ro*·beesh

What are you doing tonight?
Co będziesz robić — tso *ben*·jyesh *ro*·beech
wieczorem? — vye·*cho*·rem

What are you doing this weekend?
Co będziesz robić w — tso *ben*·jyesh *ro*·beech v
czasie weekendu? — *cha*·shye wee·*ken*·doo

Would you like	*Czy chciałbyś/*	chi *khchow*·bish/
to go (for a) …?	*chciałabyś*	khchow·*a*·bish
	iść …? m/f	eeshch …
I feel like going	*Mam ochotę*	mam o·*kho*·te
(for a) …	*pójść …*	pooysh …
coffee	*na kawę*	na *ka*·ve
dancing	*potańczyć*	po·*tan'*·chich
drink	*na drinka*	na *dreen*·ka
meal	*coś zjeść*	tsosh zyeshch
out somewhere	*gdzieś*	gjyesh
walk	*na spacer*	na *spa*·tser

My round.
Ja funduję. — ya foon·*doo*·ye

Do you know a good restaurant?
Czy znasz jakąś — chi znash *ya*·komsh
dobrą restaurację? — *do*·brom res·tow·*ra*·tsye

Do you want to come to the concert with me?
Czy chcesz pójść ze — chi khtsesh pooyshch ze
mną na koncert? — mnom na *kon*·tsert

We're having a party.
Organizujemy imprezę. — or·ga·nee·zoo·*ye*·mi eem·*pre*·ze

You should come.
Powinieneś/Powinnaś — po·vee·*nye*·nesh/po·*vee*·nash
przyjść. m/f — pshiyshch

hip-hop polish style

If you're in the mood to go clubbing in Poland chances are that your eardrums will experience a strangely dislocating phenomenon: hip-hop in Polish. The Polish hip-hop scene was born in the early '90s when American exports MC Hammer and Vanilla Ice became popular, inspiring a raft of home-grown Polish rappers. Hip-hop music is now firmly ensconced in the mainstream and is just about the only form of Polish music to permeate beyond Polish borders.

Though the lyrics might be foreign, the themes are not unfamiliar. They express the alienation and anger of the *blokersi* blo·*ker*·shee (young white working-class men) from the *bloki* blo·kee (communist-era high-rise housing estates) who've missed out on the prosperity of post-Communist Poland. If you don't speak any Polish, you won't be able to make much sense of what you hear but you should recognise the popular swearword *kurwa* koor·va ('whore' or 'slut') amid a sprinkling of American slang.

responding to invitations

odpowiadanie na zaproszenia

Sure!
Oczywiście!   o·chi·*veesh*·chye

Yes, I'd love to.
Tak, z przyjemnością.   tak z pzhi·yem·*nosh*·chyom

That's very kind of you.
To miło z twojej strony.   to *mee*·wo z *tfo*·yey *stro*·ni

Where shall we go?
Gdzie pójdziemy?   gjye *pooy*·jye·mi

No, I'm afraid I can't.
  Niestety, nie mogę.   nye·*ste*·ti nye *mo*·ge

Sorry, I can't sing/dance.
  Przepraszam, ale nie   pshe·*pra*·sham *a*·le nye
  śpiewam/tańczę.   shpye·vam/*tan'*·che

What about tomorrow?
  A może jutro?   a *mo*·zhe yoo·tro

arranging to meet

What time will we meet?
  O której godzinie   o *ktoo*·rey go·*jee*·nye
  się spotkamy?   shye spot·*ka*·mi

Where will we meet?
  Gdzie się spotkamy?   gjye shye spot·*ka*·mi

I'll pick you up.
  Przyjadę po ciebie.   pshi·*ya*·de po *chye*·bye

Are you ready?
  Czy jesteś gotowy/a? m/f   chi *yes*·tesh go·*to*·vi/va

I'm ready.
  Jestem gotowy/a. m/f   *yes*·tem go·*to*·vi/va

I'll be coming later.
  Przyjdę później.   *pshiy*·de *poozh*·nyey

Where will you be?
  Gdzie będziesz?   gjye *ben*·jyesh

If I'm not there by (nine), don't wait for me.
  Jeśli nie będzie mnie tu   *yesh*·lee nye *ben*·jye mnye too
  do (dziewiątej) to   do (jye·*vyon*·tey) to
  nie czekaj na mnie.   nye *che*·kai na mnye

Let's meet at …	*Umówmy się …*	oo·*moov*·mi shye …
(eight) o'clock	*o (ósmej)*	o (*oos*·mey)
the (entrance)	*przy (wejściu)*	pshi (*veysh*·chyoo)

OK!
Dobrze.   dob·zhe

I'll see you then.
To do zobaczenia.   to do zo·ba·che·nya

See you later/tomorrow.
Do zobaczenia/jutra.   do zo·ba·che·nya/yoo·tra

I'm looking forward to it.
Czekam na to z   che·kam na to z
niecierpliwością.   nye·chyer·plee·vosh·chyom

Sorry I'm late.
Przepraszam za   pshe·pra·sham za
spóźnienie.   spoozh·nye·nye

Never mind.
Nic nie szkodzi.   neets nye shko·jee

drugs

narkotyki

Do you have a light?
Czy masz zapalniczkę?   chi mash za·pal·neech·ke

Do you want to have a smoke?
Czy chcesz zapalić?   chi khtsesh za·pa·leech

I take … occasionally.
Czasem wezmę …   cha·sem vez·me …

I don't take drugs.
Nie zażywam narkotyków.   nye za·zhi·vam nar·ko·ti·koof

If the police are talking to you about drugs, see **police**, page 190, for useful phrases.

SOCIAL

In this chapter we've given informal verb forms. If you're not sure what this means, see the **a–z phrasebuilder**, page 24.

asking someone out

proszenie kogoś na randkę

Where would you like to go (tonight)?
Gdzie byś chciał/chciała   gjye bish *khchow/khchow*·a
pójść (dzisiaj   pooyshch (*jee*·shai
wieczorem)? m/f   vye·*cho*·rem)

Would you like to do something (tomorrow)?
Czy chciałbyś/chciałabyś   chi *khchow*·bish/khchow·*a*·bish
(jutro) coś zrobić?   (*yoo*·tro) tsosh *zro*·beech

Yes, I'd love to.
Tak, bardzo bym   tak *bar*·dzo bim
chciał/chciała. m/f   khchow/*khchow*·a

Sorry, I can't.
Przepraszam, ale nie mogę.   pshe·*pra*·sham *a*·le nye *mo*·ge

pick-up lines

podrywanie

I'll buy you a drink.
Kupię ci drinka.   koo·pye chee *dreen*·ka

You look like someone I know.
Kogoś mi   ko·gosh mee
przypomianasz.   pshi·po·*mee*·nash

You're a fantastic dancer.
Świetnie tańczysz.   shvyet·nye *tan'*·chish

He's a babe.	On jest słodki.	on yest *swod*·kee
He's hot.	On jest boski.	on yest *bo*·skee
She's a babe.	Ona jest słodka.	*o*·na yest *swod*·ka
She's hot.	Ona jest fajna	*o*·na yest *fai*·na
	foczka.	*foch*·ka
	(lit: she's a cute seal)	

Can I …?	Czy mogę …?	chi *mo*·ge …
dance with	z tobą	z *to*·bom
you	zatańczyć	za·*tan'*·chich
sit here	tu usiąść	too oo·shyonshch
take you home	odprowadzić	od·pro·*va*·jeech
	cię do domu	chye do *do*·moo

rejections

No, thank you.
Nie dziękuję. nye jyen·*koo*·ye

I'd rather not.
Raczej nie. *ra*·chey nye

I'm here with my girlfriend.
Jestem z moją dziewczyną. *yes*·tem z *mo*·yom jyev·*chi*·nom

I'm here with my boyfriend.
Jestem z moim chłopakiem. *yes*·tem z *mo*·yeem khwo·*pa*·kyem

Excuse me, I have to go now.
Przepraszam, ale pshe·pra·sham ale
muszę już iść. *moo*·she yoosh eeshch

getting closer

Offering someone *kwiaty* kfya·ti (flowers) is a common sign of a romantic interest. Your bunch of flowers – preferably *róże* roo·zhe (roses) – should contain an odd number of flowers as an even number is considered bad luck. Colour choice is of the essence too: white for innocence, yellow for jealousy and red for love is the local mantra.

I really like you.
   Bardzo cię lubię.   bar·dzo chye loo·bye

You're great.
   Jesteś cudowny/a. m/f   yes·tesh tsoo·dov·ni/na

Can I kiss you?
   Czy mogę cię pocałować?   chi mo·ge chye po·tsa·wo·vach

Do you want to come inside for a while?
   Czy chcesz wejść na   chi khtsesh veysh na
   chwilę do środka?   khvee·le do shrod·ka

Do you want a massage?
   Czy zrobić ci masaż?   chi zro·beech chee ma·sash

Would you like to stay over?
   Czy chcesz zostać na noc?   chi khtsesh zos·tach na nots

Can I stay over?
   Czy mogę zostać na noc?   chi mo·ge zos·tach na nots

I have a headache.
   Boli mnie głowa.   bo·lee mnye gwo·va

Leave me alone!
   Zostaw mnie w spokoju   zos·tav mnye v spo·ko·yoo

romance

135

If there's one area in which Polish linguistic creativity comes to the fore it's in the coining of diminutives for people's names. A whole raft of endings can be added to a person's first name by friends, family or loved ones to express affection.

The most common endings for male names are -ek ek and -uś oosh. Female names can be embellished with the endings -ka ka, -nia nya, -dzia jya or -sia shya among others. The popular name *Maria* mar·ya can be lovingly transformed into *Marysia* ma·ri·shya, *Maryśka* ma·rish·ka, *Marysieńka* ma·ri·shen ·ka, *Marychna* ma·rikh·na, *Mania* ma·nya, *Mańka* man ·ka or *Maniusia* ma·nyoo·shya, just to name a few!

sex

seks

Kiss me.	*Pocałuj mnie.*	po·*tsa*·wooy mnye
I want you.	*Pragnę ciebie.*	*prag*·ne *chye*·bye
Let's go to bed.	*Chodźmy do łóżka.*	*khoj*·mi do *woozh*·ka
Touch me here.	*Dotknij tu mnie.*	*dot*·kneey too mnye
Do you like this?	*Czy lubisz to?*	chi *loo*·beesh to
I (don't) like that.	*(Nie) Lubię tego.*	(nye) *loo*·bye *te*·go

I think we should stop now.
Myślę, że powinniśmy przestać. — *mish*·le zhe po·vi·*neesh*·mi *pshes*·tach

Do you have a (condom)?
Czy masz (prezerwatywę)? — chi mash (pre·zer·va·*ti*·ve)

Let's use a (condom).
Musimy użyć (prezerwatywę). — moo·*shee*·mi oo·zhich (pre·zer·va·*ti*·ve)

I won't do it without protection.
Nie chcę tego robić bez zabezpieczenia. — nye khtse *te*·go ro·beech bes za·bes·pye·*che*·nya

It's my first time.
To jest mój pierwszy raz.   to yest mooy *pyerf*·shi ras

It helps to have a sense of humour.
Dobre poczucie   *do*·bre po·*choo*·chye
humoru bardzo   khoo·*mo*·roo *bar*·dzo
pomaga.   po·*ma*·ga

Oh my god!   *Ach!*   akh
That's great.   *To jest cudowne.*   to yest tsoo·*dov*·ne

That was ...   *To było ...*   to *bi*·wo ...
 amazing   *niesamowite*   nye·sa·mo·*vee*·te
 romantic   *romantyczne*   ro·man·*tich*·ne
 wild   *szalone*   sha·*lo*·ne

romance

137

love

I think we're good together.
Myślę, że dobrze   *mish·le zhe dob·zhe*
nam razem.   nam ra·zem

I love you.
Kocham cię.   ko·*kham* chye

Will you …?	*Czy …?*	chi …
go out with me	*umówisz*	oo·*moo*·veesh
	się ze mną	shye ze mnom
marry me	*wyjdziesz za*	*viy*·jyesh za
(said by a man)	*mnie*	mnye
marry me	*ożenisz się*	o·*zhe*·neesh shye
(said by a	*ze mną*	ze mnom
woman)		
meet my	*poznasz moich*	*poz*·nash mo·yeekh
parents	*rodziców*	ro·*jee*·tsoof

problems

I don't think it's working out.
Nie wydaje mi się   nye vi·*da*·ye mee shye
żeby to miało sens.   zhe·bi to *myow*·o sens

Are you seeing someone else?
Czy spotykasz się   chi spo·*ti*·kash shye
z kimś innym?   z keemsh *ee*·nim

He/She is just a friend.
To tylko przyjaciel/   to *til*·ko pshi·*ya*·chyel/
przyjaciółka. m/f   pshi·ya·*chyoow*·ka

I never want to see you again.
Nie chcę się już więcej   nye khtse shye yoosh *vyen*·tsey
z tobą spotykać.   z *to*·bom spo·*ti*·kach

We'll work it out.
Zaczniemy od nowa.   zach·*nye*·mi od *no*·va

religion

religia

What's your religion?
Jakiego jesteś wyznania?   ya·*kye*·go *yes*·tesh viz·*na*·nya

I'm not religious.
Nie jestem zbyt   nye *yes*·tem zbit
religijny/a. m/f   re·lee·*geey*·ni/na

I'm ...	*Jestem ...*	*yes*·tem ...
agnostic	*agnostykiem/*	ag·nos·*ti*·kyem/
	agnostyczką m/f	ag·nos·*tich*·kom
Buddhist	*buddystą/*	bood·*dis*·tom/
	buddystką m/f	bood·*dist*·kom
Catholic	*katolikiem/*	ka·to·*lee*·kyem/
	katoliczką m/f	ka·to·*leech*·kom
Christian	*chrześcijaninem/*	khshesh·chee·ya·*nee*·nem/
	chrześcijanką m/f	khshesh·chee·*yan*·kom
Hindu	*hinduistą/*	heen·doo·*ees*·tom/
	hinduistką m/f	heen·doo·*eest*·kom
Jewish	*żydem/*	*zhi*·dem/
	żydówką m/f	zhi·*doof*·kom
Muslim	*muzułmaninem/*	moo·zoow·ma·*nee*·nem/
	muzułmanką m/f	moo·zoow·*man*·kom
Orthodox	*prawosławnym/*	pra·vo·*swav*·nim/
	prawosławną m/f	pra·vo·*swav*·nom
Protestant	*protestantem/*	pro·test·*tan*·tem/
	protestantką m/f	pro·test·*tant*·kom

I (don't) believe in ...	(Nie) Wierzę w ...	(nye) vye·zhe v ...
astrology	astrologię	a·stro·lo·gye
fate	przeznaczenie	pshez·na·che·nye
God	Boga	bo·ga
Can I ... here?	Czy mogę tu gdzieś ...?	chi mo·ge too gjyesh ...
Where can I ...?	Gdzie mogę ...?	gjye mo·ge ...
attend mass	iść na mszę	eeshch na mshe
attend a service	uczestniczyć w nabożeństwie	oo·chest·nee·chich v na·bo·zhen'ts·fye
pray	się pomodlić	shye po·mod·leech
worship	uczestniczyć w nabożeństwie	oo·chest·nee·chich v na·bo·zhenst·fye

cultural differences

I didn't mean to do anything wrong.
*Nie chciałem/am
zrobić nic złego.* m/f
nye khchow·em/am
zro·beech neets zwe·go

I didn't mean to say anything wrong.
*Nie chciałem/am
powiedzieć nic złego.* m/f
nye khchow·em/am
po·vye·jyech neets zwe·go

Is this a local or national custom?
*Czy to jest miejscowy
czy ogólnopolski zwyczaj.*
chi to yest myeys·tso·vi
chi o·gool·no·pol·skee zvi·chai

I don't want to offend you.
Nie chcę cię urazić.
nye khtse chye oo·ra·zheech

I'm not used to this.
*Nie jestem do tego
przyzwyczajony/a.* m/f
nye yes·tem do te·go
pshi·zvi·cha·yo·ni/na

Easter   *Wielkanoc*   vyel·*ka*·nots

Easter Sunday is the most important religious celebration in Poland and the culmination of *Wielki Tydzień* vyel·kee ti·jyen´ (Holy Week). The day's celebrations kick off with a *śniadanie wielkanocne* shnya·*da*·nye vyel·ka·*nots*·ne (Easter breakfast) where food (including hand-painted eggs) that has been blessed on Easter Saturday is shared. Easter Monday, known as *Dyngus* din·goos or *Lany Poniedziałek* la·ni po·nye·*jya*·wek, concludes the celebrations in a wet way as young people observe the tradition of pouring water on passers-by.

Christmas Eve   *Boże Narodzenie*   bo·zhe na·ro·*dze*·nye

Although technically the 24th of December isn't a public holiday, it's one of the most joyous celebrations in Poland. Most people fast for the whole day but when the first star shines in the sky a sumptuous supper begins. After some prayers and exchanging the Christmas greeting *Wesołych Świąt!* ve·*so*·wikh shvyont, an *opłatek* o·*pwa*·tek (a wafer symbolising bread) is eaten. This is followed by the Christmas dinner itself, where no less than 12 different dishes are served, followed by a selection of desserts.

It's around this time that children start looking expectantly towards the *choinka* kho·*een*·ka (Christmas tree) hoping that presents will finally appear under it. This miracle, however, doesn't take place until the family sing some carols together and the children are sent outside to look for *Święty Mikołaj* shvyen·ti mee·*ko*·wai (St Nicholas). With the children safely outdoors the presents magically appear under the tree.

New Year   *Nowy Rok*   no·vi rok

New Year celebrations start on New Year's Eve, which is known as *Sylwester* sil·*ves*·ter. Most people see in the New Year at large alcohol-fuelled parties but in the larger cities there are open-air celebrations in the *rynek główny* ri·nek *gwoov*·ni (main marketplace).

I'd rather not join in.

Wolałbym/Wolałabym się	vo·*low*·bim/vo·low·*a*·bim shye
nie przyłączać. m/f	nye pshi·*won*·chach

I'll try it.

Spróbuję.	sproo·*boo*·ye

I'm sorry, it's | *Przepraszam, ale* | pshe·*pra*·sham *a*·le
against my … | *to jest wbrew* | to yest vbrev
| *mojej …* | *mo*·yey …
  beliefs | *wierze* | *vye*·zhe
  religion | *religii* | re·*lee*·gyee

This is … | *To jest …* | to yest …
  different | *inne* | *ee*·ne
  fun | *fajne* | *fai*·ne
  interesting | *interesujące* | een·te·re·soo·*yon*·tse

---

what's in a name?

If you look at a Polish calendar you'll see that every day of the year has a name attached to it. These are the names of the Catholic saints whose feast days fall on a given day but, more importantly, they also indicate *imieniny* ee·mye·*nee*·ni (name days), the Polish equivalent of a birthday.

Polish babies are traditionally named after a particular saint. A child by the name of Barbara takes her name from *Święta Barbara* shvyen·ta bar·*ba*·ra (Saint Barbara), for instance. Up until the age of 13 or so the child will celebrate her *urodziny* oo·ro·*jee*·ni (birthday) on the day of her actual birth. Beyond this age she'll celebrate her *imieniny* on Saint Barbara's feast day instead, along with all the other Barbaras in Poland.

Name days are celebrated with special gatherings of family and friends. If gifts are given they're usually small and often consist of flowers or chocolates. The traditional name-day greeting is *Wszystkiego najlepszego!* fshist·*kye*·go nai·lep·*she*·go (All the best!), and a congratulatory song called *Sto Lat* sto lat (100 years) is sung wishing the person a long life. More often than not, the well-wishing is washed down with a little vodka.

When's the ...	Kiedy jest ...	kye·di yest ...
open?	otwarty/a/e? m/f/n	ot·far·ti/ta/te
gallery	galeria f	ga·le·rya
museum	muzeum n	moo·ze·oom
skansen	skansen m	skan·sen

What's in the collection?
Co jest w zbiorach? tso yest v zbyo·rakh

It's an exhibition of ...
To jest wystawa ... to yest vi·sta·va ...

What kind of art are you interested in?
Jakim rodzajem sztuki	ya·keem ro·dza·yem shtoo·kee
pan/pani się	pan/pa·nee shye
interesuje? m/f pol	een·te·re·soo·ye
Jakim rodzajem sztuki	ya·keem ro·dza·yem shtoo·kee
się interesujesz? inf	shye een·te·re·soo·yesh

What do you think of ...?
Co pan/pani myśli	tso pan/pa·nee mish·lee
o ...? m/f pol	o ...
Co myślisz o ...? inf	tso mish·leesh o ...

I'm interested in ...
Interesuję się ... een·te·re·soo·ye shye ...

I like the works of ...
Lubię prace ... loo·bye pra·tse ...

It reminds me of ...
To mi przypomina ... to mee pshi·po·mee·na ...

... art	... sztuka f	... shtoo·ka
baroque	barokowa	ba·ro·ko·va
impressionist	impresjonis-tyczna	eem·pre·syo·nees·tich·na
modern	nowoczesna	no·vo·ches·na
Renaissance	Renesansowa	re·ne·san·so·va
surrealist	surrealistyczna	soor·re·a·lees·tich·na

art

143

architecture	architektura f	ar·khee·tek·too·ra
art	sztuka f	shtoo·ka
artwork	dzieło sztuki n	jye·wo shtoo·kee
avant-garde	awangarda f	a·van·gar·da
curator	kustosz m	koos·tosh
design	projekt m	pro·yekt
etching	kwasoryt m	kva·so·rit
exhibit	wystawa f	vis·ta·va
exhibition hall	hala wystawowa f	kha·la vis·ta·vo·va
fabric	tkanina f	tka·nee·na
installation	instalacja f	een·sta·la·tsya
opening	otwarcie n	ot·far·chye
painter	malarz m	ma·lash
painting (artwork)	obraz m	o·bras
painting (technique)	malarstwo n	ma·lars·tfo
period	okres m	o·kres
permanent collection	wystawa stała f	vis·ta·va sta·wa
Polish poster school	polska szkoła plakatu f	pol·ska shko·wa pla·ka·too
Poster Museum	Muzeum Plakatu m	moo·ze·oom pla·ka·too
print	druk m	drook
sculptor	rzeźbiarz m	zhezh·byash
sculpture	rzeźba f	zhezh·ba
statue	pomnik m	pom·neek
studio	pracownia f	pra·tsov·nya
style	styl m	stil

---

superstitious poles

Keep your eyes peeled for *kominarze* ko·mee·na·zhe (chimney sweeps) on the streets. These men, clad in dusty-black overalls and sprouting a number of oddly shaped brushes and containers, look a bit like apparitions from the 19th century. Superstition has it that if you clasp a button anywhere on your clothing as soon as you see one and make a wish it will invariably be fulfilled.

In this chapter we've given informal forms. If you're not sure what this means, see the **a–z phrasebuilder**, page 24.

sporting interests

zainteresowania sportowe

What sport do you play?
Jaki sport uprawiasz?   ya·kee sport oo·*pra*·vyash

What sport do you follow?
Jakim sportem się   ya·keem *spor*·tem shye
interesujesz?   een·te·re·*soo*·yesh

I play/do ...	*Gram ...*	gram ...
I follow ...	*Interesuję się ...*	een·te·re·*soo*·ye shye ...
Alpine skiing	*narciarstwem*	nar·*chyarst*·fem
	zjazdowym	zyaz·*do*·vim
athletics	*lekkoatletyką*	le·ko·at·le·*ti*·kom
basketball	*koszykówką*	ko·shi·*koof*·kom
cycling	*kolarstwem*	ko·*larst*·fem
football (soccer)	*piłką nożną*	*peew*·kom *nozh*·nom
karate	*karate*	ka·*ra*·te
scuba diving	*nurkowaniem*	noor·ko·*va*·nyem
tennis	*tenisem*	te·*nee*·sem
volleyball	*siatkówką*	shyat·*koof*·kom

For more sports, see the **dictionary**.

koszykówka f · ko·shi·*koof*·ka
Basketball: this is a school sport. The women's national team has had some success in European competitions.

narciarstwo zjazdowe n · nar·*chyar*·stfo zyaz·*do*·ve
Alpine skiing: every winter weekend masses of keen skiers head for the mountains for their dose of adrenaline.

piłka nożna f · *peew*·ka *nozh*·na
Football: this is by far the most popular sport in Poland.

siatkówka f · shyat·*koof*·ka
Volleyball: this a very popular sport taught in primary schools as part of physical education.

żużel m · *zhoo*·zhel
Speedway: surprisingly, this is the second most-watched sport in Poland. Four drivers or motorcyclists race it out on an oval track.

I ...

cycle	*Jeżdżę na rowerze.*	yezh·je na ro·*ve*·zhe
run	*Biegam.*	*bye*·gam
walk	*Chodzę.*	*kho*·dze

Do you like (tennis)?
Czy lubisz (tenis)? · chi *loo*·beesh (*te*·nees)

Yes, very much.
Tak. Bardzo. · tak. *bar*·dzo

Not really.
Nie specjalnie. · nye spe·*tsyal*·nye

I like watching it.
Lubię oglądać. · *loo*·bye o·*glon*·dach

Who's your favourite sportsperson?
Kto jest twoim · kto yest *tfoy*·eem
ulubionym sportowcem? · oo·loo·*byo*·nim spor·*tof*·tsem

What's your favourite team?
Jaka jest twoja · *ya*·ka yest *tfo*·ya
ulubiona drużyna? · oo·loo·*byo*·na droo·*zhi*·na

going to a game

Would you like to go to a game?
Czy chcesz iść na mecz? — chi khtsesh eeshch na mech

Who are you supporting?
Komu kibicujesz? — ko·moo kee·bee·tsoo·yesh

Who's …?	*Kto …?*	kto …
playing	*gra*	gra
winning	*wygrywa*	vi·gri·va

That was a … game!	*To był … mecz!*	to biw … mech
bad	*słaby*	swa·bi
boring	*nudny*	noo·dni
great	*wspaniały*	vspa·nya·wi

playing sport

Do you want to play?
Czy chcesz grać? — chi khtsesh grach

Can I join in?
Czy mogę dołączyć? — chi mo·ge do·won·chich

That would be great.
To by było świetnie! — to bi bi·wo shvyet·nye

I can't.
Nie mogę. — nye mo·ge

I have an injury.
Mam kontuzję. — mam kon·too·zye

sport

147

Your/My point.
Punkt dla ciebie/mnie.   poonkt dla *chye*·bye/mnye

Kick/Pass it to me!
Podaj do mnie!   *po*·dai do mnye

You're a good player.
Jesteś dobrym graczem.   *yes*·tesh *do*·brim *gra*·chem

Thanks for the game.
Dziękuję za grę.   jyen·*koo*·ye za gre

Where's a good place to …?	*Gdzie jest dobre miejsce …?*	gjye yest *do*·bre myeys·tse …
fish	*do łowienia ryb*	do wo·*vye*·nya rib
go horse riding	*do jazdy konnej*	do *yaz*·di *kon*·ney
go sailboarding	*na windsurfing*	na weend·*ser*·feeng
run	*do biegania*	do bye·*ga*·nya
ski	*do jazdy na nartach*	do *yaz*·di na *nar*·takh

Where's the nearest …?	*Gdzie jest najbliższy/a?* m/f	gjye yest … nai·*blizh*·shi/sha
gym	*siłownia* f	shee·*wov*·nya
swimming pool	*basen* m	*ba*·sen
tennis court	*kort tenisowy* m	kort te·nee·*so*·vi

Do I have to be a member to attend?
Czy muszę być członkiem by wejść?   chi *moo*·she bich *chwon*·kyem bi veyshch

Is there a women-only session?
Czy jest sesja tylko dla kobiet?   chi yest *ses*·ya *til*·ko dla *ko*·byet

Where are the changing rooms?
Gdzie są szatnie?   gjye som *shat*·nye

What's the score?	*Jaki jest wynik?*	*ya*·kee yest *vi*·neek
draw/even	*remis*	*re*·mees
love (zero)	*zero*	*ze*·ro
match-point	*meczbol*	*mech*·bol
nil	*zero*	*ze*·ro

What's the charge per ...?	*Jaka jest opłata za ...?*	*ya*·ka yest o·*pwa*·ta za ...
day	*dzień*	jyen'
game	*grę*	gre
hour	*godzinę*	go·*jee*·ne
visit	*wizytę*	vee·*zi*·te

Can I hire (a) ...?	*Czy mogę wypożyczyć ...?*	chi *mo*·ge vi·po·*zhi*·chich ...
ball	*piłkę*	*peew*·ke
bicycle	*rower*	*ro*·ver
court	*kort*	kort
racquet	*rakietę*	ra·*kye*·te
kayak	*kajak*	*ka*·yak
yacht	*yacht*	yakht
skis	*narty*	*nar*·ti

skiing

na nartach

How much is a pass?
Ile kosztuje bilet? ee·le kosh·*too*·ye bee·let

Can I take lessons?
Czy mogę zamówić lekcję? chi *mo*·ge za·*moo*·veech *lek*·tsye

I'd like to hire (a) …	Chciałbym/ Chciałabym wypożyczyć … m/f	khchow·bim/ khchow·a·bim vi·po·zhi·chich …
boots	buty	boo·ti
gloves	rękawice	ren·ka·vee·tse
goggles	gogle	go·gle
poles	kijki	keey·kee
skis	narty	nar·ti
ski suit	kombinezon narciarski	kom·bee·ne·zon nar·chyar·skee

Is it possible to go …?	Czy jest możliwe aby pojechać na …?	chi yest mozh·lee·ve a·bi po·ye·khach na …
Alpine skiing	narty	nar·ti
cross-country skiing	biegówki	bye·goof·kee
snowboarding	snowboard	snow·bord
tobogganing	sanki	san·kee

What are the conditions like …?	Jakie są warunki …?	ya·kye som va·roon·kee …
at (Kasprowy)	na (Kasprowym)	na (kas·pro·vim)
on that run	na tej trasie	na tey tra·shye
higher up	tam wyżej	tam vi·zhey

Which are the … slopes?	Który zjazd jest dla …?	ktoo·ri zyazd yest dla …
beginner	początkujących	po·chont·koo·yon·tsikh
intermediate	średniozaawansowanych	shred·nyo·za·a·van·so·va·nikh
advanced	zaawansowanych	za·a·van·so·va·nikh

cable car	*kolejka linowa* f	ko·*ley*·ka lee·*no*·va
chairlift	*wyciąg*	*vi*·chyonk
	krzesełkowy m	kshe·sew·*ko*·vi
instructor	*instruktor* m	een·*strook*·tor
resort	*ośrodek*	osh·*ro*·dek
	narciarski m	nar·*chyar*·skee
ski lift	*wyciąg*	*vi*·chyonk
	narciarski m	nar·*chyar*·skee
sled	*sanki* pl	*san*·kee

soccer/football

piłka nożna

Who plays for (Legia Warszawa)?
  Kto gra w (Legii Warszawa)? kto gra v (le·gyee var·*sha*·va)

He's a great (player).
  On jest świetnym (graczem). on yest shfyet·nim (*gra*·chem)

He played brilliantly in the match against (Italy).
  On grał wspaniale w on grow fspa·*nya*·le v
  meczu z (Włochami). me·choo z (vwo·*kha*·mee)

Which team is at the top of the league?
  Która drużyna jest ktoo·ra droo·*zhi*·na yest
  na szczycie tabeli? na *shchi*·chye ta·*be*·lee

What a great/terrible team!
  Co za wspaniały/ tso za vspa·*nya*·wi/
  beznadziejny zespół! bez·na·*jyey*·ni *zes*·poow

sports talk		
What a …!	*Co za … !*	tso za …
goal	*gol*	gol
hit	*uderzenie*	oo·de·*zhe*·nye
kick	*strzał*	stshow
pass	*podanie*	po·*da*·nye
performance	*występ*	*vis*·temp

ball	piłka f	peew·ka
coach n	trener m	tre·ner
corner (kick) n	róg m	roog
expulsion	usunięcie n	oo·soo·nyen·chye
fan	kibic m	kee·beets
foul n	faul m	faool
free kick	rzut wolny m	zhoot vol·ni
goal (structure)	bramka f	bram·ka
goalkeeper	bramkarz m	bram·kash
manager	menedżer m	me·ne·jer
offside	spalony m	spa·lo·ni
penalty	rzut karny m	zhoot kar·ni
player	zawodnik m	za·vod·neek
red card	czerwona kartka f	cher·vo·na kart·ka
referee	sędzia m	sen·jya
striker	napastnik m	na·past·neek
throw in n	wrzut z autu m	vzhoot z ow·too
yellow card	żółta kartka f	zhoow·ta kart·ka

Off to see a match? Check out **going to a game**, page 147.

---

ups and down

If you're at a match and want to be vocal in the support of a particular team or howl the opposition down, try out these phrases:

Go ...!	... pany!	... pa·ni
Down with ...!	... dziady!	... jya·di
A goal for (Poland)!	(Polska) gola!	(pol·ska) go·la

hiking

wycieczki piesze

Where can I ...?	Gdzie mogę ...?	gjye *mo*·ge ...
buy supplies	kupić	*koo*·peech
	zaopatrzenie	za·o·pa·*tshe*·nye
find someone	znaleźć	*zna*·leshch
who knows	kogoś kto	*ko*·gosh kto
this area	zna okolicę	zna o·ko·*lee*·tse
get a map	dostać mapę	*dos*·tach *ma*·pe
hire hiking gear	wypożyczyć	vi·po·*zhi*·chich
	sprzęt	spshent
	turystyczny	too·ris·*tich*·ni

How ...?	Jak ...?	yak ...
high is the	długie jest	*dwoo*·gye yest
climb	podejście	po·*deysh*·chye
long is the	długi jest	*dwoo*·gee yest
trail	szlak	shlak

Do we need a guide?
Czy potrzebujemy   chi po·tshe·boo·*ye*·mi
przewodnika?   pshe·vod·*nee*·ka

Are there guided treks?
Czy są tam   chi som tam
wyznaczone szlaki?   viz·na·*cho*·ne *shla*·kee

Is it safe?
Czy to jest bezpieczne?   chi to yest bes·*pyech*·ne

Is there a hut/shelter?
Czy jest tam chatka/   chi yest tam *khat*·ka/
schronisko?   skhro·*nees*·ko

When does it get dark?
Kiedy robi się ciemno?   *kye*·di *ro*·bee shye *chyem*·no

Do we need to take ...?	Czy musimy zabrać ...?	chi moo·shee·mi za·brach ...
a sleeping bag	śpiwór	shpee·voor
a mat	materac	ma·te·rats
food	żywność	zhiv·noshch
water	wodę	vo·de

Is the track ...?	Czy droga jest ...?	chi dro·ga yest ...
(well-)marked	(dobrze) oznaczona	(dob·zhe) oz·na·cho·na
open	otwarta	ot·far·ta
scenic	widowiskowa	vee·do·vees·ko·va

Which is the ... route?	Która droga jest ...?	ktoo·ra dro·ga yest ...
easiest	najłatwiejsza	nai·wat·fyey·sha
most interesting	najciekawsza	nai·chye·kaf·sha
shortest	najkrótsza	nai·kroot·sha

Where can I find the ...?	Gdzie jest/są ...? sg/pl	gjye yest/som ...
camping ground	kamping sg	kam·peeng
nearest village	najbliższa wieś sg	nai·bleezh·sha vyesh
showers	prysznice pl	prish·nee·tse
toilets	toalety pl	to·a·le·ti

Where have you come from?

Skąd pan/pani przyszedł/przyszła? m/f pol	skont pan/pa·nee pshi·shedw/pshi·shwa
Skąd przyszedłeś/ przyszłaś? m/f	skont pshi·shed·wesh/ pshi·shwash

How long did it take?

Ile czasu to zajęło?	ee·le cha·soo to za·ye·wo

Does this path go to (Kudowa)?
   Czy ta droga prowadzi   chi ta *dro*·ga pro·*va*·jee
   do (Kudowy)?   do (koo·*do*·vi)

Can I go through here?
   Czy mogę tędy przejść?   chi *mo*·ge *ten*·di psheyshch

Is the water OK to drink?
   Czy woda jest zdatna   chi *vo*·da yest *zdat*·na
   do picia?   do *pee*·chya

I'm lost.
   Zgubiłem/am się. m/f   zgoo·*bee*·wem/wam shye

beach

plaża

Beaches along Poland's Baltic coastline are either *płatne*
pwat·ne (paying) or *dzikie jee*·kye (lit: wild, but meaning 'free
of charge') and you'll see signage to this effect. Another sign
you may see is one that reads *strzeżone* stshe·*zho*·ne (guarded),
indicating that there is a lifeguard. Facilities such as toilets are
usually present at these beaches too.

Where's the ...	*Gdzie jest ...?*	gjye yest ...
beach?		
best	*najlepsza plaża*	nai·*lep*·sha *pla*·zha
nearest	*najbliższa plaża*	nai·*bleezh*·sha *pla*·zha
nudist	*plaża dla*	*pla*·zha dla
	nudystów	noo·*dis*·toof

Is it safe to ...	*Czy tu można*	chi too *mozh*·na
here?	*bezpiecznie ...?*	bes·*pyech*·nye ...
dive	*nurkować*	noor·*ko*·vach
swim	*pływać*	*pwi*·vach

beach & pool signs		
No Diving	*Skakanie*	ska·*ka*·nye
	wzbronione	vzbro·*nyo*·ne
No Swimming	*Zakaz*	*za*·kaz
	kąpieli	kom·*pye*·lee

outdoors

What time is high/low tide?
O której godzinie — o ktoo·rey go·*jee*·nye
jest przypływ/odpływ? — yest *pshi*·pwiv/*od*·pwiv

Do we have to pay?
Czy musimy płacić? — chi moo·*shee*·mi *pwa*·cheech

How much to | *Ile kosztuje* — ee·le kosh·*too*·ye
rent a/an …? | *wypożyczenie …?* — vi·po·zhi·*che*·nye …
   chair | *krzesła* — *kshes*·wa
   umbrella | *parasola* — pa·ra·so·la

weather

pogoda

What's the weather like?
Jaka jest pogoda? — ya·ka yest po·*go*·da

What will the weather be like tomorrow?
Jaka jutro będzie pogoda? — ya·ka yoo·tro ben·jye po·*go*·da

wet sense of humour

Want to sound like a local? Here are a couple of amusing Polish idioms you can trot out in inclement weather:

Leje jak z cebra.
le·ye yak z *tse*·bra
(It's raining cats and dogs – lit: it's pouring from a bucket.)

Przemokłem/am do suchej nitki. m/f
pzhe·*mok*·wem/wam do *soo*·khey *neet*·kee
(I'm soaked to the bone – lit: to be wet right through to your dry threads.)

SOCIAL

156

It's …		
raining	Pada deszcz.	pa·da deshch
snowing	Pada śnieg.	pa·da shnyeg

It's …	Jest …	yest …
cloudy	pochmurnie	pokh·moor·nye
cold	zimno	zheem·no
fine	pogodnie	po·god·nye
freezing	lodowato	lo·do·va·to
hot	gorąco	go·ron·tso
sunny	słonecznie	swo·nech·nye
warm	ciepło	chyep·wo
windy	wietrznie	vyetzh·nye

Where can I buy a/an …?	Gdzie mogę kupić …?	gjye mo·ge koo·peech …
rain jacket	kurtkę przeciw deszczową	koort·ke pshe·cheef desh·cho·vom
umbrella	parasol	pa·ra·sol

flora & fauna

flora i fauna

What … is that?	Co to jest za …?	tso to yest za …
animal	zwierzę	zvye·zhe
flower	kwiat	kfyat
plant	roślina	rosh·lee·na
tree	drzewo	dzhe·vo

Is it …?	Czy to jest …?	chi to yest …
common	pospolite	pos·po·lee·te
dangerous	niebezpieczne	nye·bes·pyech·ne
endangered	pod ochroną	pod okh·ro·nom
poisonous	trujące	troo·yon·tse
protected	chronione	khro·nyo·ne

outdoors

157

What's it used for?
Do czego się to używa?   do *che*·go shye to oo·*zhi*·va

Can you eat the fruit?
Czy ten owoc jest jadalny?   chi ten *o*·vots yest ya·*dal*·ni

For geographical and agricultural terms, and the names of animals and plants, see the **dictionary**.

---

local animals & plants

The Polish word for 'bear', *niedźwiedź* nyej·vyej, is derived from the common Slavic words *medu* (meaning 'honey') and *ed* ('to eat'). Thus *niedźwiedź* originally meant 'honey eater'. This eumphemistic derivation came about because naming the fearful beast was once taboo. Here are some other examples of Polish flora and fauna:

bear	*niedźwiedź* m	nyej·vyej
bison	*żubr* m	zhoobr
oak	*dąb* m	domb
pine	*sosna* f	sos·na
white stork	*bocian* m	bo·chyan
wolf	*wilk* m	veelk

Breakfast might seem a bit heavy by Western standards. It usually includes bread and butter, various types of cheese, ham and eggs, washed down with tea or coffee. Around 11am morning tea is served. This generally consists of various types of sandwiches and fruit. The next and main meal of the day is dinner in the early afternoon which usually features soup, a main course and a dessert. The last meal of the day is supper which is relatively light and is served around 6 to 7pm.

basics

podstawy

breakfast	śniadanie n	shnya·da·nye
morning tea	drugie	droo·gye
	śniadanie n	shnya·da·nye
dinner (late lunch)	obiad m	o·byad
supper	kolacja f	ko·la·tsya
snack	przekąska f	pshe·kons·ka
menu	jadłospis m	ya·dwo·spees
eat	jeść	yeshch
drink v	pić	peech
I'd like ...	Chciałbym/	khchow·bim/
	Chciałabym ... m/f	khchow·a·bim ...
Please.	Proszę.	pro·she
Thank you.	Dziękuję.	jyen·koo·ye
I'm starving!	Umieram z głodu!	oo·mye·ram z gwo·doo

finding a place to eat

Your best option for dining out in Poland is a meal at a *restauracja* res·tow·*rats*·ya (restaurant). These run the gamut from unpretentious eateries to luxury establishments. A *bar mleczny* bar *mlech*·ni (lit: milk bar) is a no-frills self-service cafeteria with a large portion of the menu made up of dairy-derived dishes, as the name suggests. The place to go for coffee, snacks and light meals is a *kawiarna* ka·*vyar*·na (café).

Can you recommend a …?	*Czy może pan/ pani polecić …?* m/f	chi *mo*·zhe pan/ *pa*·nee po·*le*·cheech …
bar	*bar*	bar
café	*kawiarnię*	ka·*vyar*·nye
restaurant	*restaurację*	res·tow·*rats*·ye
self-service cafeteria	*bar mleczny*	bar *mlech*·ni

Where would you go for …?	*Dokąd byś poszedł/ poszła …?* m/f	*do*·kond bish po·shedw/ *po*·shwa …
a celebration	*by coś uczcić*	bi tsosh *ooch*·tseech
a cheap meal	*na tani posiłek*	na *ta*·nee po·*shee*·wek
local specialities	*na miejscowe specjały*	na myeys·*tso*·ve spe·*tsya*·wi

I'd like to reserve a table for …	*Chciałem/am zarezerwować stolik …* m/f	khchow·em/am za·re·zer·*vo*·vach *sto*·leek …
(two) people	*dla (dwóch) osób*	dla (dvookh) o·soob
(eight) o'clock	*na (ósmą)*	na (*oos*·mom)

Are you still serving food?
Czy można jeszcze zamawiać jedzenie? chi *mo*·zhna *yesh*·che za·*ma*·vyach ye·*dze*·nye

How long is the wait?
Jak długo trzeba czekać? yak *dwoo*·go *tshe*·ba *che*·kach

listen for ...

Już jest zamknięte.
  yoosh yest zamk·*nyen*·te | **We're closed.**

Nie ma wolnych miejsc.
  nye ma *vol*·nikh myeysts | **We're full.**

Chwileczkę.
  khfee·*lech*·ke | **One moment.**

at the restaurant

w restauracji

Leaving a *napiwek* na·*pee*·vek (tip) is advisable but not strictly necessary. Worth sampling is *bigos* bee·gos, the national dish, made from sauerkraut and a variety of meats slow-simmered together.

What would you recommend?
Co by pan/pani	tso bi pan/*pa*·nee
polecił/poleciła? m/f	po·*le*·cheew/po·le·*chee*·wa

What's in that dish?
Co jest w tym daniu?	tso yest v tim *da*·nyoo

What's that called?
Jak się to nazywa?	yak shye to na·*zi*·va

I'll have that.
Zamówię to.	za·*moo*·vye to

Does it take long to prepare?
Czy długo trwa	chi *dwoo*·go trfa
przyrządzenie tego?	pshi·zhon·*dze*·nye tego

Is it self-serve?
Czy tu jest samoobsługa?	chi too yest sa·mo·ob·*swoo*·ga

eating out

161

Is there a cover/service charge?
Czy jest opłata za wstęp/obsługę? — chi yest o·*pwa*·ta za fstemp/ob·*swoo*·ge

Is service included in the bill?
Czy obsługa jest wliczona do rachunku? — chi ob·*swoo*·ga yest vlee·*cho*·na do ra·*khoon*·koo

Are these complimentary?
Czy to jest bezpłatne? — chi to yest bes·*pwa*·tne

Could I please see the wine list?
Czy mogę prosić o listę win? — chi *mo*·ge *pro*·sheech o *lees*·te veen

I'd like (a/the) …, please.	*Proszę …*	pro·she …
children's menu	*o jadłospis dla dzieci*	o ya·*dwo*·spees dla *jye*·chee
drink list	*o spis napojów*	o spees na·*po*·yoof
half portion	*o pół porcji*	o poow *ports*·yee
local speciality	*o miejscową specjalność*	o myeys·*tso*·vom spe·*tsyal*·noshch
meal fit for a king	*o królewski posiłek*	o kroo·*lef*·skee po·*shee*·wek
menu (in English)	*o jadłospis (po angielsku)*	o ya·*dwo*·spees (po an·*gyel*·skoo)
nonsmoking	*dla niepalących*	dla nye·pa·*lon*·tsikh
smoking	*dla palących*	dla pa·*lon*·tsikh
table for (five)	*o stolik na (pięć osób)*	o *sto*·leek na (pyench o·soob)
that dish	*to danie*	to *da*·nye

I'd like it with ...	*Chciałbym/ Chciałabym to z ... m/f*	khchow·bim/ khchow·a·bim to z ...
cheese	*serem*	se·rem
chilli	*chili*	chee·lee
chilli sauce	*sosem chili*	so·sem chee·lee
garlic	*czosnkiem*	chosn·kyem
ketchup	*keczupem*	ke·choo·pem
nuts	*orzechami*	o·zhe·kha·mee
oil	*oliwą*	o·lee·vom
pepper	*pieprzem*	pyep·shem
salt	*solą*	so·lom
tomato	*sosem*	so·sem
sauce	*pomidorowym*	po·mee·do·ro·vim
vinegar	*octem*	ots·tem
I'd like it without ...	*Chciałbym/ Chciałabym to bez ... m/f*	khchow·bim/ khchow·a·bim to bes ...
cheese	*sera*	se·ra
chilli	*chili*	chee·lee
chilli sauce	*sosu chili*	so·soo chee·lee
garlic	*czosnku*	chosn·koo
ketchup	*keczupu*	ke·choo·poo
nuts	*orzechów*	o·zhe·khoof
oil	*oliwy*	o·lee·vee
pepper	*pieprzu*	pyep·shoo
salt	*soli*	so·lee
tomato	*sosu*	so·soo
sauce	*pomidorowego*	po·mee·do·ro·ve·go
vinegar	*octu*	ots·too

For other specific meal requests, see **vegetarian & special meals**, page 177.

listen for ...		
Polecam ...	po·le·tsam ...	I suggest the ...
Proszę bardzo!	pro·she bar·dzo	Here you go!
Smacznego.	smach·ne·go	Enjoy your meal.

Poland has for centuries been a cosmopolitan country, and its food has been influenced by the cuisines of its neighbours. Polish food is hearty and rich in meat, if not vegetables. Vegetarians should find *dania jarskie* da·nya yar·skye or vegetable dishes on the menu in most places. The price of a main course doesn't usually include side orders, which you should select from the *dodatki* do·dat·kee section of the menu. Below is a selection of other common menu terms:

Przekąski	pshe·kons·kee	Appetisers
Zupy	zoo·pi	Soups
Entrée	an·tre	Entrées
Sałatki	sa·wat·kee	Salads
Drugie Dania	droo·gye da·nya	Main Courses
Dania Mięsne	da·nya myens·ne	Meat Dishes
Dania Rybne	da·nya rib·ne	Fish Dishes
Drób	droob	Poultry
Dania Jarskie	da·nya yar·skye	Vegetarian Dishes
Dodatki	do·dat·kee	Side Dishes
Desery	de·se·ri	Desserts
Aperitify	a·pe·ree·tee·fi	Apéritifs
Drinki	dreen·kee	Drinks
Napoje	na·po·ye	Soft Drinks
Alkohole	al·ko·ho·le	Spirits
Piwa	pee·va	Beers
Alkohole	al·ko·ho·le	Digestifs
Poprawiające	po·pra·vya·yon·tse	
Trawienie	tra·vye·nye	
Wina ...	vee·na ...	... Wines
Musujące	moo·soo·yon·tse	Sparkling
Białe	bya·we	White
Czerwone	cher·vo·ne	Red
Deserowe	de·se·ro·ve	Dessert

For additional items, see the **menu decoder** section, p179.

at the table

Please bring (a/the) ...	Proszę o ...	pro·she o ...
bill/check	rachunek	ra·khoo·nek
cutlery	sztućce	shtooch·tse
(wine)glass	kieliszek	kye·lee·shek
	(do wina)	(do vee·na)
serviette	serwetkę	ser·vet·ke
tablecloth	obrus	o·broos

This is ...	To jest ...	to yest ...
burnt	przypalone	pshi·pa·lo·ne
(too) cold	(za) zimne	(za) zheem·ne
(too) spicy	(za) pikantne	(za) pee·kant·ne
(too) salty	(za) słone	(za) swo·ne
stale	nieświeże	nye·shvye·zhe
superb	pyszne	pish·ne
spicy	ostre	os·tre

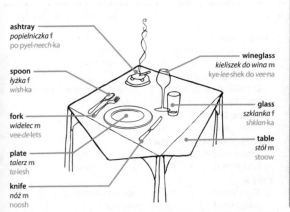

ashtray
popielniczka f
po·pyel·neech·ka

spoon
łyżka f
wish·ka

fork
widelec m
vee·de·lets

plate
talerz m
ta·lesh

knife
nóż m
noosh

wineglass
kieliszek do wina m
kye·lee·shek do vee·na

glass
szklanka f
shklan·ka

table
stół m
stoow

eating out

165

Try some of these treats while you're out and about:

gofry pl   *go*·fri
waffles with whipped cream – as delicious as they sound

obwarzanek m   ob·va·*zha*·nek
bagel – legend has it that these originated in Poland

oscypek m   os·*tsi*·pek
smoked sheep's-milk cheese – an important symbol of
Poland's culinary heritage hailing from the Tatra Mountains

placki ziemniaczane pl   *plats*·kee zhym·nya·*cha*·ne
potato pancakes – fried cakes of grated potato and egg
flavoured with onion

zapiekanki pl   za·pye·*kan*·kee
split baguette topped with cheese, mushrooms and ketchup

talking food

komentowanie posiłku

I love this dish.
To danie bardzo mi   to *da*·nye *bar*·dzo mee
smakuje.   sma·*koo*·ye

I love the local cuisine.
Uwielbiam miejscową   oo·*vyel*·byam myeys·*tso*·vom
kuchnię.   *kookh*·nye

That was delicious!
To było pyszne.   to *bi*·wo *pish*·ne

My compliments to the chef.
Proszę podziękować   *pro*·she po·jyen·*ko*·vach
kucharzowi.   koo·kha·*zho*·vee

I'm full.
Najadłem/am się   na·*yad*·wem/wam shye
do syta. m/f   do *si*·ta

methods of preparation

I'd like it ...	*Chciałbym/*	*khchow*·bim/
	Chciałabym	khchow·*a*·bim
	to ... m/f	to ...
boiled	*gotowane*	go·to·*va*·ne
deep-fried	*smażone*	sma·*zho*·ne
	w oleju	v o·*le*·yoo
fried	*usmażone*	oo·sma·*zho*·ne
grilled	*z rusztu*	z *roosh*·too
mashed	*purée*	pee·*re*
medium	*średnio*	*shred*·nyo
	przyrządzone	pshi·zhon·*dzo*·ne
rare	*lekko*	*le*·ko
	przyrządzone	pshi·zhon·*dzo*·ne
reheated	*odgrzane*	od·*gzha*·ne
steamed	*na parze*	na *pa*·zhe
well done	*dobrze*	*dob*·zhe
	przyrządzone	pshi·zhon·*dzo*·ne
without ...	*bez ...*	bes ...
I don't want it ...	*Nie chcę tego ...*	nye khtse *te*·go ...
boiled	*ugotowanego*	oo·go·to·va·*ne*·go
deep-fried	*smażonego w*	sma·zho·*ne* go v
	oleju	o·*le*·yoo
fried	*usmażonego*	oo·sma·zho·*ne*·go
grilled	*z rusztu*	z *roosh*·too
mashed	*purée*	pee·*re*
medium	*średnio*	*shred*·nyo
	przyrządzonego	pshi·zhon·dzo·*ne*·go
rare	*lekko*	*le*·ko
	przyrządzonego	pshi·zhon·dzo·*ne*·go
reheated	*odgrzanego*	od·gzha·*ne*·go
steamed	*na parze*	na *pa*·zhe
well done	*dobrze*	*dob*·zhe
	przyrządzonego	pshi·zhon·dzo·*ne*·go

eating out

nonalcoholic drinks

... water	woda f ...	vo·da ...
mineral	mineralna	mee·ne·ral·na
sparkling	gazowana	ga·zo·va·na
still	niegazowana	nye·ga·zo·va·na
(orange) juice	sok (pomarańczowy) m	sok (po·ma·ran'·cho·vi)
soft drink	napój m	na·pooy
(hot) water	(gorąca) woda f	(go·ron·tsa) vo·da
cup of tea (with lemon)	filiżanka herbaty (z cytryną)	fee·lee·zhan·ka her·ba·ti (z tsi·tri·nom)
cup of coffee/ tea ...	filiżanka kawy/ herbaty ...	fee·lee·zhan·ka ka·vi/ her·ba·ti ...
with milk	z mlekiem	z mle·kyem
without milk	bez mleka	bes mle·ka
with sugar	z cukrem	z tsoo·krem
without sugar	bez cukru	bez tsoo·kroo

anyone for coffee?

Coffee *po turecku* po too·rets·koo (lit: in the Turkish manner) is, much like its namesake, thick, black and sweet with a sludge of grounds at the bottom. It's made by putting a couple of teaspoons of coffee grounds directly into a glass and topping it up with water. This brew also goes by the name of *kawa parzona* ka·va pa·zho·na.

black coffee	czarna kawa f	char·na ka·va
decaffeinated coffee	kawa bez kafeiny f	ka·va bes ka·fe·ee·ni
iced coffee	kawa mrożona f	ka·va mro·zho·na
strong	mocna f	mots·na
strong black coffee	kawa po turecku f	ka·va po too·rets·koo
weak	słaba f	swa·ba

alcoholic drinks

(cold) beer	(zimne) piwo n	(zheem·ne) pee·vo
brandy	brandy m	bren·di
champagne	szampan m	sham·pan
cocktail	koktail m	kok·tail
Goldwasser (herbal liqueur)	goldwasser m	gold·va·ser
grape brandy	winiak m	vee·nyak
honey liqueur	krupnik m	kroop·neek

a shot of ...	kieliszek ...	kye·lee·shek ...
gin	dżinu	jee·noo
rum	rumu	roo·moo
tequila	tequili	te·kee·lee
vodka	wódki	vood·kee
whisky	whisky	wis·kee

a bottle/glass of ... wine	butelka/ kieliszek wina ...	boo·tel·ka/ kye·lee·shek vee·na ...
dessert	deserowego	de·se·ro·ve·go
red	czerwonego	cher·vo·ne·go
rosé	rose	ro·se
sparkling	musującego	moo·soo·yon·tse·go
white	białego	bya·we·go

a ... of beer	... piwa	... pee·va
glass	szklanka	shklan·ka
pint	kufel	koo·fel
small bottle	mała butelka	ma·wa boo·tel·ka
large bottle	duża butelka	doo·zha boo·tel·ka

For additional items, see the **menu decoder**, page 179, and the dictionary.

in the bar

The most popular drink by far in Poland is *wódka* vood·ka (vodka), which is served neat in 25ml or 50ml glasses (or 100ml for heavy drinkers). Only Russians or Finns can match the prodigious vodka consumption of the Poles, so pace yourself carefully if you're joining in with the locals. Some of the best brands of vodka are *Belvedere* bel·ve·der, *Wyborowa* vi·bo·ro·va and *Żubrówka* zhoo·broof·ka. *Piwo* pee·vo (beer) is also good quality and popular. Try these brands: *Tyskie* tis·kye, *Okocim* o·ko·cheem, *Lech* lekh and *Żywiec* zhi·vyets.

Excuse me!
Przepraszam!   pshe·*pra*·sham

I'm next.
Ja jestem następny w   ya *yes*·tem nas·*temp*·ni v
kolejce.   ko·*ley*·tse

I'll have (vodka).
Proszę (wódkę).   pro·she (vood·ke)

Same again, please.
Proszę jeszcze raz to samo.   pro·she yesh·che ras to sa·mo

No ice, thanks.
Proszę bez lodu.   pro·she bes lo·doo

I'll buy you a drink.
Czy mogę panu/pani   chi mo·ge pa·noo/pa·nee
kupić drinka? m/f pol   koo·peech dreen·ka
Kupię ci drinka. inf   koo·pye chee dreen·ka

listen for ...

Co mogę panu/pani/państwu podać? m/f/pl
tso mo·ge pa·noo/pa·nee/   **What are you having?**
pan'·stfoo po·dach

Myślę, że panu/i już wystarczy.
mish·le zhe pa·noo/nee   **I think you've had**
yoosh vis·tar·chi   **enough.**

What would you like?
  Co mogę dla pana/pani   tso *mo*·ge dla *pa*·na/*pa*·nee
  zamówić? m/f pol   za·*moo*·veech
  Co zamówić dla ciebie? inf   tso za·*moo*·veech dla *chye*·bye

I don't drink alcohol.
  Nie piję alkoholu.   nye *pee*·ye al·ko·*kho*·loo

It's my round.
  Ja stawiam.   ya *sta*·vyam

How much is that?
  Ile to kosztuje?   *ee*·le to kosh·*too*·ye

Do you serve meals here?
  Czy można tu coś   chi *mozh*·na too tsosh
  zjeść?   zyeshch

drinking up

The gesture for indicating inebriation is an outstretched palm
making a repeated chopping action on the side of the neck.

Cheers!
  Na zdrowie!   na *zdro*·vye

I feel fantastic!
  Czuję się wspaniale!   *choo*·ye shye fspa·*nya*·le

I think I've had one too many.
  Chyba wypiłem/am   *khi*·ba vi·*pee*·wem/wam
  o jeden za dużo. m/f   o *ye*·den za *doo*·zho

I'm feeling drunk.
  Jestem pijany/a. m/f   *yes*·tem pee·*ya*·ni/na

I feel ill.
  Niedobrze mi.   nye·*do*·bzhe mee

Where's the toilet?
  Gdzie jest ubikacja?   gje yest oo·bee·*ka*·tsya

eating out

I'm tired, I'd better go home.

Jestem zmęczony/a,	*yes*·tem zmen·*cho*·ni/na
lepiej już pójdę	*le*·pyey yoosh *pooy*·de
do domu. m/f	do *do*·moo

Can you call a taxi for me?

Czy może pan/pani	chi *mo*·zhe pan/*pa*·nee
zamówić dla mnie	za·*moo*·veech dla mnye
taksówkę? m/f pol	tak·*soof*·ke
Czy możesz zamówić	chi *mo*·zhesh za·*moo*·veech
dla mnie taksówkę? inf	dla mnye tak·*soof*·ke

I don't think you should drive.

Nie powinien/powinna	nye po·*vee*·nyen/po·*vee*·na
pan/pani kierować. m/f pol	pan/*pa*·nee kye·ro·vach
Nie powinieneś/	nye po·vee·*nye*·nesh/
powinnaś kierować. m/f inf	po·*veen*·nash kye·ro·vach

---

vodka reader

There can be no doubt that Poles love their *wódka* vood·ka. They even claim to have invented the beverage, much to the disapproval of their Russian neighbours. Polish vodka comes in a number of different colours and flavours. *Żubrówka* zhoo·*broof*·ka (bison vodka) is so called because it's flavoured with grass from the Biełowieża Forest on which bison feed.

bimber m	*beem*·ber	moonshine (illegally brewed vodka)
jałowcówka f	ya·wov·*tsoof*·ka	juniper-berry vodka
jarzębiak m	ya·*zhem*·byak	rowanberry vodka
śliwowica f	shlee·vo·*vee*·tsa	plum brandy
wiśniówka f	vish·*nyoof*·ka	cherry vodka
Żubrówka f	zhoo·*broof*·ka	bison vodka

For vodka-drinking etiquette see the box on page 128.

buying food

kupowanie żywności

What's the local speciality?
Co jest miejscową
specjalnością?
tso yest myeys·*tso*·vom
spe·tsyal·*nosh*·chyom

What's that?
Co to jest?
tso to yest

Can I taste it?
Czy mogę spróbować?
chi *mo*·ge sproo·*bo*·vach

Can I have a bag, please?
Czy mogę prosić o torbę?
chi *mo*·ge *pro*·sheech o *tor*·be

I don't need a bag, thanks.
Dziękuję, ale nie
potrzebuje torby.
jyen·*koo*·ye *a*·le nye
po·tshe·*boo*·ye *tor*·bi

How much (is a kilo of cheese)?
Ile kosztuje
(kilogram sera)?
ee·le kosh·*too*·ye
(kee·*lo*·gram *se*·ra)

I'd like …	Proszę …	pro·she …
(20) decagrams/ (200) grams	(20) deko	(dva·jyesh·chya) de·ko
half a dozen	sześć	sheshch
a dozen	dwanaście	dva·nash·chye
half a kilo	pół kilo	poow kee·lo
a kilo	kilo	kee·lo
(two) kilos	(dwa) kilo	(dva) kee·lo
a bottle	butelkę	boo·tel·ke
a jar	słoik	swo·yeek
a packet	paczkę	pach·ke
a piece	kawałek	ka·vow·ek
(three) pieces	(trzy) kawałki	(tshi) ka·vow·kee
(five) pieces	(pięć) kawałków	(pyench) ka·vow·koof
a slice	plasterek	plas·te·rek
(two) slices	(dwa) plasterki	(dva) plas·ter·kee
(six) slices	(sześć) plasterków	(sheshch) plas·ter·koof
a tin	puszkę	poosh·ke
(just) a little	(tylko) trochę	(til·ko) tro·khe
more	więcej	vyen·tsey
some …	kilka …	keel·ka …
that one	tamten	tam·ten
this one	ten	ten

For an explanation of the *deko* de·ko unit of measurement and why nouns change their form with numbers, see **numbers & amounts,** pages 34 and 36.

see **numbers & amounts,** pages 34 and 36.

how would you like that?		
cooked	gotowany m	go·to·va·ni
cured	konserwowany m	kon·ser·vo·va·ni
dried	suszony m	soo·sho·ni
fresh	świeży m	shvye·zhi
frozen	mrożony m	mro·zho·ni
raw	surowy m	soo·ro·vi
smoked	wędzony m	ven·dzo·ni

FOOD

174

Less.	Mniej.	mney
A bit more.	Trochę więcej.	tro·khe vyen·tsey
Enough.	Wystarczy.	vis·tar·chi
Please.	Proszę.	pro·she
Please give me …	Proszę …	pro·she …
Thank you.	Dziękuję.	jyen·koo·ye
That's delicious!	To jest pyszne.	to yest pish·ne

Do you have …?	Czy …?	chi …
anything	jest coś	yest tsosh
cheaper	tańszego	tan'·she·go
other kinds	są inne rodzaje	som ee·ne ro·dza·ye

Where can I find	Gdzie mogę	gjye mo·ge
the … section?	znaleźć dział …?	zna·leshch jyow …
dairy	z nabiałem	z na·bya·wem
fish	rybny	rib·ni
frozen goods	z mrożon-kami	z mro·zhon·ka·mee
fruit and	owocowo-	o·vo·tso·vo·
vegetable	warzywny	va·zhiv·ni
meat	z mięsem	z myen·sem
poultry	z drobiem	z dro·byem

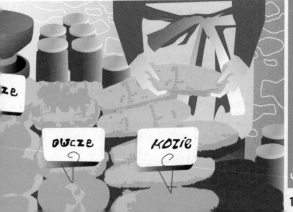

cooking utensils

Could I please	Czy mogę	chi mo·ge
borrow a ...?	pożyczyć ...?	po·zhi·chich ...
I need a ...	Potrzebuję ...	po·tshe·boo·ye ...
chopping	deskę do	des·ke do
board	krojenia	kro·ye·nya
frying pan	patelnię	pa·tel·nye
knife	nóż	noozh
saucepan	garnek	gar·nek

For more cooking implements, see the **dictionary**.

some salt with that?

In Polish culture *chleb* khlep (bread) and *sól* sool (salt) have a special symbolic status. They're symbols of fertility and good fortune, but perhaps most importantly, of *gościnność* gosh·chee·noshch (hospitality). After a traditional Polish wedding, the bride and groom visit the bride's parents and are welcomed with a gift of bread and salt. According to a tradition that's no longer widely observed, the bride's mother is supposed to say:

Co wolisz: chleb, sól czy pana młodego?
tso vo·lesh khlep sool chi pa·na mwo·de·go
(Which would you prefer: the bread, the salt or your young man?)

To which the bride should reply (though perhaps not in these days of relative gender equality):

Wolę chleb, sól i pana młodego, żeby zarobić na niego.
vo·le khlep sool ee pa·na mwo·de·go zhe·bi za·ro·beech na nye·go
(I'd like the bread, the salt and my young man to earn the money to pay for them.)

vegetarian & special meals
potrawy wegetariańskie i specjalne

ordering food

Is there a (vegetarian) restaurant near here?

Czy jest tu gdzieś		chi yest too gjyesh
restauracja		re·stow·*ra*·tsya
(wegetariańska)?		(ve·ge·ta·*ryan'*·ska)

I don't eat …	*Nie jadam …*	nye *ya*·dam …
Could you	*Czy można*	chi *mo*·zhna
prepare a meal	*przygotować*	pshi·go·*to*·vach
without …?	*jedzenie bez …?*	ye·*dze*·nye bes …
butter	*masła*	*ma*·swa
eggs	*jajek*	*yai*·ek
fish	*ryb*	rib
fish/meat	*wywaru rybnego/*	vi·*va*·roo rib·*ne*·go/
stock	*mięsnego*	myens·*ne*·go
pork	*wieprzowiny*	vye·psho·*vee*·ni
poultry	*drobiu*	*dro*·byoo
(red) meat	*(czerwonego)*	(cher·vo·*ne*·go)
	mięsa	*myen*·sa

Is this …?	*Czy to jest …?*	chi to yest …
decaffeinated	*bez kofeiny*	bes ko·fe·*ee*·ni
free-range	*hodowli*	ho·*dov*·lee
	naturalnej	na·too·*ral*·ney
genetically	*modyfikowane*	mo·di·fee·ko·*va*·ne
modified	*genetycznie*	ge·ne·*tich*·nye
gluten-free	*bezglutenowe*	bes·gloo·te·*no*·ve
low in fat/sugar	*z niską*	z *nees*·kom
	zawartością	za·var·*tosh*·chyom
	tłuszczu/	*twoosh*·choo/
	cukru	*tsoo*·kro
organic	*organiczne*	or·ga·*neech*·ne
salt-free	*bez soli*	bes *so*·lee

special diets & allergies

I'm on a special diet.
Jestem na specjalnej diecie.
yes·tem na spe·tsyal·ney dye·chye

I'm vegan/vegetarian.
Jestem weganem/ wegetarianinem.
yes·tem ve·ga·nem/ ve·ge·ta·rya·nee·nem

I'm allergic to …	*Mam uczulenie na …*	mam oo·choo·le·nye na …
dairy produce	*produkty mleczne*	pro·dook·ti mlech·ne
eggs	*jajka*	yai·ka
gelatine	*żelatynę*	zhe·la·ti·ne
gluten	*gluten*	gloo·ten
honey	*miód*	myood
MSG	*glutaminian sodu*	gloo·ta·mee·nyan so·doo
nuts	*orzechy*	o·zhe·khi
peanuts	*orzeszki ziemne*	o·zhesh·kee zhyem·ne
seafood	*owoce morza*	o·vo·tse mo·zha
shellfish	*małże*	mow·zhe

To explain your dietary restrictions with reference to religious beliefs, see **beliefs & cultural differences**, page 139.

menu decoder
słownik kulinarny

This guide to Polish food is in Polish alphabetical order (shown below). It's designed to help you get the most out of your Polish culinary experiences by helping you find your way around menus and markets. Note that adjectives are given in the masculine form only – for more information on how to make the feminine and neuter forms of adjectives, see the **a–z phrasebuilder**, page 17.

A a	Ą ą	B b	C c	Ć ć	D d	E e	Ę ę
F f	G g	H h	I i	J j	K k	L l	Ł ł
M m	N n	Ń ń	O o	Ó ó	P p	R r	S s
Ś ś	T t	U u	W w	Y y	Z z	Ź ź	Ż ż

A

agrest ⓜ *a*-grest *gooseberry*

alkoholowy ⓜ al-ko-ho-*lo*-vi *alcoholic*

ananas ⓜ a-*na*-nas *pineapple*

arbuz ⓜ *ar*-boos *watermelon*

awokado ⓝ a-vo-*ka*-do *avocado*

B

babka ⓕ *bap*-ka *a sweet spongy yeast cake traditionally baked at Easter*

bakalie ⓕ pl ba-*ka*-lye *dried fruit & nuts*

bakłażan ⓜ ba-*kwa*-zhan *eggplant*

baleron ⓜ ba-*le*-ron *smoked neck of pork (a kind of ham)*

banan ⓜ *ba*-nan *banana*

baranina ⓕ ba-ra-*nee*-na *lamb • mutton*

bar mleczny ⓜ bar *mlech*-ni *'milk bar' – self-service cafeteria-style eatery*

barszcz ⓜ barshch *borshch (beetroot soup) – there are many variations on this theme*

barszcz biały ⓜ barshch *bya*-wi *'white borshch', not actually a beetroot soup but a thick sourish wheat & potato-starch soup flavoured with marjoram*

barszcz czerwony ⓜ barshch cher-*vo*-ni *beetroot soup sometimes served with dumplings, hard-boiled egg slices or beans – a favourite winter food*

barszcz ukraiński ⓜ barshch oo-kra-*yeen*ˈ-skee *beetroot soup with beans & potatoes*

barszcz zabielany ⓜ barshch za-bye-*la*-ni *beetroot soup with sour cream*

barszcz z pasztecikiem ⓜ barshch z pash-te-*chyee*-kyem *beetroot soup with a savoury pastry filled with mincemeat*

barszcz z uszkami ⓜ barshch z *oosh*-ka-mee *beetroot soup with small, ravioli-style dumplings stuffed with meat*

bawarka ⓕ ba-*var*-ka *tea with milk*

bazylia ⓕ ba-*zil*-ya *basil*

bażant ⓜ *ba*-zhant *pheasant*

befsztyk ⓜ *bef*-shtik *beef steak*

— tatarski ta-*tar*-skee *raw minced sirloin served with onion, raw egg yolk & often chopped pickled dill cucumber*

bigos ⓜ *bee*-gos *sauerkraut, cabbage & meat (including game) stew, slow simmered with prunes & mushrooms & flavoured with red wine – generally considered the Polish national dish*

bimber ⓜ *beem*-ber Polish moonshine, ie home-distilled vodka

bita śmietana ⓕ *bee*-ta shmye-*ta*-na whipped cream

bitki wołowe pl *beet*-kee-va-*wo*-ve beef cutlets

bliny pl *blee*-ni small thick pancakes made from wheat or buckwheat flour & leavened with yeast

boczek ⓜ *bo*-chek bacon – served either fried or boiled or baked in a chunk

botwinka ⓕ bot-*feen*-ka soup made from the stems & leaves of baby beetroot – often includes a sliced hard-boiled egg

brokuł ⓜ *bro*-koow broccoli

brukselka ⓕ brook-*sel*-ka Brussels sprouts

bryndza ⓕ *brin*-dza ewe's-milk cheese

bryzol ⓜ *bri*-zol grilled beef steak

brzoskwinia ⓕ bzhosk-*fee*-nya peach

budyń ⓜ *boo*-din´ milk-based cream dessert – available in commercially pre-pared packets in a range of flavours including strawberry, chocolate & vanilla

— z szynki z shin-kee mashed potato, ham & egg pie

bukiet z jarzyn ⓜ *boo*-kyet z ya-zhin cooked vegetables served as a side dish

bulion ⓜ *boo*-lyon broth

bułeczka ⓕ boo-*wech*-ka small bread roll

bułka ⓕ *boow*-ka white bread roll

buraczki ⓜ pl boo-*rach*-kee chopped or grated braised beetroot & sometimes apple – served as a side dish with meat

burak ⓜ *boo*-rak beetroot

C

cebula ⓕ tse-*boo*-la onion

chili ⓝ *chee*-lee chilli

chleb ⓜ khlep bread

— razowy ra-*zo*-vi dark rye bread

chłodnik ⓜ khwod-neek baby beetroot soup with yogurt & fresh vegetables – served cold, in summer only

chrzan ⓜ khshan horseradish

ciasto ⓝ *chyas*-to batter • cake • dough

ciastko ⓝ *chyast*-ko biscuit • cookie • pastry • small cake

cielęcina ⓕ chye-len-*chee*-na veal

cocktail ⓜ *kok*-tail cocktail

cukier ⓜ *tsoo*-kyer sugar

cukierek ⓜ tsoo-*kye*-rek candy • sweets

cukinia ⓕ tsoo-*kee*-nya courgette • zucchini

ćwikła ⓕ *chfeek*-wa boiled & grated beetroot with horseradish – a typical accompaniment to roast or smoked meat & sausages

cykoria ⓕ tsi-*kor*-ya endive

cynaderki pl tsi-na-*der*-kee kidneys

cynamon ⓜ tsi-*na*-mon cinnamon

cytryna ⓕ tsi-*tri*-na lemon

czarna kawa ⓕ *char*-na *ka*-va black coffee

czarna porzeczka ⓕ *char*-na po-*zhech*-ka blackcurrant

czereśnia ⓕ che-*resh*-nya cherry

czosnek ⓜ *chos*-nek garlic

D

dania jarskie pl *da*-nya *yar*-skye vegetarian dishes

dania mięsne pl *da*-nya *myens*-ne meat dishes

danie ⓝ *da*-nye dish

deser ⓜ *de*-ser dessert

desery pl de-*se*-ri desserts

dodatki pl do-*dat*-kee side dishes

dorsz ⓜ dorsh cod

drożdżówka ⓕ drozh-*joof*-ka brioche (sweet yeast bun)

drób ⓜ droob poultry

drugie danie ⓝ *droo*-gye *da*-nye main course

drugie śniadanie ⓝ *droo*-gye shnya-*da*-nye morning tea

duszony ⓜ doo-*sho*-ni stewed

dynia ⓕ *di*-nya pumpkin

dziczyzna ⓕ jyee-*chis*-na game

dżem ⓜ jem jam

F

farsz ⓜ farsh stuffing

fasola ⓕ fa-*so*-la beans

— szparagowa shpa-ra-*go*-va green string beans

— po bretońsku po bre-*ton*´-skoo baked beans in tomato sauce

faszerowany ⑩ fa-she-ro-*va*-ni *stuffed*

figa ① *fee*-ga *fig*

filet cielęcy ⑩ *fee*-let chye-*len*-tsi
veal escalope

flaczki/flaki pl *flach*-kee/*fla*-kee *seasoned
tripe & vegetables cooked in bouillon*

flądra ① *flon*-dra *flounder*

frytki pl *frit*-kee *chips • French fries*

G

galareta/galaretka ① ga-la-*re*-ta/
ga-la-*ret*-ka *meat or fish encased in
aspic – a typical Polish appetiser • sweet
flavoured jelly*

gęś ⑤ gensh *goose*

— **pieczona** pye-*cho*-na *roast goose*

gofry pl *go*-fri *thick rectangular waffles
served with toppings such as whipped
cream, chocolate or jam*

golonka ① go-*lon*-ka *boiled pigs' hocks
often served with sauerkraut or puréed
yellow peas*

gołąbki pl go-*womb*-kee *cabbage leaves
stuffed with minced beef & rice*

gotowany ⑩ go-to-*va*-ni *boiled*

— **na parze** na *pa*-zhe *steamed*

goździki pl gozh-*jee*-kee *cloves*

grahamka ① gra-*kham*-ka
small wholemeal roll

grejpfrut ⑩ *greyp*-froot *grapefruit*

groch ⑩ grokh *lentils*

— **włoski** *vwos*-kee *chickpea*

grochówka ① gro-*khoof*-ka *lentil soup*

groszek ⑩ *gro*-shek *green peas*

gruszka ① *groosh*-ka *pear*

grzaniec z piwa ⑩ *gzha*-nyets z *pee*-va
mulled beer

grzaniec z wina ⑩ *gzha*-nyets z *vee*-na
mulled wine

grzanka ① *gzhan*-ka *toast*

grzyby (marynowane) pl
gzhi-bi (ma-ri-no-*va*-ne)
(marinated) wild mushrooms

gulasz ⑩ *goo*-lash *goulash*

H

herbata ① her-*ba*-ta *tea*

— **bez cukru** bes *tsoo*-kroo
tea without sugar

— **z cukrem** z *tsoo*-krem
tea with sugar

— **z cytryną** z tsi-*tri*-nom *tea with a slice
of lemon*

— **ziołowa** zhyo-*wo*-va *herbal tea*

herbatniki pl her-bat-*nee*-kee *biscuits*

homar ⑩ *ho*-mar *lobster*

I

imbir ⑩ *eem*-beer *ginger*

indyk ⑩ *een*-dik *turkey*

J

jabłecznik ⑩ ya-*bvech*-neek
apple strudel

jabłko ⑩ *yabw*-ko *apple*

jadłodajnia ① ya-dwo-*dai*-nya *restaurant*

jadłospis ⑩ ya-dwo-*spees* *menu*

jagnię ⑩ *yag*-nye *lamb*

jagoda ① ya-*go*-da *blueberry*

jajecznica ① ya-yech-*nee*-tsa
scrambled eggs

jajka pl *yai*-ka *eggs*

— **na boczku** na *boch*-koo
bacon & eggs

— **na szynce** na *shin*-tse *ham & eggs*

— **sadzone** sa-*dzo*-ne *fried eggs*

jajko ⑩ *yai*-ko *egg*

— **na miękko** na *myen*-ko
soft-boiled egg

— **na twardo** na *tfar*-do
hard-boiled egg

— **w majonezie** v ma-yo-*ne*-zhe
hard-boiled egg in mayonnaise

jarski ⑩ *yar*-skee *vegetarian*

jarzębiak ⑩ ya-*zhem*-byak *vodka
flavoured with rowanberry*

jarzyny pl ya-*zhi*-ni *vegetables*

jogurt ⑩ yo-*goort* *yogurt*

K

kabanos ⓜ ka-*ba*-nos *thin dry smoked pork sausage*

kaczka ⓕ *kach*-ka *duck*
— **pieczona** pye-*cho*-na *roast duck*
— **z jabłkami** z yabw-*ka*-mee *roast duck stuffed with apples*

kajzerka ⓕ kai-*zer*-ka *small white round roll*

kalafior ⓜ ka-*la*-fyor *cauliflower*

kanapka ⓕ ka-*nap*-ka *sandwich*

kapusta ⓕ ka-*poos*-ta *cabbage*
— **kiszona/kwaszona** kee-*sho*-na/kfa-*sho*-na *sauerkraut*

kapuśniak ⓜ ka-*poosh*-nyak *sauerkraut soup*

karp ⓜ karp *carp*
— **po grecku** po *grets*-koo *carp served cold in an onion & tomato sauce*
— **w galarecie** v ga-la-*re*-chye *carp in aspic*
— **z wody** z *vo*-di *boiled carp*

karta dań ⓕ *kar*-ta dan' *menu*

karta win ⓕ *kar*-ta veen *wine list*

kartofel ⓜ kar-*to*-fel *potato*

kartoflanka ⓕ kar-to-*flan*-ka *potato & vegetable soup*
— **z grzybami** z gzhi-*ba*-mee *potato & vegetable soup with mushrooms*

kasza ⓕ *ka*-sha *cereals • gruel • porridge*
— **gryczana** gri-*cha*-na *buckwheat served as a cereal*
— **jęczmienna** yench-*myen*-na *pearl barley*
— **manna** *ma*-na *semolina served as a cereal*

kawa ⓕ *ka*-va *coffee*
— **neska** *nes*-ka *instant coffee*
— **z ekspresu** z eks-*pre*-soo *espresso coffee*
— **ze śmietanką** ze shmye-*tan*-kom *coffee with cream*
— **z mlekiem** z *mle*-kyem *coffee with milk*

kawiarnia ⓕ ka-*vyar*-nya *café*

kawior ⓜ *ka*-vyor *caviar*

keks ⓜ keks *fruit cake*

kieliszek ⓜ kye-*lee*-shek *glass (for wine & spirits)*

kiełbasa ⓕ kyew-*ba*-sa *sausage*
— **z rożna** z *rozh*-na *spit-roasted sausage*
— **z rusztu** z *roosh*-too *grilled or barbecued sausage*

kisiel ⓜ *kee*-shyel *jelly-type dessert made with potato starch*

klopsiki/klopsy pl klop-*shee*-kee/ *klop*-si *meatballs made with ground beef, pork or veal or a combination of these*

kluski pl *kloos*-kee *dumplings • noodles*

kminek ⓜ *kmee*-nek *caraway seeds*

knedle pl *kned*-le *dumplings stuffed with plums, cherries or apples*

koktajl ⓜ *kok*-tail *milkshake*

kolacja ⓕ ko-*lats*-ya *evening meal*

kołduny pl kow-*doo*-ni *savoury dumplings*

kompot ⓜ *kom*-pot *fruit compote*

konfitury pl kon-fee-*too*-ri *preserves*

koniak ⓜ *ko*-nyak *brandy*

koper/koperek ⓜ *ko*-per/ko-*pe*-rek *dill*

kopytka ⓕ ko-*pit*-ka *potato dumplings similar to gnocchi*

korniszony pl kor-nee-*sho*-ni *small pickled gherkins*

kotlet ⓜ *kot*-let *chop*
— **cielęcy** chye-*len*-tsi *veal cutlet or chop*
— **de volaille** de vo-*lail* *chicken breast fillet fried in breadcrumbs*
— **mielony** mye-*lo*-ni *mincemeat patty fried in breadcrumbs*
— **schabowy** skha-*bo*-vi *pork chop fried in breadcrumbs*

krewetki pl kre-*vet*-kee *prawns • shrimps*

krokiet ⓜ *kro*-kyet *croquette*

królik ⓜ *kroo*-leek *rabbit*

krupnik ⓜ *kroop*-neek *barley, meat & vegetable soup • honey liqueur*

kukurydza ⓕ koo-koo-*ri*-dza *corn • maize*

kurczak ⓜ *koor*-chak *chicken*
— **pieczony** pye-*cho*-ni *roast chicken*
— **z rożna** z *rozh*-na *spit-roasted chicken*

L

leszcz ⓜ *leshch* bream
likier ⓜ *lee·kyer* liqueur
lody pl *lo·di* ice cream

Ł

łosoś ⓜ *wo·sosh* salmon
— **wędzony** *ven·dzo·ni*
smoked salmon

M

majeranek ⓜ *ma·ye·ra·nek* marjoram
mak ⓜ *mak* poppy seeds
makaron ⓜ *ma·ka·ron* macaroni · pasta
makowiec ⓜ *ma·ko·vyets* poppy-seed
strudel
makrela ⓕ *ma·kre·la* mackerel
malina ⓕ *ma·lee·na* raspberry
małże pl *mow·zhe* mussels
mandarynka ⓕ *man·da·rin·ka* mandarin
marchew ⓕ *mar·khef* carrot
marchewka z groszkiem ⓕ
mar·khef·ka z grosh·kyem
boiled carrots with green peas
margaryna ⓕ *mar·ga·ri·na* margarine
marynowany ⓜ *ma·ri·no·va·ni*
marinated
masło ⓜ *mas·wo* butter
mąka ⓕ *mon·ka* flour
melba ⓕ *mel·ba* ice cream with fruit &
whipped cream
mielony *mye·lo·ni* minced
mięso ⓜ *myen·so* meat
— **mielone** *mye·lo·ne* mincemeat
migdał ⓜ *meeg·dow* almond
miód ⓜ *myood* honey
— **pitny** *peet·ni* mead
mizeria ⓕ *mee·zer·ya*
sliced fresh cucumber in sour cream
mleko ⓝ *mle·ko* milk
morela ⓕ *mo·re·la* apricot

N

nabiał ⓜ *na·byow* dairy produce
nadzienie ⓝ *na·jye·nye* stuffing
nadziewany ⓜ *na·jye·va·ni* stuffed
naleśniki pl *na·lesh·nee·kee*
crêpes · pancakes
— **z dżemem** *z je·mem* pancakes
with jam
— **z serem** *z se·rem* pancakes stuffed
with sweetened white soft cheese
nalewka ⓕ *na·lef·ka* homemade spirit
made from vodka flavoured with
herbs & berries
napiwek ⓜ *na·pee·vek* tip
napój ⓜ *na·pooy* nonalcoholic drink
nóżki w galarecie pl *noosh·kee v
ga·la·re·chye* jellied pigs' knuckles

O

obiad firmowy ⓜ *o·byad feer·mo·vi*
set menu
obiady domowe pl *o·bya·di do·mo·ve*
home-cooked set meals
obwarzanek ⓜ *ob·va·zha·nek*
ring-shaped pretzel
ogórek ⓜ *o·goo·rek* cucumber
— **kiszony/kwaszony** *kee·sho·ni/
kfa·sho·ni* dill cucumber
oliwki pl *o·leef·kee* olives
omlet ⓜ *om·let* omelette
— **z dżemem** *z je·mem* omelette
with jam
— **z pieczarkami** *z pye·char·ka·mee*
omelette with mushrooms
orzech ⓜ *o·zhekh* nut · walnut
— **kokosowy** *ko·ko·so·vi* coconut
— **laskowy** *las·ko·vi* hazelnut
— **włoski** *vwos·kee* walnut
orzeszek ziemny ⓜ *o·zhe·shek zhyem·ni*
peanut
oscypek/oszczypek ⓜ *os·tsi·pek/
osh·chi·pek* ewe's-milk cheese
ostrygi pl *os·tri·gee* oysters
owoc ⓜ *o·vots* fruit

owoce i orzechy pl o-vo-tse ee o-zhe-khi
fruit & nuts

owoce morza pl o-vo-tse mo-zha seafood

ozór ⓜ o-zoor tongue

P

panierowany ⓜ pa-nye-ro-va-ni crumbed

papryka ⓕ pap-ri-ka bell pepper •
capsicum

parówka ⓕ pa-roof-ka frankfurter

parówki z musztardą pl pa-roof-kee z
moosh-tar-dom boiled frankfurters
served with mustard

pasztecik ⓜ pash-te-cheek savoury pastry
stuffed with minced meat

pasztet z drobiu ⓜ pash-tet z drob-yoo
chicken pâté

pączek ⓜ pon-chek doughnut

pieczarka pl pye-char-ka mushroom

pieczarki z patelni pl pye-char-kee z
pa-tel-nee fried button mushrooms

pieczeń ⓕ pye-chen' roasted
— **cielęca** chye-len-tsa roast veal
— **wieprzowa** vye-psho-va roast pork
— **wołowa** vo-wo-va roast beef

pieczony ⓜ pye-cho-ni baked • roasted

pieprz ⓜ pyepsh pepper (condiment)

piernik ⓜ pyer-neek gingerbread –
traditionally made in Toruń & Gdańsk

pierogi pl pye-ro-gee ravioli-like dumplings
made from noodle dough, commonly
stuffed with mincemeat, sauerkraut,
mushroom, cheese & potato
— **leniwe** le-nee-ve dumplings filled
with curd cheese
— **ruskie** roos-kye dumplings filled with
soft, white cheese & potatoes
— **z jagodami** z ya-go-da-mee
dumplings filled with blueberries
— **z kapustą i grzybami** z ka-poos-tom
ee gzhi-ba-mee dumplings filled with
sauerkraut & wild mushrooms
— **z mięsem** z myen-sem dumplings
filled with mincemeat
— **z serem** z se-rem dumplings filled
with soft, white cheese

pierożki pl pye-rozh-kee a smaller version
of **pierogi**

pietruszka ⓕ pyet-roosh-ka parsley

pikantny ⓜ pee-kant-ni spicy

piwo ⓝ pee-vo beer
— **beczkowe** bech-ko-ve draught beer
— **butelkowe** boo-tel-ko-ve
bottled beer

placki kartoflane/ziemniaczane pl
plats-kee kar-to-fla-ne/zhyem-na-cha-ne
fried potato pancakes

polędwica ⓕ po-len-dvee-tsa sirloin
— **pieczona** pye-cho-na roasted
sirloin steak

pomarańcza ⓕ po-ma-ran'-cha orange

pomidor ⓜ po-mee-dor tomato

por ⓜ por leek

porzeczka ⓕ po-zhech-ka currant

posiłek ⓜ po-shee-wek meal

potrawa ⓕ po-tra-va course • dish

potrawy jarskie pl po-tra-vi yar-skye
vegetarian dishes

poziomka ⓕ po-zhyom-ka
wild stawberry

przekąska ⓕ pshe-kons-ka snack

przekąski pl pshe-kons-kee
appetisers • hors d'oeuvres

przyprawy pl pshi-pra-vi spices

przystawki pl pshis-taf-kee
accompaniments • side dishes

pstrąg ⓜ pstrong trout

pyzy pl pi-zi steamed potato dumplings

R

rachunek ⓜ ra-khoo-nek bill

rak ⓜ rak crayfish

restauracja ⓕ res-tow-ra-tsya
restaurant

rodzynka ⓕ ro-jin-ka raisin

rolmops ⓜ rol-mops marinated herring

rosół ⓜ ro-soow beef or chicken soup
— **z makaronem** z ma-ka-ro-nem
bouillon with noodles

rum ⓜ room rum

rumsztyk ⓜ room-shtik rump steak

ryba ① *ri*-ba *fish*
— **w galarecie** v ga-la-*re*-chye *in aspic*
ryż ⑩ rizh *rice*
rzodkiewka ① zhod-*kyef*-ka *radish*

S

sałata ① sa-*wa*-ta *lettuce*
sałatka ① sa-*wat*-ka *salad*
— **jarzynowa** ya-zhi-*no*-va *salad made with potato, vegetables & mayonnaise*
— **owocowa** o-vo-*tso*-va *fruit salad*
— **z pomidorów** z po-mee-*do*-roof *tomato salad*
sardynka ① sar-*din*-ka *sardine*
schab ⑩ skhab *loin of pork*
— **pieczony** pye-*cho*-ni *roasted pork flavoured with prunes*
seler ⑩ *se*-ler *celery*
ser ⑩ ser *cheese*
— **biały** *bya*-wi *white medium-soft cheese*
— **topiony** to-*pyo*-ni *cheese spread*
— **żółty** *zhoow*-ti *hard cheese*
serdelki pl ser-*del*-kee *sausages similar to frankfurters but thicker*
sernik ⑩ *ser*-neek *cheesecake*
serwetka ① ser-*vet*-ka *napkin*
siekany ⑩ shye-*ka*-ni *chopped*
słodki ⑩ *swod*-kee *sweet*
smażony ⑩ sma-*zho*-ni *fried*
sok ⑩ sok *juice*
— **owocowy** o-vo-*tso*-vi *fruit juice*
— **pomidorowy** po-mee-do-*ro*-vi *tomato juice*
sól ① sool *salt*
sos ⑩ sos *gravy • sauce*
— **chrzanowy** khsha-*no*-vi *horseradish sauce*
— **grzybowy** gzhi-*bo*-vi *mushroom sauce*
— **pomidorowy** po-mee-do-*ro*-vi *sauce made from tomatoes*
specjalność zakładu ① spe-*tsyal*-noshch za-*kwa*-doo *speciality of the house*
spis potraw ⑩ spees *po*-traf *menu*

stek ⑩ stek *steak*
surowy ⑩ soo-*ro*-vi *raw • uncooked*
surówka ① soo-*roof*-ka *vegetable salad*
— **z kiszonej kapusty** z kee-*sho*-ney ka-*poos*-ti *sauerkraut, sometimes served with chopped apple & onion*
szampan ⑩ *sham*-pan *champagne*
szarlotka ① shar-*lot*-ka *apple cake*
szaszłyk ⑩ *shash*-wik *shish kebab*
szczupak ⑩ *shchoo*-pak *pike*
szklanka ① *shklan*-ka *glass (for tea, water, soft drinks)*
sznycel ⑩ *shni*-tsel *escalope • schnitzel*
szparagi pl shpa-*ra*-gee *asparagus*
szpinak ⑩ *shpee*-nak *spinach*
szprotki pl *shprot*-kee *sprats (small herrings)*
sztuka mięsa ① *shtoo*-ka *myen*-sa *boiled beef served with horseradish*
szynka ① *shin*-ka *ham*

Ś

śledź ⑩ shlej *herring*
— **w oleju** v o-*le*-yoo *herring in oil with onion*
— **w śmietanie** v shmye-*ta*-nye *herring in sour cream*
śliwka ① *shleef*-ka *plum*
śliwowica ① shlee-vo-*vee*-tsa *plum brandy*
śmietana ① shmye-*ta*-na *sour cream*
śmietanka ① shmye-*tan*-ka *cream*

T

talerz ⑩ *ta*-lesh *plate*
tatar ⑩ *ta*-tar *minced sirloin served raw with onion, raw egg yolk & often chopped dill cucumber*
tort ⑩ tort *cream cake*
truskawka ① troos-*kaf*-ka *strawberry*
truskawkowy ⑩ troos-kaf-*ko*-vi *strawberry*
tuńczyk ⑩ toon´-*chik *tuna*
twaróg ⑩ *tfa*-roog *cottage cheese*
tymianek ⑩ ti-*mya*-nek *thyme*

W

wafle pl *vaf*·le *sweet wafer biscuits*

warzywa pl va·*zhi*·va *vegetables*

wątróbka ① von·*troop*·ka *liver*

wędzony ⓜ ven·*dzo*·ni *smoked*

węgorz ⓜ *ven*·gosh *eel*
— **wędzony** ven·*dzo*·ni *smoked eel*

w galarecie v ga·la·*re*·chye *in aspic • jellied*

widelec ⓜ vee·*de*·lets *fork*

wieprzowina ① vye·psho·*vee*·na *pork*

winiak ⓜ *vee*·nyak *grape brandy*

wino ⓝ *vee*·no *wine*
— **białe** *bya*·we *white wine*
— **czerwone** cher·*vo*·ne *red wine*
— **słodkie** *swod*·kye *sweet wine*
— **wytrawne** vi·*trav*·ne *dry wine*

winogrono ⓝ vee·no·*gro*·no *grape*

wiśnia ① *veesh*·nya *cherry*

wiśniówka ① veesh·*nyoof*·ka *cherry-flavoured vodka*

woda ① *vo*·da *water*
— **mineralna** mee·ne·*ral*·na *mineral water*

wołowina ① vo·wo·*vee*·na *beef*

wódka ① *vood*·ka *vodka*
— **myśliwska** mish·*leef*·ska *vodka flavoured with juniper berries*

Z

zając ⓜ *za*·yonts *hare*

zakąski ① pl za·*kons*·kee *appetisers • hors d'oeuvres • starters*

zapiekanka ① za·pye·*kan*·ka *half a bread roll filled with cheese & mushrooms, baked & served hot*

ziemniak ⓜ *zhyem*·nyak *potato*

ziemniaki pl zhyem·*nya*·kee *potatoes*

zioła pl *zhyo*·wa *herbs*

zioło ⓝ *zhyo*·wo *herb*

zrazy zawijane pl *zra*·zi za·vee·*ya*·ne *beef rolls in a sour-cream sauce stuffed with mushrooms and/or bacon*

z rożna z *rozh*·na *spit-roasted*

z rusztu z *roosh*·too *grilled*

zsiadłe mleko ⓝ *zshyad*·we *mle*·ko *sour milk (similar in taste to buttermilk & drunk with vegetable dishes)*

zupa ① *zoo*·pa *soup*
— **cebulowa** tse·boo·*lo*·va *onion soup*
— **fasolowa** fa·so·*lo*·va *bean soup*
— **grochowa** gro·*kho*·va *lentil soup*
— **grzybowa** gzhi·*bo*·va *mushroom soup*
— **jarzynowa** ya·zhi·*no*·va *vegetable soup*
— **mleczna** *mlech*·na *semolina, rice or spaghetti cooked in milk & sweetened as a breakfast food*
— **ogórkowa** o·goor·*ko*·va *pickled dill cucumber soup*
— **owocowa** o·vo·*tso*·va *sweet chilled fruit soup*
— **pomidorowa** po·mee·do·*ro*·va *tomato soup*
— **rybna** *rib*·na *fish soup*
— **szczawiowa** shcha·*vyo*·va *sorrel soup*
— **ziemniaczana** zhyem·nya·*cha*·na *potato soup*

Ż

żeberka pl zhe·*ber*·ka *ribs*

żubrówka ① zhoo·*broof*·ka *'bison vodka' – vodka flavoured with grass from the Białowieża forest on which bison feed*

żurek ⓜ *zhoo*·rek *sour rye-flour soup with smoked pork sausage*

żytnia (wódka) ① *zhit*·nya (*vood*·ka) *dry vodka*

emergencies

niebezpieczeństwa

Help!	*Na pomoc!*	na *po*·mots
Stop!	*Stój!*	stooy
Go away!	*Odejdź!*	o·deyj
Thief!	*Złodziej!*	zwo·jyey
Fire!	*Pożar!*	po·zhar
Watch out!	*Uważaj!*	oo·*va*·zhai

Call the police!
Zadzwoń po policję!   *zad*·zvon' po po·*lee*·tsye

Call a doctor!
Zadzwoń po lekarza!   *zad*·zvon' po le·*ka*·zha

Call an ambulance!
Zadzwoń po karetkę!   *zad*·zvon' po ka·*ret*·ke

It's an emergency.
To nagły wypadek.   to *nag*·wi vi·*pa*·dek

There's been an accident.
Tam był wypadek.   tam biw vi·*pa*·dek

I've been injured.
Jestem ranny/a. **m/f**   *yes*·tem *ra*·ni/na

Could you please help?
Czy może pan/pani   chi *mo*·zhe pan/*pa*·nee
mi pomóc? **m/f**   mee *po*·moots

signs		
Szpital	*shpee*·tal	**Hospital**
Policja	po·*lee*·tsya	**Police**
Komisariat	ko·mee·*sar*·yat	**Police Station**
Policji	po·*lee*·tsyee	
Oddział Nagłych	od·jyow *na*·gwikh	**Emergency**
Wypadków	vi·*pad*·koof	**Department**

essentials

187

Can I use your phone?
Czy mogę użyć telefon?   chi *mo*·ge *oo*·zhich te·*le*·fon

I'm going to call the police.
Wezwę policję.   vez·ve po·*lee*·tsye

I'm lost.
Zgubiłem/am się. m/f   zgoo·*bee*·wem/wam shye

Where are the toilets?
Gdzie są toalety?   gjye som to·a·*le*·ti

She's having a baby.
Ona rodzi dziecko.   o·na ro·jee *jyet*·sko

He/She is having a/an …	*On/Ona ma …*	on/*o*·na ma …
allergic reaction	*reakcje alergiczną*	re·*ak*·tsye a·ler·*geech*·nom
asthma attack	*atak astmy*	a·tak *ast*·mi
epileptic fit	*atak epilepsji*	a·tak e·pee·*lep*·syee
heart attack	*atak serca*	a·tak *ser*·tsa

Is it safe …?	*Czy jest bezpiecznie …?*	chi yest bes·*pyech*·nye …
at night	*w nocy*	v *no*·tsi
for gay men/ lesbians	*dla gejów/ lesbijek*	dla *ge*·yoof/ les·*bee*·yek
for travellers	*dla podróżnych*	dla po·*droozh*·nikh
for women	*dla kobiet*	dla *ko*·byet
on your own	*w pojedynkę*	v po·ye·*din*·ke

police

Where's the police station?
Gdzie jest posterunek policji?   gje yest pos·te·*roo*·nek po·*lee*·tsyee

I want to report an offence.
Chciałem/am zgłosić przestępstwo. m/f   khchow·em/am *zgwo*·sheech pshe·*stempst*·fo

I've been ...	*Zostałem/am ...* m/f	zo·*stow*·em/am ...
He's been ...	*On został ...*	on *zos*·tow ...
She's been ...	*Ona została ...*	o·na zos·*tow*·a ...
assaulted	*napadnięty/a* m/f	na·pad·*nyen*·ti/ta
attacked by	*zaatakowany/a*	za·a·ta·ko·*va*·ni/na
a dog	*przez psa* m/f	pshes psa
raped	*zgwałcony/a* m/f	zgvow·*tso*·ni/na
robbed	*okradziony/a* m/f	o·kra·*jyo*·ni/na
He tried to	*On próbował*	on proo·*bo*·vow
... me.	*... mnie.*	... mnye
She tried to	*Ona próbowała*	o·na proo·bo·*va*·wa
... me.	*... mnie.*	... mnye
assault	*napaść na*	na·pashch na
rape	*zgwałcić*	zgvow·cheech
rob	*okraść*	o·krashch

It was him.
  To był on.   to biw on

It was her.
  To była ona.   to *bi*·wa o·na

I have insurance.
  Mam ubezpieczenie.   mam oo·bes·pye·*che*·nye

My ... was stolen.
  Mój ... został skradziony. m   mooy ... *zos*·tow skra·*jyo*·ni
  Moja ... została skradziona. f *mo*·ya ... zos·*tow*·a skra·*jyo*·na
  Moje zostało ... skradzione. n *mo*·ye ... zos·*tow*·o skra·*jyo*·ne

My ... were stolen.
  Moje ... zostały   *mo*·ye ... zos·*tow*·i
  skradzione.   skra·*jyo*·ne

mind your p's

When a Pole has turned over a new leaf and has decided to eschew bad habits in favour of a clean and healthy lifestyle, he or she might say *Nie robię nic na 'p'!* nye *ro*·bye neets na pe. This literally translates as 'I'm not doing anything beginning with a "p".' What they have in mind is the following trinity: *nie piję, nie palę, nie pierdolę* nye *pee*·ye nye *pa*·le nye pyer·*do*·le, which means 'no smoking, no drinking and no bonking'.

I've lost my …	*Zgubiłem/am …* m/f	zgoo·*bee*·wem/wam …
backpack	*plecak*	*ple*·tsak
bag	*torbę*	*tor*·be
credit card	*kartę*	*kar*·te
	kredytową	kre·di·*to*·vom
handbag	*torebkę*	to·*rep*·ke
jewellery	*biżuterię*	bee·zhoo·*ter*·ye
money	*pieniądze*	pye·*nyon*·dze
papers	*dokumenty*	do·koo·*men*·ti
travellers	*czeki*	*che*·kee
cheques	*podróżne*	po·*droozh*·ne
passport	*paszport*	*pash*·port
wallet	*portfel*	*port*·fel

I (don't) understand.
(Nie) Rozumiem. (nye) ro·*zoo*·myem

Could I please have a/an (English) interpreter?
Czy mogę prosić o chi *mo*·ge *pro*·sheech o
(angielskiego) (an·gyel·*skye*·go)
tłumacza? twoo·*ma*·cha

What am I accused of?
O co jestem oskarżony/a? m/f o tso *yes*·tem os·kar·*zho*·ni/na

I'm sorry.
Przepraszam. pshe·*pra*·sham

I didn't realise I was doing anything wrong.
Nie zdawałem/am sobie nye zda·*vow*·em/am *so*·bye
sprawy, że robię *spra*·vi zhe *ro*·bye
coś złego. m/f tsosh *zwe*·go

190

I didn't do it.
  Ja tego nie   ya *te*·go nye
  zrobiłem/am. m/f   zro·*bee*·wem/wam

Can I pay an on-the-spot fine?
  Czy mogę zapłacić   chi *mo*·ge za·*pwa*·cheech
  karę miejscu?   *ka*·re na *myeys*·tsoo

Can I make a phone call?
  Czy mogę zadzwonić?   chi *mo*·ge za·*dzvo*·neech

the police may say …

Jest pan/pani	yest pan/*pa*·nee	**You're charged**
oskarżony/a	os·kar·*zho*·ni/na	**with …**
o … m/f	o …	
On/Ona jest	on/o·na yest	**He/She is**
oskarżony/a	os·kar·*zho*·ni/na	**charged with …**
o … m/f	o …	
brak wizy	brak *vee*·zi	**not having a visa**
kradzież	*kra*·jyesh	**theft**
kradzież	*kra*·jyesh	**shoplifting**
sklepową	skle·*po*·vom	
napad	*na*·pad	**assault**
posiadanie	po·shya·*da*·nye	**possession**
(nielegalnych	(nye·le·*gal*·nikh	**(of illegal**
substancji)	soob·*stan*·tsyee)	**substances)**
przekroczenie	pshe·kro·*che*·nye	**overstaying**
okresu pobytu	o·*kre*·soo po·*bi*·too	**a visa**
poza termin	*po*·za *ter*·meen	
ważności wizy	vazh·*nosh*·chee *vee*·zi	
zakłócenie	za·kwoo·*tse*·nye	**disturbing**
spokoju	spo·*ko*·yoo	**the peace**
To jest mandat	to yest *man*·dat	**It's a … fine.**
za …	za …	
nadmierną	nad·*myer*·nom	**speeding**
prędkość	*prend*·koshch	
parkowanie	par·ko·*va*·nye	**parking**

I want to contact my consulate.

Chcę się skontaktować z — khtse shye skon·tak·*to*·vach z
moim konsulatem. — mo·yeem kon·soo·*la*·tem

Can I have a lawyer (who speaks English)?

Czy mogę prosić o — chi mo·ge pro·sheech o
prawnika (który mówi — prav·*nee*·ka (*ktoo*·ri *moo*·vee
po angielsku). — po an·*gyel*·skoo)

I want to contact my embassy.

Chcę się skontaktować — khtse shye skon·tak·*to*·vach
z moją ambasadą. — z mo·yom am·ba·*sa*·dom

This drug is for personal use.

To lekarstwo jest do — to le·*karst*·fo yest do
użytku osobistego. — oo·*zhit*·koo o·so·bees·*te*·go

I have a prescription for this drug.

Mam receptę na to — mam re·*tsep*·te na to
lekarstwo. — le·*karst*·fo

---

damned if you do ...

The number one Polish swearword is probably *cholera!* kho·*le*·ra, which is roughly equivalent to 'shit!' or 'damn it!' The etymology of this word is pretty self-explanatory: it's also the name of the disease cholera. As swearwords go it's fairly innocous and you won't see too many raised eyebrows should you be provoked into spitting it out yourself. When used as part of the expression *ty cholero!* ti kho·*le*·ro (lit: you cholera) it's pretty similar in meaning to 'you bastard!' in English.

Another useful word if the chips are down is *Szkoda!* *shko*·da. This literally means 'harm' or 'damage', but when used as an exclamation it means 'What a pity!' Coincidentally (or not, some might argue), the once-maligned Czech make of car Škoda has the same pronunciation as this Polish exclamation of despair.

doctor

lekarz

Where's the nearest ...?	*Gdzie jest najbliższy/a/e ...? m/f*	gjye yest nai·*bleezh*·shi/sha/she ...
dentist	*dentysta* m	den·*tis*·ta
doctor	*lekarz* m	le·kash
emergency department	*pogotowie ratunkowe* n	po·go·*to*·vye ra·toon·*ko*·ve
hospital	*szpital* m	*shpee*·tal
medical centre	*ośrodek zdrowia* m	o·*shro*·dek *zdro*·vya
optometrist	*okulista* m	o·koo·*lees*·ta
outpatient clinic	*ambulatorium* n	am·boo·la·*tor*·yoom
(night) pharmacist	*apteka (nocna)* f	ap·*te*·ka (*nots*·na)

I need a doctor (who speaks English).
Szukam lekarza (który mówi po angielsku).
shoo·kam le·*ka*·zha (*ktoo*·ri moo·vee po an·*gyel*·skoo)

Could I see a female doctor?
Czy mogę się widzieć z lekarzem kobietą?
chi *mo*·ge shye *vee*·jyech z le·*ka*·zhem ko·*bye*·tom

Could the doctor come here?
Czy lekarz może tutaj przyjść?
chi *le*·kash *mo*·zhe *too*·tai pshiyshch

Is there an after-hours emergency number?
Czy jest numer do nagłych wypadków po godzinach pracy?
chi yest *noo*·mer do *nag*·wikh vi·*pad*·koof po go·*jee*·nakh *pra*·tsi

I've run out of my medication.
Skończyły mi się lekarstwa.
skon·*chi*·wi mee shye le·*karst*·fa

Co panu/pani dolega? m/f
  tso *pa*·noo/*pa*·nee do·*le*·ga **What's the problem?**

Gdzie boli?
  gjye *bo*·lee **Where does it hurt?**

Czy ma pan/pani temperaturę? m/f
  chi ma pan/*pa*·nee **Do you have a temperature?**
  tem·pe·ra·*too*·re

Jak długo jest pan/pani w tym stanie? m/f
  yak *dwoo*·go yest **How long have you been**
  pan/*pa*·nee v tim *sta*·nye **like this?**

Czy już kiedyś pan/pani to miał/miała? m/f
  chi yoosh *kye*·dish **Have you had this before?**
  pan/*pa*·nee to
  myow/*myow*·a

Jak długo pan/pani podróżuje? m/f
  yak *dwoo*·go pan/*pa*·nee **How long are you**
  po·droo·*zhoo*·ye **travelling for?**

Czy jest pan/pani aktywny/a seksualnie? m/f
  chi yest pan/*pa*·nee **Are you sexually active?**
  ak·*tiv*·ni/na sek·soo·*al*·nye

Czy miał/miała pan/pani seks bez zabezpieczenia? m/f
  chi myow/*myow*·a **Have you had unprotected**
  pan/*pa*·nee seks bes **sex?**
  za·bes·pye·*che*·nya

Czy pan/pani …? m/f   chi pan/*pa*·nee …   **Do you …?**
  pije   *pee*·ye   **drink**
  pali   *pa*·lee   **smoke**
  zażywa   za·*zhi*·va   **take drugs**
  narkotyki   nar·ko·*ti*·kee

Czy …?   chi …   **Are you …?**
  ma pan/pani   ma pan/*pa*·nee   **allergic to**
  na coś alergię m/f   na tsosh a·*ler*·gye   **anything**
  zażywa pan/   za·*zhi*·va pan/   **on medication**
  pani leki m/f   *pa*·nee *le*·kee

Musi pan/pani iść do szpitala. m/f

    moo·shee pan/*pa*·nee   **You need to be admitted to**
    eeshch do shpee·*ta*·la   **hospital.**

*Powinien/Powinna pan/pani iść do kontroli po powrocie
do domu.* m/f

    po·*vee*·nyen/po·*vee*·na   **You should have it checked**
    pan/*pa*·nee eeshch do   **when you go home.**
    kon·*tro*·lee po pov·*ro*·chye
    do *do*·moo

Powinien/Powinna pan/pani wrócić do domu na leczenie. m/f

    po·*vee*·nyen/po·*vee*·na   **You should return home for**
    pan/*pa*·nee *vroo*·cheech   **treatment.**
    do *do*·moo na le·*che*·nye

This is my usual medicine.

    To jest lekarstwo które   to yest le·*karst*·fo *ktoo*·re
    zazwyczaj zażywam.   zaz·*vi*·chai za·*zhi*·vam

What's the correct dosage?

    Jaka jest prawidłowa   *ya*·ka yest pra·vee·*dwo*·va
    dawka?   *daf*·ka

My child weighs (20 kilos).

    Moje dziecko waży   mo·ye *jyets*·ko va·zhi
    (dwadzieścia kilogramów).   (dva·*jyesh*·chya kee·lo·*gra*·moof)

Please use a new syringe.

    Proszę użyć nową   *pro*·she oo·zhich *no*·vom
    strzykawkę.   stshi·*kaf*·ke

I have my own syringe.

    Mam własną strzykawkę.   mam *vwas*·nom stshi·*kaf*·ke

I don't want a blood transfusion.

    Nie chcę transfuzji krwi.   nye khtse trans·*foo*·zyee krfee

I've been	Byłem/am	bi·wem/wam
vaccinated	szczepiony/a	shche·pyo·ni/na
against ...	na ... m/f	na ...
hepatitis A/B/C	żółtaczkę	zhoow·tach·ke
	typu A/B/C	ti·poo a/be/tse
tetanus	tężec	ten·zhets
typhoid	tyfus	ti·foos

I need new ...	Potrzebuję	po·tshe·boo·ye
	nowe ...	no·ve ...
contact lenses	soczewki	so·chef·kee
	kontaktowe	kon·tak·to·ve
glasses	okulary	o·koo·la·ri

My prescription is ...
Moja recepta jest ... — mo·ya re·tsep·ta yest ...

How much will it cost?
Ile to będzie kosztowało? — ee·le to ben·jye kosh·to·va·wo

Can I have a receipt for my insurance?
Czy mogę prosić o — chi mo·ge pro·sheech o
rachunek dla mojego — ra·khoo·nek dla mo·ye·go
ubezpieczenia? — oo·bes·pye·che·nya

---

doctor, doctor!

The correct way of addressing a male doctor or dentist is
panie doktorze pa·nye dok·to·zhe. The female equivalent is
pani doktor pa·nee dok·tor.

symptoms & conditions

objawy chorób i stan zdrowia

I'm sick.
Jestem chory/a. m/f — yes·tem kho·ri/ra

My friend is (very) sick.
Mój kolega jest (bardzo) — mooy ko·le·ga yest (bar·dzo)
chory. m — kho·ri
Moja koleżanka jest — mo·ya ko·le·zhan·ka yest
(bardzo) chora. f — (bar·dzo) kho·ra

My child is (very) sick.
Moje dziecko jest (bardzo)   mo·ye jyets·ko yest (bar·dzo)
chore.   kho·re

I've been injured.
Jestem ranny/a. m/f   yes·tem ra·ni/na

I've been vomiting.
Miałem/am wymioty. m/f   myow·em/am vi·myo·ti

He/She has been injured.
On/Ona jest ranny/a. m/f   on/o·na yest ra·ni/na

He/She has been vomiting.
On/Ona miała wymioty.   on/o·na myow/myow·a vi·myo·ti

It hurts here.
Tutaj boli.   too·tai bo·lee

I'm dehydrated.
Jestem odwodniony/a. m/f   yes·tem od·vod·nyo·ni/na

I can't sleep.
Nie mogę spać.   nye mo·ge spach

I can't eat.
Nie mogę jeść.   nye mo·ge yeshch

I feel depressed.
Jestem w depresji.   yes·tem v de·pres·yee

I feel dizzy.
Kręci mi się w głowie.   kren·chee mee shye v gwo·vye

I feel shivery.
Mam dreszcze.   mam dresh·che

I feel nauseous.
Mam mdłości.   mam mdwosh·chee

I feel hot and cold.
Mam dreszcze.   mam dresh·che

I feel ...	*Czuję się ...*	choo·ye shye ...
anxious	*zaniepokojony/a* m/f	za·nye·po·ko·yo·ni/na
better	*lepiej*	le·pyey
strange	*dziwnie*	jeev·nye
weak	*słaby/a* m/f	swa·bi/ba
worse	*gorzej*	go·zhey

Poles generally say *ręka* ren·ka for both 'hand' and 'arm'. The word *ramię* ra·mye can be used specifically to refer to the hand though. Similarly, the word *noga* no·ga refers to both the leg and foot, but you can you use the word *stopa* sto·pa to single out the part below the ankle.

I think it's the medication I'm on.

Myślę, że to z powodu	mish·le zhe to s po·vo·doo
lekarstw, które zażywam.	le·karstf ktoo·re za·zhi·vam

I'm on medication for …

Biorę leki na … byo·re le·kee na …

He/She is on medication for …

On/Ona bierze leki na … on/o·na bye·zhe le·kee na …

I have (a/an) …

Mam … mam …

He/She has (a/an) …

On/Ona ma … on/o·na ma …

I've recently had (a/an) …

Niedawno	nye·dav·no
miałem/am … m/f	myow·em/am …

He/She has recently had (a/an) …

On/Ona niedawno	on/o·na nye·dav·no
miał/miała …	myow/myow·a …

asthma	*astma* f	*ast*·ma
cold n	*przeziębienie* n	pshe·zhyem·*bye*·nye
constipation	*zatwardzenie* n	zat·far·*dze*·nye
cough n	*kaszel* m	*ka*·shel
diabetes	*cukrzyca* f	tsook·*shi*·tsa
diarrhoea	*rozwolnienie* n	roz·vol·*nye*·nye
fever	*gorączka* f	go·*ronch*·ka
headache	*ból głowy* m	bool *gwo*·vi
nausea	*mdłości* f pl	*mdwosh*·chee
pain n	*ból* m	bool
sore throat	*ból gardła* m	bool *gar*·dwa

women's health

(I think) I'm pregnant.
(Myślę, że) Jestem w ciąży.   *(mish*·le zhe) *yes*·tem f *chyon*·zhi

I'm on the pill.
Jestem na środkach   *yes*·tem na *shrod*·kakh
antykoncepcyjnych.   an·ti·kon·tsep·*tsiy*·nikh

I haven't had my period for (six) weeks.
Nie miałam okresu   nye *myow*·am o·*kre*·soo
przez (sześć) tygodni.   pshes (sheshch) ti·*god*·nee

I've noticed a lump here.
Zauważyłam tutaj guz.   za·oo·va·*zhi*·wam *too*·tai goos

Do you have something for (period pain)?
Czy jest coś na   chi yest tsosh na
(bóle okresowe)?   (*boo*·le o·kre·*so*·ve)

---

the doctor may say ...

Czy używa pani środki antykoncepcyjne?
chi oo·*zhi*·va *pa*·nee   **Are you using**
shrod·kee   **contraception?**
an·ti·kon·tsep·*tsiy*·ne

Czy ma pani menstruację?
chi ma *pa*·nee   **Are you**
men·stroo·*a*·tsye   **menstruating?**

Czy jest pani w ciąży?
chi yest *pa*·nee v *chyon*·zhi   **Are you pregnant?**

Kiedy ostatni raz miała pani okres?
kye·di os·*tat*·nee ras *myow*·a   **When did you last have**
pa·nee o·kres   **your period?**

Jest pani w ciąży.
yest *pa*·nee v *chyon*·zhi   **You're pregnant.**

health

199

I have a …	Mam …	mam …
urinary tract infection	zapalenie dróg moczowych	za·pa·le·nye droog mo·cho·vikh
yeast infection	infekcję grzybiczą	een·fek·tsye gzhi·bee·chom
I need (a/the) …	Chciałem/am … m/f	khchow·em/am …
contraception	środki antykoncepcyjne	shrod·kee an·ti·kon·tsep·tsiy·ne
morning-after pill	pigułkę aborcyjną	pee·goow·ke a·bor·tsiy·nom
pregnancy test	test ciążowy	test chyon·zho·vi

allergies

I have a skin allergy.
Mam alergię skórną. mam a·ler·gye skoor·nom

I'm allergic to …	Mam alergię na …	mam a·ler·gye na …
He/She is allergic to …	On/Ona ma alergię na …	on/o·na ma a·ler·gye na …
antibiotics	antybiotyki	an·ti·byo·ti·kee
antiinflammatories	leki przeciwzapalne	le·kee pshe·cheef·za·pal·ne
aspirin	aspirynę	as·pee·ri·ne
bees	pszczoły	pshcho·wi
codeine	kodeinę	ko·de·ee·ne
penicillin	penicylinę	pe·nee·tsi·lee·ne
pollen	pyłek	pi·wek
sulphur-based drugs	leki na bazie siarki	le·kee na ba·zhye shyar·kee
inhaler	inhalator m	een·kha·la·tor
injection	zastrzyk m	zast·shik
antihistamines	antyhistaminy pl	an·ti·hees·ta·mee·ni

For a list of food-related allergies, see **special diets & allergies**, page 178.

alternative treatments

I don't use (Western medicine).
Nie stosuję   nye sto·*soo*·ye
(medycyny zachodniej).   (me·di·*tsi*·ni za·*khod*·nyey)

Can I see	*Czy mogę się*	chi *mo*·ge shye
someone who	*skonsultować z*	skon·sool·*to*·vach z
practises ...?	*kimś kto*	keemsh kto
	praktykuje ...?	prak·ti·*koo*·ye ...
acupuncture	*akupunkturę*	a·koo·poonk·*too*·re
naturopathy	*naturopatię*	na·too·ro·*pa*·tye
reflexology	*refleksologię*	re·fle·kso·*lo*·gye

take the plunge

Look closely at a map of Poland and you'll see a number of towns with the word *Zdrój* zdrooy (mineral spa) tacked onto them, eg *Krynica-Zdrój* kri·*nee*·tsa·zdrooy. Poland has a long tradition of *uzdrowisko* ooz·dro·*vees*·ko (mineral spa towns), which draw visitors from all over Europe.

Polish spas are not merely places for a spot of R&R or pampering, however. They're celebrated for the curative powers of their *woda mineralna* vo·da mee·ne·*ral*·na (mineral water). The health-conscious flock to them to undertake *leczenie* le·*che*·nye (treatment) for a wide spectrum of ailments – anything from obesity to orthopaedic disorders. The varying composition of the waters means that spa towns specialise in the treatment of particular *choroba* kho·*ro*·ba (diseases).

Polish mineral spas offer an elaborate range of treatments. You can 'take the waters' at a *pijalnia* pee·*yal*·nya (pump room), selecting from a 'menu' of waters, or you can opt for a *błoto lecznicze* bwo·to lech·*nee*·che (therapeutic mud wrap) or a *masaż* ma·sash (massage). More adventurous souls can choose from a smorgasbord of new-age treatments including electrotherapy, light therapy, magnetotherapy, fonotherapy, inhalation therapy, cryotherapy, kinesitherapy and mechanotherapy.

parts of the body

My ... hurts.
Boli mnie ...   *bo·lee mnye ...*

I can't move my ...
Nie mogę ruszać ...   nye *mo·*ge *roo·*shach ...

I have a cramp in my ...
Mam skurcz w ...   mam skoorch v ...

My ... is/are swollen.
Mam spuchnięty/ą/e ... **m/f/n&pl**   mam spookh·*nyen·*ti/tom/te .

For other parts of the body, see the **dictionary**.

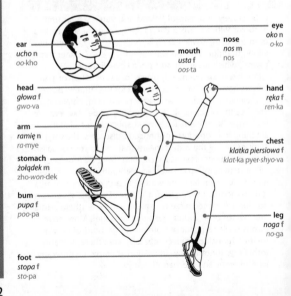

ear
ucho n
*oo·*kho

eye
oko n
*o·*ko

nose
nos m
nos

mouth
usta f
*oos·*ta

head
głowa f
*gwo·*va

hand
ręka f
*ren·*ka

arm
ramię n
*ra·*mye

chest
klatka piersiowa f
*klat·*ka pyer·*shyo·*va

stomach
żołądek m
*zho·won·*dek

bum
pupa f
*poo·*pa

leg
noga f
*no·*ga

foot
stopa f
*sto·*pa

pharmacist

I need something for (a headache).

Chciałem/am coś na
(ból głowy). m/f

khchow·em/am tsosh na
(bool gwo·vi)

Do I need a prescription for (antihistamines)?

Czy potrzebuję receptę
na (środek
antyhistaminowy)?

chi po·tshe·boo·ye re·tsep·te
na (shro·dek
an·ti·hees·ta·mee·no·vi)

I have a prescription.

Mam receptę.

mam re·tsep·te

How many times a day?

Ile razy dziennie?

ee·le ra·zi jye·nye

Will it make me drowsy?

Czy będę po tym
ospały/a? m/f

chi ben·de po tim
os·pa·wi/wa

---

the pharmacist may say ...

Dwa/Trzy razy dziennie. dva/tshi ra·zi jye·nye	**Twice/Three times a day.**
Przed jedzeniem. pshet ye·dze·nyem	**Before eating.**
W czasie jedzenia. v cha·shye ye·dze·nya	**With food.**
Po jedzeniu. po ye·dze·nyoo	**After eating.**
Czy pan/pani zażywał/zażywała to już kiedyś? m/f chi pan/pa·nee za·zhi·vow/ za·zhi·va·wa to yoosh kye·dish	**Have you taken this before?**
Musi pan/pani dokończyć tę serię. moo·shee pan/pa·nee do·kon'·chich te ser·ye	**You must complete the course.**

health

203

antiseptic	środki	shrod·kee
	odkażające pl	od·ka·zha·yon·tse
contraceptives	środki	shrod·kee
	antykoncepcyjne pl	an·ti·kon·tsep·tsiy·ne
painkillers	środki	shrod·kee
	przeciwbólowe pl	pshe·cheef·boo·lo·ve
rehydration salts	sóle fizjologiczne pl	so·le fee·zyo·lo·geech·ne

For more pharmaceutical items, see the **dictionary**.

dentist

dentysta

I have a …	Mam …	mam …
broken tooth	złamany ząb	zwa·ma·ni zomb
cavity	dziurę w zębie	jyoo·re v zem·bye
toothache	ból zęba	bool zem·ba

I need (a/an) …	Chciałem/am… m/f	khchow·em/am…
anaesthetic	znieczulenie	znye·choo·le·nye
filling	plombę	plom·be

I've lost a filling.
Wypadła mi plomba. vi·pad·wa mee plom·ba

My dentures are broken.
Moja proteza zębowa mo·ya pro·te·za zem·bo·va
jest pęknięta. yest penk·nyen·ta

My gums hurt.
Bolą mnie dziąsła. bo·lom mnye jyon·swa

I don't want it extracted.
Nie chcę go wyrywać. nye khtse go vi·ri·vach

---

the dentist may say …

Proszę otworzyć szeroko.
pro·she ot·vo·zhich she·ro·ko **Open wide.**

Proszę popłukać.
pro·she pop·woo·kach **Rinse.**

Polish nouns in the **dictionary** have their gender indicated by ⓜ (masculine), ⓕ (feminine) or ⓝ (neuter). If it's a plural noun, you'll also see pl, but you won't see a gender marker as all plural nouns in this dictionary belong to the general (genderless) plural category (refer to the **a–z phrasebuilder** for more on this). When a word that could be either a noun or a verb has no gender indicated, it's a verb. For added clarity, certain words are marked as adjectives a or verbs v. Adjectives, however, are given in the masculine form only. Both nouns and adjectives are provided in the nominative case only. For information on case and gender, refer to the **a–z phrasebuilder**.

A

aboard *na pokładzie* na po·*kwa*·jye
abortion *aborcja* ⓕ a·*bor*·tsya
abroad *za granicą* za gra·*nee*·tsom
accident *wypadek* ⓜ vi·*pa*·dek
accommodation *nocleg* ⓜ *nots*·leg
account (bill) *konto* ⓝ *kon*·to
acid (drug) *LSD* ⓜ el·es·de
acid rain *kwaśny deszcz* ⓜ *kfash*·ni deshch
activist *aktywista* ⓜ ak·ti·*vees*·ta
actor *aktor/aktorka* ⓜ/ⓕ *ak*·tor/ak·*tor*·ka
adaptor *zasilacz* ⓜ za·*shee*·lach
addiction *nałóg* ⓜ *na*·woog
address *adres* ⓜ *a*·dres
administration *administracja* ⓕ a·dmee·nee·*stra*·tsya
admission (price) *wstęp* ⓜ fstemp
admit (let in) v *wpuszczać* fpoosh·chach
adult *dorosły* ⓜ do·*ro*·swi
advertisement *reklama* ⓕ re·*kla*·ma
advice *rada* ⓕ *ra*·da
aeroplane *samolot* ⓜ sa·*mo*·lot
Africa *Afryka* ⓕ a·*fri*·ka
after *po* · *za* po · za
afternoon *popołudnie* ⓝ po·po·*wood*·nye
aftershave *woda po goleniu* ⓕ *vo*·da po go·*le*·nyoo
again *znowu* zno·voo
age *wiek* ⓜ vyek
(three days) ago *(trzy dni) temu* (tshi dnee) *te*·moo
agree *zgodzić się* zgo·jeech shye
agriculture *rolnictwo* ⓝ rol·*neetst*·fo

agritourist farm *gospodarstwo agroturystyczne* ⓝ gos·po·*darst*·fo a·gro·too·ris·*tich*·ne
AIDS *AIDS* ⓜ ayds
air *powietrze* ⓝ po·*vye*·tshe
air conditioning *klimatyzacja* ⓕ klee·ma·ti·*za*·tsya
airline *linia lotnicza* ⓕ *lee*·nya lot·*nee*·cha
airmail *poczta lotnicza* ⓕ *poch*·ta lot·*nee*·cha
airplane *samolot* ⓜ sa·*mo*·lot
airport *lotnisko* ⓝ lot·*nees*·ko
airport tax *opłata lotniskowa* ⓕ o·*pwa*·ta lot·nees·*ko*·va
aisle (on plane) *przejście (w samolocie)* ⓝ *psheysh*·chye (v sa·mo·*lo*·chye)
alarm clock *budzik* ⓜ *boo*·jeek
alcohol *alkohol* ⓜ al·*ko*·khol
allergy *alergia* ⓕ a·*ler*·gya
almond *migdał* ⓜ *meeg*·dow
almost *prawie* *pra*·vye
alone *samotny* sa·*mot*·ni
already *już* yoosh
altar *ołtarz* ⓜ *ow*·tazh
altitude *wysokość* ⓕ vi·*so*·koshch
always *zawsze* *zaf*·she
ambassador *ambasador* ⓜ am·ba·*sa*·dor
amber *bursztyn* ⓜ *boorsh*·tin
ambulance *karetka pogotowia* ⓕ ka·*ret*·ka po·go·*to*·vya
anaemia *anemia* ⓕ a·*ne*·mya
anarchist *anarchista* ⓜ a·nar·*khees*·ta
ancient *starożytny* sta·ro·*zhit*·ni
and *i* ee
angry *zły* zwi

animal *zwierzę* ⓝ *zvye*-zhe
ankle *kostka* ⓕ *kos*-tka
another (a different one) *inny ee*-ni
another (one more) *jeszcze jeden*
  yesh-che *ye*-den
answer n *odpowiedź* ⓕ od-*po*-vyej
answer *odpowiadać* od-po-*vya*-dach
ant *mrówka* ⓕ *mroof*-ka
antibiotics *antybiotyki* pl an-ti-byo-*ti*-kee
antique *antyk* ⓜ *an*-tik
antiseptic *środek odkażający* ⓜ
  shro-dek od-ka-zha-*yon*-tsi
any (some) *jakiś ya*-keesh
any (whichever) *dowolny* do-*vol*-ni
apartment *mieszkanie* ⓝ myesh-*ka*-nye
apple *jabłko* ⓝ *yabw*-ko
appointment *spotkanie* ⓝ spot-*ka*-nye
apricot *morela* ⓕ mo-*re*-la
April *kwiecień* ⓜ *kfye*-chen´
Aquarius *Wodnik* ⓜ *vod*-neek
architect *architekt* ⓜ ar-*khee*-tekt
architecture *architektura* ⓕ
  ar-khee-tek-*too*-ra
Aries *Baran* ⓜ *ba*-ran
arm (body) *ręka* ⓕ *ren*-ka
arrest *aresztować* a-resh-to-*vach*
arrivals (general) *przyjazdy* pl pshi-*yaz*-di
arrivals (plane) *przyloty* pl pshi-*lo*-ti
arrive *przyjechać* pshi-*ye*-khach
art *sztuka* ⓕ *shtoo*-ka
art gallery *galeria sztuki* ⓕ
  ga-*ler*-ya *shtoo*-kee
artist *artysta/artystka* ⓜ/ⓕ
  ar-*tis*-ta/ar-*tis*-tka
Art nouveau *sztuka secesyjna* ⓕ
  shtoo-ka se-tse-*siy*-na
ashtray *popielniczka* ⓕ po-pyel-*neech*-ka
Asia *Azja* ⓕ *az*-ya
ask (a question) *pytać pi*-tach
ask (for something) *prosić* pro-*sheech*
aspirin *aspiryna* ⓕ as-pee-*ri*-na
asthma *astma* ⓕ *ast*-ma
at *przy* · w pshi · v
athletics *lekkoatletyka* ⓕ lek-ko-at-le-*ti*-ka
August *sierpień* ⓜ *shyer*-pyen´
aunt *ciotka* ⓕ *chyot*-ka
Australia *Australia* ⓕ ows-*tra*-lya
automated teller machine (ATM)
  bankomat ⓜ ban-*ko*-mat
autumn *jesień* ⓕ *ye*-shyen´
avenue *aleja* ⓕ a-*le*-ya
avocado *awokado* ⓝ a-vo-*ka*-do
awful *okropny* o-*krop*-ni

B

B&W (film) *panchromatyczny*
  pan-khro-ma-*tich*-ni
baby *niemowlę* ⓝ nye-*mov*-le
baby food *odżywka dla niemowląt* ⓕ
  od-*zhif*-ka dla nye-*mov*-lont
baby powder *zasypka dla niemowląt* ⓕ
  za-*sip*-ka dla nye-*mov*-lont
babysitter *opiekunka do dziecka* ⓕ
  o-pye-*koon*-ka do *jye*-tska
back (body) *plecy* pl *ple*-tsi
back (position) *tył* ⓜ tiw
backpack *plecak* ⓜ *ple*-tsak
bacon *boczek* ⓜ *bo*-chek
bad *zły* zwi
bag *torba* ⓕ *tor*-ba
baggage *bagaż* ⓜ *ba*-gash
baggage allowance *dopuszczalna ilość*
  bagażu ⓕ do-poosh-*chal*-na ee-loshch
  ba-*ga*-zhoo
baggage claim *odbiór bagażu* ⓜ
  od-byoor ba-*ga*-zhoo
bakery *piekarnia* ⓕ pye-*kar*-nya
balance (account) *stan konta* ⓜ
  stan *kon*-ta
balcony *balkon* ⓜ *bal*-kon
ball (sport) *piłka* ⓕ *peew*-ka
ballet *balet* ⓜ *ba*-let
Baltic Sea *Morze Bałtyckie* ⓝ
  mo-zhe bow-*tits*-kye
banana *banan* ⓜ *ba*-nan
band (music) *zespół* ⓜ *zes*-poow
bandage *bandaż* ⓜ *ban*-dash
Band-Aid *plaster* ⓜ *plas*-ter
bank (money) *bank* ⓜ bank
bank account *konto bankowe* ⓝ
  kon-to ban-*ko*-ve
banknote *banknot* ⓜ *bank*-not
baptism *chrzest* ⓜ khshest
bar *bar* ⓜ bar
barber *fryzjer* ⓜ *friz*-yer
baseball *baseball* ⓜ *beys*-bol
basketball *koszykówka* ⓕ ko-shi-*koof*-ka
bath *kąpiel* ⓕ *kom*-pyel
bathing suit *strój kąpielowy* ⓜ
  strooy kom-pye-*lo*-vi
bathroom *łazienka* ⓕ wa-*zhyen*-ka
battery (general) *bateria* ⓕ ba-*te*-rya
battery (car) *akumulator* ⓜ
  a-koo-moo-*la*-tor
be *być* bich
beach *plaża* ⓕ *pla*-zha

beach volleyball *siatkówka plażowa* ①
shyat·koof·ka pla·zho·va
bean *fasola* ① fa·so·la
beautician *kosmetyczka* ① kos·me·tich·ka
beautiful *piękny* pyenk·ni
beauty salon *salon kosmetyczny* ⓜ
sa·lon kos·me·tich·ni
because *ponieważ* po·nye·vash
bed *łóżko* ⓝ woozh·ko
bed linen *pościel* ① posh·chyel
bedroom *sypialnia* ① si·pyal·nya
bee *pszczoła* ① pshcho·wa
beef *wołowina* ① vo·wo·vee·na
beer *piwo* ⓝ pee·vo
before *przed* pshet
beggar *żebrak/żebraczka* ⓜ/①
zhe·brak/zhe·brach·ka
behind *za* za
Belarus *Białoruś* ① bya·wo·roosh
Belgium *Belgia* ① bel·gya
Berlin *Berlin* ⓜ ber·leen
beside *obok* o·bok
best *najlepszy* nai·lep·shi
bet *zakład* ⓜ za·kwad
bet *zakładać się* za·kwa·dach shye
better *lepszy* lep·shi
between *między* myen·dzi
Bible *biblia* ① bee·blya
bicycle *rower* ⓜ ro·ver
big *duży* doo·zhi
bigger *większy* vyenk·shi
biggest *największy* nai·vyenk·shi
bike *rower* ⓜ ro·ver
bike chain *łańcuch rowerowy* ⓜ
wan'·tsookh ro·ve·ro·vi
bike path *ścieżka rowerowa* ①
shchyezh·ka ro·ve·ro·va
bill (restaurant) *rachunek* ⓜ ra·khoo·nek
binoculars *lornetka* ① lor·net·ka
bird *ptak* ⓜ ptak
birth certificate *akt urodzenia* ⓝ
akt oo·ro·je·nya
birthday *urodziny* pl oo·ro·jee·ni
biscuit *herbatnik* ⓜ her·bat·neek
bison *żubr* ⓜ zhoobr
bite (dog etc) n *ugryzienie* ⓝ
oo·gri·zhye·nye
bite (insect) n *ukąszenie* ⓝ
oo·kon·she·nye
bitter *gorzki* gosh·kee
black *czarny* char·ni
bladder *pęcherz* ⓜ pen·khesh
blanket *koc* ⓜ kots

blind a *ślepy* shle·pi
blister *odcisk* ⓜ od·cheesk
blood *krew* ① kref
blood group *grupa krwi* ① groo·pa krfee
blue *niebieski* nye·byes·kee
board (plane, ship) v *wchodzić na
pokład* ⓜ fkho·jeech na po·kwad
boat *łódź* ① wooj
body *ciało* ⓝ chya·wo
boiled *gotowany* go·to·va·ni
bone *kość* ① koshch
book *książka* ① ksyonzh·ka
book (make a booking) *rezerwować*
re·zer·vo·vach
booked out *wyprzedany* vi·pshe·da·ni
book shop *księgarnia* ① kshyen·gar·nya
boots (footwear) *buty* pl boo·ti
border *granica* ① gra·nee·tsa
bored *znudzony* znoo·dzo·ni
boring *nudny* noo·dni
borrow *pożyczać* po·zhi·chach
bottle *butelka* ① boo·tel·ka
bottle opener *otwieracz do butelek* ⓜ
ot·fye·rach do boo·te·lek
bottle shop *sklep monopolowy* ⓜ
sklep mo·no·po·lo·vi
bottom (body) *tyłek* ⓜ ti·wek
bottom (position) *dno* ⓝ dno
bowl (plate) *miska* ① mee·ska
box *pudełko* ⓝ poo·dew·ko
boy *chłopiec* ⓜ khwo·pyets
boyfriend *chłopak* ⓜ khwo·pak
bra *biustonosz* ⓜ byoo·sto·nosh
brakes *hamulce* pl ha·mool·tse
brandy *winiak* ⓜ vee·nyak
Bratislava *Bratysława* ① bra·ti·swa·va
brave *odważny* ⓜ od·vazh·ni
bread *chleb* ⓜ khlep
break *złamać* zwa·mach
break down *psuć się* psooch shye
breakfast *śniadanie* ⓝ shnya·da·nye
breast (body) *pierś* ① pyersh
breathe *oddychać* ot·di·khach
bribe *łapówka* ① wa·poof·ka
bribe *przekupywać* pshe·koo·pi·vach
bridge (structure) *most* ⓜ most
briefcase *teczka* ① tech·ka
bring *przynosić* pshi·no·sheech
broccoli *brokuł* ⓜ bro·koow
brochure *broszura* ① bro·shoo·ra
broken *połamany* po·wa·ma·ni
broken down *zepsuty* zep·soo·ti
brother *brat* ⓜ brat

brown *brązowy* bron·zo·vi
bruise *siniak* ① shee·nyak
brush *szczotka* ① shchot·ka
bucket *wiadro* ① vya·dro
Buddhist *buddysta* ⓜ bood·*dis*·ta
budget *budżet* ⓜ boo·jet
buffet *bufet* ⓜ boo·fet
bug *pluskwa* ① ploosk·fa
build *budować* boo·do·vach
builder *budowniczy* ⓜ boo·dov·*nee*·chi
building *budynek* ⓜ boo·di·nek
burn *poparzenie* ⓝ po·pa·*zhe*·nye
burnt *spalony* spa·lo·ni
bus (city) *autobus* ⓜ ow·to·boos
bus (intercity) *autokar* ⓜ ow·to·kar
business *firma* ⓜ feer·ma
business class *klasa biznesowa* ①
  kla·sa beez·ne·so·va
businessperson *biznesmen* ⓜ
  beez·nes·men
business trip *podróż służbowa* ①
  pod·roosh swoozh·bo·va
busker *grajek uliczny* ⓜ
  gra·yek oo·leech·ni
bus station *dworzec autobusowy* ⓜ
  dvo·zhets ow·to·boo·so·vi
bus stop *przystanek* ⓜ pshi·*sta*·nek
busy (of person) *zajęty* za·yen·ti
busy (street, etc) *ruchliwy* rookh·*lee*·vi
but *ale* a·le
butcher *rzeźnik* ⓜ zhezh·neek
butcher's shop *sklep mięsny* ⓜ
  sklep myens·ni
butter *masło* ⓝ mas·wo
butterfly *motyl* ⓜ mo·til
button *guzik* ⓜ goo·zheek
buy *kupować* koo·po·vach

C

cabbage *kapusta* ① ka·*poos*·ta
café *kawiarnia* ① ka·vyar·nya
cafeteria *stołówka* ① sto·*woof*·ka
cake *ciasto* ⓝ chyas·to
cake shop *cukiernia* ① tsoo·*kyer*·nya
calculator *kalkulator* ⓜ kal·koo·*la*·tor
calendar *kalendarz* ⓜ ka·*len*·dash
call (phone) v *dzwonić* dzvo·neech
camera *aparat* ⓜ a·pa·rat
camera shop *sklep fotograficzny* ⓜ
  sklep fo·to·gra·*feech*·ni
camp *obozować* o·bo·zo·vach

camping ground *kamping* ⓜ kam·peeng
camping store *sklep turystyczno-*
  sportowy ⓜ sklep too·ris·*tich*·no-
  spor·to·vi
can (have permission) *móc* moots
can (know how to) *umieć* oo·myech
can (manage to do something) *potrafić*
  po·*tra*·feech
Canada *Kanada* ① ka·*na*·da
cancel *unieważniać* oo·nye·*vazh*·nyach
cancer *rak* ⓜ rak
Cancer *Rak* ⓜ rak
candle *świeca* ① shvye·tsa
candy *cukierek* ⓜ tsoo·*kye*·rek
canoeing *kajakarstwo* ⓝ ka·ya·*karst*·fo
can opener *otwieracz do konserw* ⓜ
  ot·*fye*·rach do kon·serf
Capricorn *Koziorożec* ⓜ ko·zhyo·ro·zhets
capsicum *papryka* ① pa·*pri*·ka
car *samochód* ⓜ sa·mo·khoot
caravan *przyczepa kampingowa* ①
  pshi·*che*·pa kam·peen·go·va
cards (playing) *karty kar*·ti
car hire *wypożyczalnia samochodów* ①
  vi·po·zhi·*chal*·nya sa·mo·kho·doof
car park *parking* ⓜ par·keeng
Carpathian mountains *Karpaty* kar·pa·ti
car registration *rejestrowanie*
  samochodu ⓝ re·ye·stro·*va*·nye
  sa·mo·kho·doo
carrot *marchewka* ① mar·*khef*·ka
carry *nosić no*·sheech
carton *karton* ⓜ kar·ton
cash *gotówka* ① go·*toof*·ka
cash (a cheque) *zrealizować czek*
  zre·a·lee·zo·vach chek
cashier *kasjer/kasjerka* ⓜ/①
  kas·yer/kas·*yer*·ka
cash register *kasa fiskalna* ①
  ka·sa fees·*kal*·na
casino *kasyno* ① ka·*si*·no
cassette *kaseta* ① ka·se·ta
castle *zamek* ⓜ za·mek
cat *kot* ⓜ kot
cathedral *katedra* ① ka·te·dra
Catholic *katolik* ⓜ ka·to·leek
cauliflower *kalafior* ⓜ ka·*la*·fyor
cave *jaskinia* ① yas·kee·nya
CD *CD* ⓝ tse·de
cell phone *telefon komórkowy* ⓜ
  te·*le*·fon ko·moor·ko·vi
cemetery *cmentarz* ⓜ tsmen·tash

cent *cent* ⓜ tsent
centimetre *centymetr* ⓜ tsen·*ti*·metr
centre *środek* ⓜ *shro*·dek
ceramics *ceramika* ⓕ tse·ra·*mee*·ka
cereal (breakfast) *płatki śniadaniowe* pl *pwat*·kee shnya·da·*nyo*·ve
certificate (education) *dyplom* ⓜ *dip*·lom
certificate (general) *zaświadczenie* ⓝ za·shvyad·*che*·nye
chain *łańcuch* ⓜ *wan'*·tsookh
chair *krzesło* ⓝ *kshes*·wo
chairlift (skiing) *wyciąg krzesełkowy* ⓜ *vi*·chyonk kshe·sew·*ko*·vi
champagne *szampan* ⓜ *sham*·pan
chance (opportunity) *szansa* ⓕ *shan*·sa
change *zmiana* ⓕ *zmya*·na
change (coins) *reszta* ⓕ *resh*·ta
change (money) *rozmieniać* roz·*mye*·nyach
changing room *szatnia* ⓕ *shat*·nya
charming *uroczy* oo·*ro*·chi
chat up *pogadać* po·*ga*·dach
cheap *tani* *ta*·nee
cheat *oszust* ⓜ *o*·shoost
check (banking) *czek* ⓜ chek
check (bill) *sprawdzenie* ⓝ sprav·*dze*·nye
check *sprawdzać* sprav·*dzach*
check-in (desk) *zameldowanie* ⓝ za·mel·do·*va*·nye
cheese *ser* ⓜ ser
chef *szef kuchni* ⓜ shef *kookh*·nee
chemist (pharmacist) *farmaceuta* ⓜ far·ma·*tsew*·ta
chemist (pharmacy) *apteka* ⓕ ap·*te*·ka
cheque (banking) *czek* ⓜ chek
cherry *czereśnia* ⓕ che·*resh*·nya
chess *szachy* pl *sha*·khi
chessboard *szachownica* ⓕ sha·khov·*nee*·tsa
chest (body) *klatka piersiowa* ⓕ *klat*·ka pyer·*shyo*·va
chestnut *kasztanowiec* ⓜ kash·ta·*no*·vyets
chewing gum *guma do żucia* ⓕ *goo*·ma do *zhoo*·chya
chicken *kurczak* ⓜ *koor*·chak
child *dziecko* ⓝ *jye*·tsko
child-minding service *usługi opieki nad dzieckiem* pl oos·*woo*·gee o·*pye*·kee nad *jyets*·kyem
children *dzieci* pl *jye*·chee

child seat *siedzenie dla dziecka* ⓝ shye·*dze*·nye dla *jyets*·ka
China *Chiny* pl *khee*·ni
chiropractor *kręgarz* ⓜ *kren*·gash
chocolate *czekolada* ⓕ che·ko·*la*·da
choose *wybierać* vi·*bye*·rach
chopsticks *pałeczki* pa·*wech*·kee
Christian *chrześcijanin* ⓜ khshesh·chee·*ya*·neen
Christian name *imię* ⓝ *ee*·mye
Christmas *Boże Narodzenie* ⓝ *bo*·zhe na·ro·*dze*·nye
Christmas Day *Dzień Bożego Narodzenia* ⓝ jyen' bo·*zhe*·go na·ro·*dze*·nya
Christmas Eve *Wigilia* ⓕ vee·*gee*·lya
church *kościół* ⓜ *kosh*·chyoow
cider *napój jabłkowy* ⓜ *na*·pooy yabw·*ko*·vi
cigar *cygaro* ⓝ tsi·*ga*·ro
cigarette *papieros* ⓜ pa·*pye*·ros
cigarette lighter *zapalniczka* ⓕ za·pal·*neech*·ka
cinema *kino* ⓝ *kee*·no
circus *cyrk* ⓜ tsirk
citizenship *obywatelstwo* ⓝ o·bi·va·*telst*·fo
city *miasto* ⓝ *myas*·to
city centre *centrum* ⓝ *tsen*·troom
classical *klasyczny* ⓜ kla·*sich*·ni
clean a *czysty* *chi*·sti
clean v *sprzątać* spshon·*tach*
cleaning *sprzątanie* ⓝ spshon·*ta*·nye
client *klient* ⓜ *klee*·yent
cliff *urwisko* ⓝ oor·*vee*·sko
climb *wspinać się* vspee·*nach* shye
cloakroom *szatnia* ⓕ *sha*·tnya
clock *zegar* ⓜ *ze*·gar
close a *bliski* *blees*·kee
close v *zamykać* za·*mi*·kach
closed *zamknięty* zam·*knyen*·ti
clothing *ubranie* ⓝ oo·*bra*·nye
clothing store *sklep odzieżowy* ⓜ sklep o·jye·*zho*·vi
cloud *chmura* ⓕ *khmoo*·ra
clutch (car) *sprzęgło* ⓝ *spshen*·gwo
coach (bus) *autokar* ⓜ *ow*·to·kar
coach (trainer) *trener* ⓜ *tre*·ner
coach *trenować* tre·*no*·vach
coast *wybrzeże* ⓝ vi·*bzhe*·zhe
coat *płaszcz* ⓜ pwashch
cocaine *kokaina* ⓕ ko·ka·*ee*·na
cockroach *karaluch* ⓜ ka·ra·*lookh*

cocktail *koktajl* ⓜ *kok*·tail
cocoa *kakao* ⓝ ka·*ka*·o
coconut *kokos* ⓜ *ko*·kos
coffee *kawa* ⓕ *ka*·va
coins *monety* pl mo·*ne*·ti
cold (illness) *katar* ⓜ *ka*·tar
cold *zimno* ⓝ *zhee*·mno
cold *zimny* zheem·ni
(have a) cold *być przeziębionym*
  bich pshe·zhyem·*byo*·nim
colleague *współpracownik/*
  współpracowniczka ⓜ/ⓕ
  fspoow·pra·*tsov*·neek/
  fspoow·pra·*tsov*·neech·ka
collect call *rozmowa opłacona*
  przez odbierającego ⓕ roz·*mo*·va
  o·pwa·*tso*·na pshes od·bye·ra·*yon*·tse·go
college *uniwersytet* ⓜ oo·nee·ver·*si*·tet
colour *kolor* ⓜ *ko*·lor
comb *grzebień* ⓜ *gzhe*·byen'
come (by mechanised means)
  przyjść pshiyshch
come (on foot) *przychodzić* pshi·*kho*·jeech
comedy *komedia* ⓕ ko·*me*·dya
comfortable *wygodny* vi·*god*·ni
commission *prowizja* ⓕ pro·*vee*·zya
communion *komunia* ⓕ ko·*moo*·nya
communist *komunista* ⓜ ko·moo·*nees*·ta
company (firm) *firma* ⓕ *feer*·ma
compass *kompas* ⓜ *kom*·pas
complain *skarżyć się* skar·zhich shye
complaint *skarga* ⓕ *skar*·ga
complimentary (free) *bezpłatny*
  bes·*pwa*·tni
computer *komputer* ⓜ kom·*poo*·ter
computer game *gra komputerowa* ⓕ
  gra kom·poo·te·*ro*·va
concert *koncert* ⓜ *kon*·tsert
concussion *wstrząs mózgu* ⓜ
  vstshons *mooz*·goo
conditioner (hair) *odżywka*
  (do włosów) ⓕ od·*zhif*·ka (do *vwo*·soof)
condom *kondom* ⓜ *kon*·dom
conference (big) *konferencja* ⓕ
  kon·fe·*ren*·tsya
conference (small) *narada* ⓕ na·*ra*·da
confession (religious) *spowiedź* ⓕ
  spo·vyej
confirm (a booking) *potwierdzać*
  pot·*fyer*·dzach
conjunctivitis *zapalenie spojówek* ⓝ
  za·pa·*le*·nye spo·*yoo*·vek

connection (transport) *połączenie* ⓝ
  po·won·*che*·nye
conservative *konserwatywny*
  kon·ser·va·*tiv*·ni
constipation *zatwardzenie* ⓝ
  zat·far·*dze*·nye
consulate *konsulat* ⓜ kon·*soo*·lat
contact lenses *soczewki kontaktowe* pl
  so·*chef*·kee kon·tak·*to*·ve
contraceptives *środki antykoncepcyjne* pl
  shrod·kee an·ti·kon·tsep·*tsiy*·ne
contract *kontrakt* ⓜ *kon*·trakt
convenience store
  sklep wielobranżowy ⓜ
  sklep vye·lo·bran·*zho*·vi
convent *klasztor* ⓜ *klash*·tor
cook *kucharz* ⓜ *koo*·khash
cook *gotować* go·*to*·vach
cookie *herbatnik* ⓜ her·*ba*·tneek
cooking *gotowanie* ⓝ go·to·*va*·nye
cool (groovy) *fajny* fai·ni
cool (temperature) *chłodny* khwo·dni
corkscrew *korkociąg* ⓜ kor·ko·chyong
corn *kukurydza* ⓕ koo·koo·*ri*·dza
corner *róg* ⓜ roog
corrupt a *zepsuty* ⓐ ze·*psoo*·ti
corruption *korupcja* ⓕ ko·*roop*·tsya
cost *koszt* ⓜ kosht
cost *kosztować* ⓕ kosh·*to*·vach
cotton *bawełna* ⓕ ba·*vew*·na
cotton balls *waciki* pl va·*chee*·kee
cotton buds *pałeczki higieniczne* pl
  pa·*wech*·kee hee·gye·*neech*·ne
couchette *kuszetka* ⓕ koo·*shet*·ka
cough *kaszel* ⓜ *ka*·shel
cough *kaszleć* kash·lech
cough medicine *lekarstwo na kaszel* ⓝ
  le·*karst*·fo na *ka*·shel
count *liczyć* lee·chich
counter (at bar) *lada* ⓕ *la*·da
country *kraj* ⓜ krai
countryside *okolica* ⓕ o·ko·*lee*·tsa
coupon *kupon* ⓜ *koo*·pon
courgette *cukinia* ⓕ tsoo·*kee*·nya
court (legal) *sąd* ⓜ sond
court (tennis) *kort* ⓜ kort
couscous *kuskus* ⓜ *koos*·koos
cover charge *opłata za wejście do baru* ⓕ
  o·*pwa*·ta za *veysh*·chye do *ba*·roo
cow *krowa* ⓕ *kro*·va
cracker *krakers* ⓜ *kra*·kers
crafts *rękodzieła* ⓝ ren·ko·*jye*·wa
crash *wypadek* ⓜ vi·*pa*·dek
crazy *szalony* sha·*lo*·ni

cream (food) *śmietana* ① shmye-*ta*-na
cream (lotion) *krem* ⑩ krem
crèche *przedszkole* ⑪ pshet-*shko*-le
credit *kredyt* ⑩ *kre*-dit
credit card *karta kredytowa* ①
  kar-ta kre-di-*to*-va
cricket (sport) *krykiet* ⑩ *kri*-kyet
crop (riding) *bicz* ⑩ beech
cross (religious) *krzyż* ⑩ kshish
crowded *zatłoczony* za-two-*cho*-ni
crystal *kryształ* ⑩ *krish*-tow
cucumber *ogórek* ⑩ o-*goo*-rek
cup *filiżanka* ① fee-lee-*zhan*-ka
cupboard *szafka kuchenna* ①
  shaf-ka koo-*khe*-na
currency exchange *kantor* ⑩ *kan*-tor
current (electricity) *prąd* ⑩ pront
current affairs *sprawy bieżące* pl
  spra-vi bye-*zhon*-tse
curry *curry* ① *ka*-ri
custom *zwyczaj* ⑩ *zvi*-chai
customs *urząd celny* ⑩ oo-*zhont* *tsel*-ni
cut *skaleczenie* ⑪ ska-le-*che*-nye
cut *ciąć* chyonch
cutlery *sztućce* shtooch-tse
CV *życiorys* ⑩ zhi-*chyo*-ris
cycle (ride) v *jeździć na rowerze*
  yezh-jeech na ro-*ve*-zhe
cycling *jazda na rowerze* ①
  yaz-da na ro-*ve*-zhe
cyclist *rowerzysta* ⑩ ro-ve-*zhi*-sta
cystitis *zapalenie pęcherza* ⑪
  za-pa-*le*-nye pen-*khe*-zha
Czech (language) *(język) czeski*
  (yen-zik) *che*-skee
Czech Republic *Czechy* pl *che*-khi

D

dad *tata* ⑩ *ta*-ta
daily *codzienny* tso-*jye*-ni
dance *taniec* ⑩ *ta*-nyets
dance *tańczyć* tan'-chich
dancing *tańce* pl tan'-tse
dangerous *niebezpieczny*
  nye-bes-*pyech*-ni
dark *ciemny* chyem-ni
date (appointment) *randka* ① *rand*-ka
date (day) *data* ① *da*-ta
date (fruit) *daktyl* ⑩ *dak*-til
date (go out with) *chodzić (z kimś)*
  kho-jeech (z keemsh)

date of birth *data urodzenia* ①
  da-ta oo-ro-*dze*-nya
daughter *córka* ① *tsoor*-ka
dawn *świt* ⑩ shveet
day *dzień* ⑩ jyen´
day after tomorrow *pojutrze* ⑪
  po-*yoo*-tshe
day before yesterday *przedwczoraj* ⑪
  pshet-*fcho*-rai
dead *martwy* *mart*-fi
deaf *głuchy* *gwoo*-khi
deal (cards) *rozdawać* roz-*da*-vach
December *grudzień* ⑩ groo-*jyen´*
decide *decydować* de-tsi-*do*-vach
deep (water) *głęboki* gwem-*bo*-kee
deforestation *ogołocenie z lasów* ⑪
  o-go-wo-*tse*-nye z la-*soof*
degrees (temperature) *stopnie* pl
  sto-pnye
delay *opóźnienie* ⑪ o-poozh-*nye*-nye
delicatessen *delikatesy* pl de-lee-ka-*te*-si
deliver *dostarczyć* dos-*tar*-chich
democracy *demokracja* ① de-mo-*kra*-tsya
demonstration (rally) *demonstracja* ①
  de-mon-*stra*-tsya
Denmark *Dania* ① *da*-nya
dental dam (safe sex) *lateksowe gumy*
  do koferdamu pl la-tek-*so*-ve *goo*-mi do
  ko-fer-*da*-moo
dental floss *nić dentystyczna* ①
  neech den-tis-*ti*-chna
dentist *dentysta* ⑩ den-*tis*-ta
deodorant *dezodorant* ⑩ de-zo-*do*-rant
depart *odjeżdżać* od-*yezh*-jach
department store *dom towarowy* ⑩
  dom to-va-*ro*-vi
departure (by air) *odlot* ⑩ *od*-lot
departure (by land) *odjazd* ⑩ *od*-yazd
departure gate *brama odlotów* ①
  bra-ma od-*lo*-toof
deposit *depozyt* ⑩ de-*po*-zit
derailleur *przerzutka* ① pshe-*zhoot*-ka
descendant *potomek* ⑩ po-*to*-mek
design *projekt* ⑩ *pro*-yekt
dessert *deser* ⑩ *de*-ser
destination *miejsce przeznaczenia* ⑪
  myeys-tse pshez-na-*che*-nya
details *detale* pl de-*ta*-le
diabetes *cukrzyca* ① tsook-*shi*-tsa
diaper *pieluszka* ① pye-*loosh*-ka
diaphragm (contraceptive)
  spirala antykoncepcyjna ①
  spee-*ra*-la an-ti-kon-tsep-*tsiy*-na

diarrhoea *rozwolnienie* ⓝ roz-vol-*nye*-nye
diary *notatnik* ⓜ no-*tat*-neek
dice *kostki do gry* pl *kos*-tkee do gri
dictionary *słownik* ⓜ *swov*-neek
die *umierać* oo-*mye*-rach
diet *dieta* ① *dye*-ta
different *różny* roozh-ni
difficult *trudny* trood-ni
digital *cyfrowy* tsi-*fro*-vi
dining car *wagon restauracyjny* ⓜ *va*-gon res-tow-ra-*tsiy*-ni
dinner *kolacja* ① ko-*la*-tsya
direct *bezpośredni* bes-po-*shred*-nee
direct-dial *rozmowa bezpośrednia* ① roz-*mo*-va bes-po-*shred*-nya
direction *kierunek* ⓜ kye-*roo*-nek
director *dyrektor* ⓜ di-*re*-ktor
dirty *brudny* brood-ni
disabled *niepełnosprawny* nye-pew-no-*sprav*-ni
disco *dyskoteka* ① dis-ko-*te*-ka
discount *zniżka* ① zneesh-ka
discrimination *dyskryminacja* ① dis-kree-mee-*na*-tsya
disease *choroba* ① kho-*ro*-ba
dish (food) *potrawa* ⓝ po-*tra*-va
dish (plate) *talerz* ⓜ *ta*-lesh
disk (CD-ROM) *dysk kompaktowy* ⓜ disk kom-pak-*to*-vi
disk (floppy) *dyskietka* ① dis-*kyet*-ka
diving *nurkowanie* ⓝ noor-ko-*va*-nye
diving equipment *sprzęt do nurkowania* ⓜ spshent do noor-ko-*va*-nya
divorced *rozwiedziony* roz-vye-*jyo*-ni
dizzy *zawrotny* za-*vrot*-ni
do *robić* ro-beech
doctor *lekarz* ⓜ *le*-kash
dog *pies* ⓜ pyes
dole *zasiłek* ⓜ za-*shee*-wek
doll *lalka* ① *lal*-ka
dollar *dolar* ⓜ *do*-lar
door *drzwi* jvee
dope (drugs) *narkotyki* nar-ko-*ti*-kee
double *podwójny* pod-*vooy*-ni
double bed *łóżko małżeńskie* ⓝ *woozh*-ko mow-*zhen'*-skye
double room *pokój dwuosobowy* ⓜ *po*-kooy dvoo-o-so-*bo*-vi
down *na dół* ⓜ na doow
downhill *zjazd* ⓜ zyazd
dozen *tuzin* ⓜ *too*-zheen
drama *dramat* ⓜ *dra*-mat

dream *sen* ⓜ sen
dress *sukienka* ① soo-*kyen*-ka
dried *suszony* soo-*sho*-ni
dried fruit *suszony owoc* ⓜ soo-*sho*-ni *o*-vots
drink *napój* ⓜ na-pooy
drink *pić* peech
drink (alcoholic) *drink* ⓜ dreenk
drive *kierować* kye-ro-vach
drivers licence *prawo jazdy* ⓝ *pra*-vo yaz-di
drug (illicit) *narkotyk* ⓜ nar-ko-tik
drug (medicinal) *lek* ⓜ lek
drug dealer *handlarz narkotyków* ⓜ *hand*-lash nar-ko-*ti*-koof
drugs (illicit) *narkotyki* nar-ko-*ti*-kee
drug trafficking *przemyt narkotyków* ⓜ pshe-mit nar-ko-*ti*-koof
drug user *narkoman* ⓜ nar-*ko*-man
drum *bęben* ⓜ *bem*-ben
drums (kit) *perkusja* ① per-*koo*-sya
drunk *pijany* pee-*ya*-ni
dry *suchy* soo-khi
dry (clothes) *suszyć* soo-shich
dry (oneself) *wycierać* vi-*chye*-rach
duck *kaczka* ① *kach*-ka
dummy (pacifier) *smoczek* ⓜ *smo*-chek
duty-free *bezcłowy* bes-*tswo*-vi
DVD *DVD* ⓜ dee-*vee*-dee

E

each *każdy* kazh-di
ear *ucho* ⓝ oo-kho
early *wcześnie* vchesh-nye
earn *zarabiać* za-ra-byach
earplugs *zatyczki do uszu* pl za-*tich*-kee do oo-shoo
earrings *kolczyki* pl kol-*chi*-kee
earth *ziemia* ① *zhye*-mya
earthquake *trzęsienie ziemi* ⓝ tshen-*shye*-nye zhye-mee
east *wschód* ⓜ vskhood
Easter *Wielkanoc* ① vyel-*ka*-nots
easy *łatwy* ① *wa*-tfi
eat *jeść* yeshch
economy class *klasa oszczędnościowa* ① *kla*-sa osh-chend-nosh-*chyo*-va
ecstasy (drug) *ekstaza* ① eks-*ta*-za
eczema *egzema* ① eg-*ze*-ma
editor *redaktor* ⓜ re-*dak*-tor
education *oświata* ① osh-*vya*-ta
egg *jajko* ⓝ *yai*-ko

election *wybory* pl vi-*bo*-ri
electrician *elektryk* ⓜ e-*lek*-trik
electricity *elektryczność* ⓕ
e-lek-*trich*-noshch
elevator *winda* ⓕ *veen*-da
email *email* ⓜ e-*mail*
embarrassed *zakłopotany*
za-kwo-po-*ta*-ni
embassy *ambasada* ⓕ am-ba-*sa*-da
emergency *nagły przypadek* ⓜ
na-gwi pshi-*pa*-dek
employee *pracownik* ⓜ pra-*tsov*-neek
employer *pracodawca* ⓜ pra-tso-*daf*-tsa
empty *pusty* poos-ti
end *koniec* ⓜ *ko*-nyets
endangered species *zagrożone gatunki*
za-gro-*zho*-ne ga-*toon*-kee
engaged (phone) *zajęty* za-*yen*-ti
engaged (to be married)
zaręczony za-ren-*cho*-ni
engagement (to marry)
zaręczyny za-ren-*chi*-ni
engine *silnik* ⓜ *sheel*-neek
engineer *inżynier* ⓜ een-*zhi*-nyer
engineering *inżynieria* ⓕ een-zhi-*nyer*-ya
England *Anglia* ⓕ *an*-glya
English (language/nationality)
angielski an-*gyel*-skee
enjoy (oneself) *cieszyć się* chye-shich shye
enough *dosyć* do-*sich*
enter *wejść* veyshch
entertainment guide
informator rozrywkowy ⓜ
een-for-*ma*-tor roz-rif-*ko*-vi
entry *wejście* ⓝ *veysh*-chye
envelope *koperta* ⓕ ko-*per*-ta
environment *środowisko* ⓝ
shro-do-*vees*-ko
epilepsy *padaczka* ⓕ pa-*dach*-ka
equality *równość* ⓕ *roov*-noshch
equipment *sprzęt* ⓜ spshent
estate agency *agencja handlu*
nieruchomościami ⓕ a-*gen*-tsya
han-dloo nye-roo-kho-mosh-*chya*-mee
euro *euro* ⓝ *ew*-ro
Europe *Europa* ⓕ ew-*ro*-pa
European Union *Unia Europejska* ⓕ
oo-nya ew-ro-*pey*-ska
euthanasia *eutanazja* ⓕ ew-ta-*na*-zya
evening *wieczór* ⓜ *vye*-choor
every *każdy* kazh-di
everyone *każdy* kazh-di
everything *wszystko* fshist-ko

exactly *dokładnie* do-*kwa*-dnye
example *przykład* ⓜ *pshi*-kwad
excellent *doskonały* dos-ko-*na*-wi
excess baggage *nadbagaż* ⓜ
nad-*ba*-gash
exchange *wymiana* ⓕ vi-*mya*-na
exchange *wymieniać* vi-*mye*-nyach
exchange rate *kurs wymiany* ⓜ
koors vi-*mya*-ni
excluded *wyłączony* vi-won-*cho*-ni
exhaust (car) *wydech* ⓜ *vi*-dekh
exhibition *wystawa* ⓕ vis-*ta*-va
exit *wyjście* ⓝ *viysh*-chye
expensive *drogi* dro-gee
experience *doświadczenie* ⓝ
dosh-vyad-*che*-nye
exploitation *wyzysk* ⓜ *vi*-zisk
export permit *zezwolenie eksportowe* ⓝ
zez-vo-*le*-nye eks-por-*to*-ve
express *ekspresowy* eks-pre-*so*-vi
express mail *list ekspresowy* ⓜ
leest eks-pre-*so*-vi
extension (visa) *przedłużenie* ⓝ
pshe-dwoo-*zhe*-nye
eye *oko* ⓝ *o*-ko

F

fabric *materiał* ⓜ ma-*ter*-yow
face *twarz* ⓕ tfash
face cloth *myjka* ⓕ *miy*-ka
factory *fabryka* ⓕ fa-*bri*-ka
factory worker *robotnik* ⓜ ro-*bot*-neek
fall (autumn) *jesień* ⓕ ye-shyen'
fall (down) *upadać* oo-*pa*-dach
family *rodzina* ⓕ ro-*jee*-na
family name *nazwisko* ⓝ naz-*vees*-ko
famous *sławny* swav-ni
fan (machine) *wentylator* ⓜ ven-ti-*la*-tor
fan (sport, politics) *kibic* ⓜ *kee*-beets
far *daleki* da-*le*-kee
fare *taryfa* ⓕ ta-*ri*-fa
farm n *gospodarstwo rolne* ⓝ
gos-po-*darst*-fo rol-ne
farmer *rolnik* ⓜ *rol*-neek
fashion *moda* ⓕ *mo*-da
fast *szybki* shib-kee
fat *tłusty* twoos-ti
father *ojciec* ⓜ oy-chyets
father-in-law *teść* ⓜ teshch
faucet *kran* ⓜ kran
fault (someone's) *wina* ⓕ *vee*-na
faulty *wadliwy* vad-*lee*-vi

F

213

fax machine *faks* ⓜ faks
February *luty* ⓜ loo·ti
feed *karmić* kar·meech
feel (touch) *czuć* chooch
feeling (physical) *uczucie* ⓝ oo·choo·chye
feelings *uczucia* pl oo·choo·chya
female *żeński* zhen'·skee
fence *płot* ⓜ pwot
fencing (sport) *szermierka* ⓕ sher·myer·ka
ferry n *prom* ⓜ prom
festival *festiwal* ⓜ fes·tee·val
fever *gorączka* ⓕ go·ronch·ka
few *kilka* keel·ka
fiancé *narzeczony* ⓜ na·zhe·cho·ni
fiancée *narzeczona* ⓕ na·zhe·cho·na
fig *figa* ⓕ fee·ga
fight *walka* ⓕ val·ka
fill *wypełnić* vi·pew·neech
fillet *filet* ⓜ fee·let
film (camera/cinema) *film* ⓜ feelm
film speed *czułość filmu* ⓕ choo·woshch feel·moo
find *znaleźć* zna·lezhch
fine *ładny* wad·ni
fine n *kara* ⓕ ka·ra
finger *palec* ⓜ pa·lets
finish (end) *koniec* ⓜ ko·nyets
finish (in sport) *meta* ⓕ me·ta
finish *kończyć* kon'·chich
Finland *Finlandia* ⓕ feen·lan·dya
fire (general) *ogień* ⓜ o·gyen'
fire (inferno) *pożar* ⓜ po·zhar
firewood *drewno opałowe* ⓝ drev·no o·pa·wo·ve
first *pierwszy* pyerf·shi
first-aid kit *apteczka pierwszej pomocy* ⓕ ap·tech·ka pyerf·shey po·mo·tsi
first class *pierwsza klasa* ⓕ pyerf·sha kla·sa
first name *imię* ⓝ ee·mye
fish *ryba* ⓕ ri·ba
fishing *rybołówstwo* ⓝ ri·bo·woos·tfo
fishmonger *handlarz ryb* ⓜ han·dlash rib
flag *flaga* ⓕ fla·ga
flash (camera) *flesz* ⓜ flesh
flashlight *latarka* ⓕ la·tar·ka
flat (apartment) *mieszkanie* ⓝ myesh·ka·nye
flat *płaski* pwas·kee
flea *pchła* ⓕ pkhwa
flight *lot* ⓜ lot

flood *powódź* ⓕ po·vooj
floor *podłoga* ⓕ pod·wo·ga
floor (storey) *piętro* ⓝ pyen·tro
florist *kwiaciarnia* ⓕ kvya·chyar·nya
flour *mąka* ⓕ mon·ka
flower *kwiat* ⓜ kvyat
flu *grypa* ⓕ gri·pa
flute *flet* ⓜ flet
fly *mucha* ⓕ moo·kha
fly *latać* la·tach
foggy *mglisty* mglees·ti
follow *iść za* eeshch za
food *żywność* ⓕ zhiv·noshch
foot (body) *stopa* ⓕ sto·pa
football (soccer) *piłka nożna* ⓕ peew·ka nozh·na
footpath *ścieżka* ⓕ shchyesh·ka
foreign *zagraniczny* za·gra·nee·chni
forest *las* ⓜ las
forever *na zawsze* na zaf·she
forget *zapomnieć* za·pom·nyech
forgive *przebaczyć* pshe·ba·chich
fork *widelec* ⓜ vee·de·lets
fortnight *dwa tygodnie* dva ti·go·dnye
foul (soccer) n *faul* ⓜ fa·ool
foyer *foyer* ⓜ foo·a·ye
fragile *kruchy* ⓜ kroo·khi
France *Francja* ⓕ fran·tsya
free (available) *wolny* vol·ni
free (gratis) *bezpłatny* bes·pwat·ni
free (not bound) *wolny* vol·ni
freeze *zamrażać* za·mra·zhach
fresh *świeży* shfye·zhi
Friday *piątek* ⓜ pyon·tek
fridge *lodówka* ⓕ lo·doof·ka
fried *smażony* sma·zho·ni
friend *przyjaciel/przyjaciółka* ⓜ/ⓕ pshi·ya·chyel/pshi·ya·choow·ka
from *od* · z od · z
frost *mróz* ⓜ mrooz
frozen *mrożony* mro·zho·ni
fruit *owoc* ⓜ o·vots
fry *smażyć* sma·zhich
frying pan *patelnia* ⓕ pa·tel·nya
full *pełny* pew·ni
full-time *w pełnym wymiarze godzin* v pew·nim vi·mya·zhe go·jeen
fun *zabawa* ⓕ za·ba·va
(have) fun *mieć frajdę* myech frai·de
funeral *pogrzeb* ⓜ pog·zheb
funny *zabawny* za·bav·ni
furniture *meble* pl me·ble
future *przyszłość* ⓕ pshish·woshch

G

game *gra* ① gra
garage *garaż* ⓜ ga-razh
garbage *śmieci* pl shmye-chee
garbage can *pojemnik na śmieci* ⓜ
    po-yem-neek na shmye-chee
garden *ogród* ⓜ o-grood
gardener *ogrodnik* ⓜ o-grod-neek
gardening *ogrodnictwo* ⓝ
    o-grod-neetst-fo
garlic *czosnek* ⓜ chos-nek
garnet *granat* ⓜ gra-nat
gas (for cooking) *gaz* ⓜ gaz
gas (petrol) *benzyna* ① ben-zi-na
gastroenteritis
    choroba przewodu pokarmowego ①
    kho-ro-ba pshe-vo-doo po-kar-mo-ve-go
gate (airport, etc) *wejście* ⓝ veysch-chye
gauze *gaza* ① ga-za
gay (homosexual) *gej* gey
gearbox *skrzynia biegów* ①
    skshi-nya bye-goof
Gemini *Bliźnięta* pl bleezh-nyen-ta
Germany *Niemcy* pl nyem-tsi
get *dostać* dos-tach
get off (bus, train) *wysiadać* vi-shya-dach
gift *prezent* ⓜ pre-zent
gig *koncert* ⓜ kon-tsert
gin *dżin* ⓜ jeen
girl *dziewczyna* ① jyev-chi-na
girlfriend *dziewczyna* ① jyev-chi-na
give *dać* dach
given name *imię* ⓝ ee-mye
glandular fever *mononukleoza*
    zakaźna ① mo-no-noo-kle-o-za
    za-kazh-na
glass (drinking) *szklanka* ① shklan-ka
glasses (spectacles) *okulary* pl o-koo-la-ri
glassware *wyroby szklane* pl
    vi-ro-bi shkla-ne
gloves *rękawiczki* pl ren-ka-veech-kee
glue *klej* ⓜ kley
go (by mechanised means) *jechać*
    ye-khach
go (on foot) *iść* eeshch
goal (sport) *gol* ⓜ gol
goalkeeper *bramkarz* ⓜ bram-kash
goat *koza* ① ko-za
god (general) *bóg* ⓜ boog
goggles (skiing) *gogle* pl go-gle

goggles (swimming) *okulary do*
    pływania pl o-koo-la-ri do pwi-va-nya
gold *złoto* ⓝ zwo-to
golf ball *piłeczka golfowa* ①
    pee-wech-ka gol-fo-va
golf course *pole golfowe* ⓝ
    po-le gol-fo-ve
good *dobry* do-bri
goodbye *do widzenia* do vee-dze-nya
go out *wychodzić* vi-kho-jeech
go out with (date) *mieć randkę z*
    myech rand-ke z
government *rząd* ⓜ zhond
gram *gram* ⓜ gram
grandchild *wnuk/wnuczka* ⓜ/①
    vnook/vnooch-ka
grandfather *dziadek* ⓜ jya-dek
grandmother *babcia* ① bab-chya
grapes *winogrona* pl vee-no-gro-na
grass (lawn) *trawa* ① tra-va
grateful *wdzięczny* ⓜ vjyench-ni
grave *grób* ⓜ groob
great (fantastic) *wspaniały* vspa-nya-wi
green *zielony* zhye-lo-ni
greengrocer *sklep warzywny* ⓜ
    sklep va-zhiv-ni
grey *szary* sha-ri
grocery *sklep spożywczy* ⓜ
    sklep spo-zhiv-chi
groundnut *orzeszek ziemny* ⓜ
    o-zhe-shek zhyem-ni
grow *rosnąć* ros-nonch
guarantee *gwarancja* ① gva-ran-tsya
guess *zgadywać* zga-di-vach
guesthouse *pensjonat* ⓜ pen-syo-nat
guide (person) *przewodnik* ⓜ
    pshe-vod-neek
guidebook *przewodnik* ⓜ pshe-vod-neek
guide dog *pies przewodnik* ⓜ
    pyes pshe-vod-neek
guided tour *wycieczka z*
    przewodnikiem ① vi-chyech-ka z
    pshe-vod-nee-kyem
guilty *winny* vee-ni
guitar *gitara* ① gee-ta-ra
gum *guma* ① goo-ma
gun *pistolet* ⓜ pees-to-let
gym (place) *siłownia* ① shee-wov-nya
gymnastics *gimnastyka* ① geem-nas-ti-ka
gynaecologist *ginekolog* ⓜ gee-ne-ko-log

H

hair *włosy* pl vwo·si
hairbrush *szczotka do włosów* ①
  shchot·ka do vwo·soof
haircut *strzyżenie* ⑩ stshi·zhe·nye
hairdresser *fryzjer* ⑩ fri·zyer
halal *halal* ⑩ ha·lal
half *połówka* ① po·woof·ka
hallucination *halucynacja* ①
  ha·loo·tsi·na·tsya
ham *szynka* ① shin·ka
hammer *młotek* ⑩ mwo·tek
hammock *hamak* ⑩ ha·mak
hand *ręka* ① ren·ka
handbag *torebka* ① to·rep·ka
handball *piłka ręczna* ①
  peew·ka rench·na
handicraft *rękodzielnictwo* ⑩
  ren·ko·jyel·neetst·fo
handkerchief *chusteczka* ①
  khoos·tech·ka
handmade *ręcznie robiony*
  rench·nye ro·byo·ni
handsome *przystojny* pshi·stoy·ni
happy *szczęśliwy* shchen·shlee·vi
harassment *napastowanie* ⑩
  na·pas·to·va·nye
harbour *port* ⑩ port
hard (not soft) *twardy* ⑩ tfar·di
hard-boiled *ugotowany na twardo*
  oo·go·to·va·ni na tfar·do
hardware store *sklep metalowy* ⑩
  sklep me·ta·lo·vi
hashish *haszysz* ⑩ ha·shish
hat *kapelusz* ⑩ ka·pe·loosh
have *mieć* myech
hay fever *katar sienny* ⑩ ka·tar shye·ni
hazelnut *orzech laskowy* ⑩
  o·zhekh las·ko·vi
he *on* on
head *głowa* ① gwo·va
headache *ból głowy* ⑩ bool gwo·vi
headlights *reflektory* pl re·fle·kto·ri
health *zdrowie* ⑩ zdro·vye
hear *słyszeć* swi·shech
hearing aid *aparat słuchowy* ⑩
  a·pa·rat swoo·kho·vi
heart *serce* ⑩ ser·tse
heart attack *atak serca* ⑩ a·tak ser·tsa
heart condition *stan serca* ⑩ stan ser·tsa
heat *upał* ⑩ oo·pow

heated *podgrzewany* pod·gzhe·va·ni
heater *grzejnik* ⑩ gzhey·neek
heating *ogrzewanie* ⑩ o·gzhe·va·nye
heavy (weight) *ciężki* ⑩ chyensh·kee
helmet *kask* ⑩ kask
help *pomoc* ① po·mots
help *pomagać* po·ma·gach
hepatitis *żółtaczka* ① zhoow·tach·ka
her (possessive) *jej* yey
herb *zioło* ⑩ zhyo·wo
herbalist *zielarz* ⑩ zhye·lash
here *tutaj* too·tai
heroin *heroina* ① he·ro·ee·na
herring *śledź* ⑩ shlej
high (height) *wysoki* vi·so·kee
highchair *wysokie krzesełko dla dziecka* ⑩
  vi·so·kye kshe·sew·ko dla jye·tska
high school *gimnazjum* ⑩
  geem·na·zyoom
highway *szosa* ① sho·sa
hike *wędrować* ven·dro·vach
hiking *wędrówka* ① ven·droof·ka
hiking boots *buty turystyczne* pl
  boo·ti too·ris·tich·ne
hill *wzgórze* ⑩ vzgoo·zhe
Hindu *Hindus/Hinduska* ⑩/①
  heen·doos/heen·doos·ka
hire *wynajmować* vi·nai·mo·vach
his *jego* ye·go
historical *historyczny* khees·to·rich·ni
history *historia* ① khees·to·rya
hitchhike *autostop* ⑩ ow·to·stop
HIV *HIV* ⑩ heev
hockey *hokej na trawie* ⑩
  ho·key na tra·vye
holiday *święto* ⑩ shvyen·to
holidays *wakacje* pl va·ka·tsye
home *dom* ⑩ dom
homeless *bezdomny* bes·dom·ni
homemaker *gospodyni domowa* ①
  gos·po·di·nee do·mo·va
homeopathy *homeopatia* ①
  ho·me·o·pa·tya
homesick *tęsknota za domem* ①
  tensk·no·ta za do·mem
homosexual *homoseksualista* ⑩
  ho·mo·sek·soo·a·lees·ta
honey *miód* ⑩ myood
honeymoon *miesiąc miodowy* ⑩
  mye·shonts myo·do·vi
horoscope *horoskop* ⑩ ho·ros·kop
horse *koń* ⑩ koń

horse racing *wyścigi konne* pl
vish-*chee*-gee ko-ne
horse riding *jazda konna* ① yaz-da ko-na
hospital *szpital* ⑩ shpee-tal
hospitality *gościnność* ①
gosh-*chee*-noshch
hot *gorący* go-*ron*-tsi
hotel *hotel* ⑩ ho-tel
hot water *ciepła woda* ① chyep-wa vo-da
hot water bottle *termofor* ⑩ ter-mo-for
hour *godzina* ① go-*jee*-na
house *dom* ⑩ dom
how *jak* yak
how much *ile* ee-le
hug *przytulić* pshi-*too*-leech
huge *olbrzymi* ol-*bzhi*-mee
humanities *nauki humanistyczne* pl
na-oo-kee khoo-ma-nees-*tich*-ne
human resources *dział kadr* ⑩ jyow kadr
human rights *prawa człowieka* pl
pra-va chwo-*vye*-ka
hundred *sto* ⑩ sto
hungry *głodny* gwo-dni
hunting *polowanie* ⑩ po-lo-*va*-nye
(in a) hurry *w pośpiechu* v posh-*pye*-khoo
hurt *zranić* *zra*-neech
husband *mąż* ⑩ monzh

I

I *Ja* ya
ice *lód* ⑩ lood
ice axe *czekan* ⑩ che-kan
ice cream *lody* pl lo-di
ice-cream parlour *lodziarnia* ①
lo-*jyar*-nya
ice hockey *hokej na lodzie* ⑩
ho-key na lo-jye
identification *identyfikacja* ①
ee-den-ti-fee-*ka*-tsya
identification card (ID)
dowód tożsamości ⑩
do-vood tozh-sa-*mosh*-chee
idiot *idiota/idiotka* ⑩/①
ee-dyo-ta/ee-*dyot*-ka
if *jeśli* yesh-lee
ill *chory* kho-ri
immigration *imigracja* ①
ee-mee-*gra*-tsya
important *ważny* vazh-ni
impossible *niemożliwy* nye-mozh-*lee*-vi
in *w* v

included *wliczony* vlee-*cho*-ni
income tax *podatek dochodowy* ⑩
po-*da*-tek do-kho-*do*-vi
India *Indie* pl een-dye
indicator *wskaźnik* ⑩ vskazh-neek
indigestion *niestrawność* ①
nye-*strav*-noshch
indoor *w pomieszczeniu* ⑩
v po-myesh-*che*-nyoo
industry *przemysł* ⑩ pshe-misw
infection *infekcja* ① een-*fek*-tsya
inflammation *zapalenie* ⑩ za-pa-*le*-nye
influenza *grypa* ① gri-pa
information *informacja* ①
een-for-*mats*-ya
in front of *przed* pshet
ingredient *składnik* ⑩ skwad-neek
inject *wstrzykiwać* vstshi-*kee*-vach
injection *zastrzyk* ⑩ zast-shik
injured *ranny* ra-ni
injury *rana* ① ra-na
inner tube *dętka* ① dent-ka
innocent *niewinny* nye-*vee*-ni
insect *owad* ⑩ o-vad
insect repellant *środek na owady* ⑩
shro-dek na o-*va*-di
inside *wewnątrz* vev-nontsh
instructor *instruktor* ⑩ een-*strook*-tor
insurance *ubezpieczenie* ⑩
oo-bes-pye-*che*-nye
interesting *interesujący*
een-te-re-soo-*yon*-tsi
intermission *przerwa* ① psher-va
international *międzynarodowy*
myen-dzi-na-ro-*do*-vi
internet *internet* ⑩ een-ter-net
internet café *kawiarnia internetowa* ①
ka-*vyar*-nya een-ter-ne-*to*-va
interpreter *tłumacz/tłumaczka* ⑩/①
twoo-mach/twoo-*mach*-ka
invite *zapraszać* za-*pra*-shach
Ireland *Irlandia* ① eer-*lan*-dya
iron (for clothes) *żelazko* ⑩ zhe-*las*-ko
island *wyspa* ① vis-pa
Israel *Izrael* ⑩ eez-ra-el
it *to • ono* ⑩ to/o-no
IT *informatyka* ① een-for-ma-*ti*-ka
Italy *Włochy* pl vwo-khi
itch *swędzenie* ⑩ sven-*dze*-nye
itinerary *trasa podróży* ①
tra-sa po-droo-zhi
IUD *spirala* ① spee-*ra*-la

J

jacket *kurtka* ① *koort*·ka
jail *więzienie* ① vyen·*zhye*·nye
jam *dżem* ⓜ jem
January *styczeń* ⓜ *sti*·chen´
Japan *Japonia* ① ya·*po*·nya
jar *słoik* ⓜ *swo*·yeek
jealous *zazdrosny* zaz·*dros*·ni
jeans *dżinsy* pl *jeen*·si
jet lag *jetlag* ⓜ *jet*·lag
jewellery *biżuteria* ① bee·zhoo·*ter*·ya
Jewish *żydowski* zhi·*dof*·skee
job *praca* ① *pra*·tsa
jogging *bieganie* ⓝ bye·*ga*·nye
joke *żart* ⓜ zhart
journalist *dziennikarz* ⓜ jye·*nee*·kash
journey *podróż* ① *po*·droosh
judge *sędzia* ① *sen*·jya
juice *sok* ⓜ sok
July *lipiec* ⓜ *lee*·pyets
jump *skakać* *ska*·kach
jumper (sweater) *sweter* ⓜ *sve*·ter
June *czerwiec* ⓜ *cher*·vyets

K

kayaking *kajakarstwo* ⓝ ka·ya·*karst*·fo
ketchup *keczup* ⓜ *ke*·choop
key (door etc) *klucz* ⓜ klooch
keyboard *klawiatura* ① kla·vya·*too*·ra
kick *kopać* *ko*·pach
kidney *nerka* ① *ner*·ka
kill *zabić* *za*·beech
kilogram *kilogram* ⓜ kee·*lo*·gram
kilometre *kilometr* ⓜ kee·*lo*·metr
kind (nice) *miły* *mee*·wi
kindergarten *przedszkole* ⓝ
   pshet·*shko*·le
king *król* ⓜ krool
kiosk *kiosk* ⓜ kyosk
kiss *pocałunek* ⓜ po·tsa·*woo*·nek
kiss *całować* tsa·*wo*·vach
kitchen *kuchnia* ① *kookh*·nya
Kiyev *Kijów* ⓜ *kee*·yoof
knee *kolano* ⓝ ko·*la*·no
knife *nóż* ⓜ noosh
know (be acquainted with) *znać* znach
know (be aware of) *wiedzieć* *vye*·jyech
kosher *koszerny* ko·*sher*·ni

L

labourer *robotnik* ⓜ ro·*bot*·neek
lace (fabric) *koronka* ① ko·*ron*·ka
lake *jezioro* ⓝ ye·*zhyo*·ro
lamb (meat) *jagnięcina* ①
   yag·nyen·*chee*·na
land *ziemia* ① *zhye*·mya
landlady *właścicielka* ①
   vwash·chee·*chyel*·ka
landlord *właściciel* ⓜ vwash·chee·chyel
language *język* ⓜ *yen*·zik
large *duży* *doo*·zhi
last (final) *ostatni* os·*tat*·nee
last (previous) *poprzedni* po·*pshed*·nee
late *późno* *poozh*·no
later *później* *poozh*·nyey
laugh *śmiać się* shmyach shye
laundrette *pralnia samoobsługowa* ①
   pral·nya sa·mo·ob·swoo·*go*·va
laundry (clothes) *bielizna do prania* ①
   bye·*leez*·na do *pra*·nya
laundry (place) *pralnia* ① *pral*·nya
laundry (room) *pralnia* ① *pral*·nya
law *prawo* ⓝ *pra*·vo
lawyer *prawnik* ⓜ *prav*·neek
laxative *środek przeczyszczający* ⓜ
   shro·dek pshe·chish·cha·*yon*·tsi
lazy *leniwy* le·*nee*·vi
leaf *liść* ⓜ leeshch
learn *uczyć się* oo·chich shye
leather *skóra* ① *skoo*·ra
lecturer *wykładowca* ⓜ vik·wa·*dof*·tsa
ledge *występ* ⓜ *vis*·temp
left (direction) *lewy* ⓜ *le*·vi
left-luggage office
   przechowalnia bagażu ①
   pshe·kho·*val*·nya ba·*ga*·zhoo
leg (body) *noga* ① *no*·ga
legal *prawny* *prav*·ni
lemon *cytryna* ① tsi·*tri*·na
lemonade *lemoniada* ① le·mo·*nya*·da
lens (camera) *obiektyw* ⓜ o·*byek*·tif
lentil *soczewica* ① so·che·*vee*·tsa
Leo *Lew* ⓜ lev
lesbian *lesbijka* ① les·*beey*·ka
less *mniej* mnyey
letter (mail) *list* ⓜ leest
liar *kłamca* ⓜ *kwam*·tsa
Libra *Waga* ① *va*·ga
librarian *bibliotekarz* ⓜ beeb·lyo·*te*·kash
library *biblioteka* ① beeb·lyo·*te*·ka
lice *wszy* pl vshi

licence *licencja* ① lee·tsen·tsya
lie (not stand) *leżeć* le·zhech
lie (not tell the truth) *kłamać* kwa·mach
life *życie* ① zhi·chye
life jacket *kamizelka ratunkowa* ①
  ka·mee·zel·ka ra·toon·ko·va
lift (elevator) *winda* ① veen·da
light *światło* ⓝ shvyat·wo
light (colour) *jasny* yas·ni
light (weight) *lekki* le·kee
light bulb *żarówka* ① zha·roof·ka
light meter *światłomierz* ⓜ
  shvya·two·myesh
like *lubić* loo·beech
lime (fruit) *limona* ① lee·mo·na
linen (material) *len* ⓜ len
linen (sheets) *pościel* ① posh·chyel
linguist *lingwista* ⓜ leen·gvees·ta
lip balm *szminka ochronna* ①
  shmeen·ka o·khro·na
lips *wargi* pl var·gee
lipstick *szminka* ① shmeen·ka
liquor store *sklep monopolowy* ⓜ
  sklep mo·no·po·lo·vi
listen *słuchać* swoo·khach
Lithuania *Litwa* ① lee·tfa
little (quantity) *trochę* tro·khe
little (size) *mały* ma·wi
live (life) *żyć* zhich
live (somewhere) *mieszkać* myesh·kach
liver *wątroba* ① von·tro·ba
local *miejscowy* myeys·tso·vi
lock *zamek* ⓜ za·mek
lock *zamykać na klucz*
  za·mi·kach na klooch
locked *zamknięty* zam·knyen·ti
lollies *cukierki* pl tsoo·kyer·kee
long *długi* dwoo·gee
look *patrzeć* pat·shech
look after *opiekować się*
  o·pye·ko·vach shye
look for *szukać* shoo·kach
lookout *punkt widokowy* ⓜ
  poonkt vee·do·ko·vi
loose *luźny* loozh·ni
lose *tracić* tra·cheech
lost *zgubiony* zgoo·byo·ni
lost-property office *biuro rzeczy
  znalezionych* ⓝ byoo·ro zhe·chi
  zna·le·zhyo·nikh
(a) lot *dużo* doo·zho
loud *głośny* gwosh·ni
love *miłość* ① mee·woshch

love *kochać* ko·khach
lover *kochanek* ⓜ ko·kha·nek
low *niski* nees·kee
lubricant *smar* ⓜ smar
luck *szczęście* shchen·shchye
lucky *szczęśliwy* shchen·shlee·vi
luggage *bagaż* ⓜ ba·gash
luggage locker *schowek na bagaż* ⓜ
  skho·vek na ba·gash
lump *guz* ⓜ goos
lunch *lunch* ⓜ lanch
lung *płuco* ⓝ pwoo·tso
luxury *luksusowy* look·soo·so·vi

M

machine *maszyna* ① ma·shi·na
magazine *magazyn* ⓜ ma·ga·zin
mail (letters) *list* ⓜ leest
mail (postal system) *poczta* ① poch·ta
mail *przysyłać* pshis·wach
mailbox *skrzynka pocztowa* ①
  skshin·ka poch·to·va
main *główny* gwoov·ni
main road *główna ulica* ①
  gwoov·na oo·lee·tsa
make *robić* ro·beech
make-up *makijaż* ⓜ ma·kee·yash
man *mężczyzna* ⓜ menzh·chiz·na
manager (business) *kierownik* ⓜ
  kye·rov·neek
manager (sport) *menedżer* ⓜ me·ne·jer
mandarin *mandarynka* ① man·da·rin·ka
mango *mango* ⓝ man·go
manual worker *robotnik* ⓜ ro·bo·tneek
many *dużo* doo·zho
map (of country) *mapa* ① ma·pa
map (of town) *plan* ⓜ plan
March *marzec* ⓜ ma·zhets
margarine *margaryna* ① mar·ga·ri·na
marijuana *marihuana* ①
  ma·ree·khoo·a·na
marital status *stan cywilny* ⓜ
  stan tsi·veel·ni
market *rynek* ⓜ ri·nek
marriage *małżeństwo* ① mow·zhen'·stfo
married (of man) *żonaty* zho·na·ti
married (of woman) *zamężna*
  za·men·zhna
marry *poślubić* po·shloo·beech
mass (Catholic) *msza* ① msha
massage *masaż* ⓜ ma·sash

masseur/masseuse *masażysta/masażystka* ⓜ/ⓕ
ma·sa·*zhi*·sta/ma·sa·*zhis*·tka
mat *mata* ⓕ *ma*·ta
match (sports) *mecz* ⓜ mech
matches (for lighting) *zapałki* pl
za·*pow*·kee
mattress *materac* ⓜ ma·*te*·rats
May *maj* ⓜ mai
maybe *być może* bich *mo*·zhe
mayor *burmistrz* ⓜ *boor*·meestsh
me *mi* mee
meal *posiłek* ⓜ po·*shee*·wek
measles *odra* ⓕ *od*·ra
meat *mięso* ⓝ *myen*·so
mechanic *mechanik* ⓜ me·*kha*·neek
medicine (medication) *lekarstwo* ⓝ
le·*karst*·fo
medicine (study/profession)
medycyna ⓕ me·di·*tsi*·na
meditation *medytacja* ⓕ me·di·*ta*·tsya
meet (first time) *zapoznać* za·*poz*·nach
meet (get together) *spotkać* *spot*·kach
melon *melon* ⓜ *me*·lon
member *członek* ⓜ *chwo*·nek
memory card/stick *karta pamięci* ⓕ
kar·ta pa·*myen*·chee
menstruation *menstruacja* ⓕ
men·stroo·*a*·tsya
menu *jadłospis* ⓜ ya·*dwo*·spees
message *wiadomość* ⓕ vya·*do*·moshch
metal *metal* ⓜ *me*·tal
metre *metr* ⓜ metr
metro (train) *metro* ⓝ *me*·tro
metro station *stacja metra* ⓕ
sta·tsya *me*·tra
microwave oven *kuchenka
mikrofalowa* ⓕ koo·*khen*·ka
mee·kro·fa·*lo*·va
midday *południe* ⓝ po·*wood*·nye
midnight *północ* ⓕ *poow*·nots
migraine *migrena* ⓕ mee·*gre*·na
military *wojsko* ⓝ *voy*·sko
milk *mleko* ⓝ *mle*·ko
milk bar *bar mleczny* ⓜ bar *mlech*·ni
millimetre *milimetr* ⓜ mee·*lee*·metr
million *milion* ⓜ *meel*·yon
mineral water *woda mineralna* ⓕ
vo·da mee·ne·*ral*·na
minibus *minibus* ⓜ mee·nee·*boos*
Minsk *Mińsk* ⓜ meen'sk
minute *minuta* ⓕ mee·*noo*·ta
mirror *lustro* ⓝ *loos*·tro

miscarriage *poronienie* ⓝ po·ro·*nye*·nye
Miss *panna* ⓕ *pa*·na
miss (feel absence of) *odczuwać brak*
od·*choo*·vach brak
miss (not catch train etc) *spóźnić się*
spoozh·neech shye
mistake *pomyłka* ⓕ po·*miw*·ka
mix *mieszać* *mye*·shach
mobile phone *telefon komórkowy* ⓜ
te·*le*·fon ko·moor·*ko*·vi
modem *modem* ⓜ *mo*·dem
modern *nowoczesny* no·vo·*ches*·ni
moisturiser *krem nawilżający* ⓜ
krem na·veel·zha·*yon*·tsi
monastery *klasztor* ⓜ *klash*·tor
Monday *poniedziałek* ⓜ po·nye·*jya*·wek
money *pieniądze* pl pye·*nyon*·dze
monk *mnich* ⓜ mneekh
month *miesiąc* ⓜ *mye*·shonts
monument *pomnik* ⓜ *pom*·neek
moon *księżyc* ⓜ *kshyen*·zhits
more *więcej* *vyen*·tsey
morning *rano* ⓝ *ra*·no
Moscow *Moskwa* ⓕ *mosk*·fa
mosque *meczet* ⓜ *me*·chet
mosquito *komar* ⓜ *ko*·mar
mosquito coil *spirala na komary* ⓕ
spee·*ra*·la na ko·*ma*·ri
mosquito net *moskitiera* ⓕ
mos·kee·*tye*·ra
motel *motel* ⓜ *mo*·tel
mother *matka* ⓕ *mat*·ka
mother-in-law (wife's mother)
teściowa ⓕ tesh·*chyo*·va
mother-in-law (husband's mother)
świekra ⓕ *shwyek*·ra
motorbike *motor* ⓜ *mo*·tor
motorboat *motorówka* ⓕ mo·to·*roof*·ka
motorway *autostrada* ⓕ ow·to·*stra*·da
mountain *góra* ⓕ *goo*·ra
mountain bike *rower górski* ⓜ
ro·ver *goor*·skee
mountaineering *wycieczka
wysokogórska* ⓕ vi·*chyech*·ka
vi·so·ko·*goor*·ska
mountain lodge *schronisko górskie* ⓝ
skhro·*nees*·ko *goor*·skye
mouse *mysz* ⓜ mish
mouth *usta* pl *oos*·ta
movie *film* ⓜ feelm
Mr *pan* ⓜ pan
Mrs *pani* ⓕ *pa*·nee
Ms *pani* ⓕ *pa*·nee

mud *błoto* ⓝ bwo·to
muesli *muesli* ⓝ moos·lee
mum *mama* ⓕ ma·ma
mumps *świnka* ⓕ shfeen·ka
murder *morderca* ⓜ mor·der·tsa
murder *mordować* mor·do·vach
muscle *mięsień* ⓜ myen·shyen'
museum *muzeum* ⓝ moo·ze·oom
mushroom *grzyb* ⓜ gzhib
music *muzyka* ⓕ moo·zi·ka
musician *muzyk* ⓜ moo·zik
Muslim *muzułmanin* ⓜ
  moo·zoow·ma·neen
mussel *małż* ⓜ mowzh
mustard *musztarda* ⓕ moosh·tar·da
mute *niemy* nye·mi
my *mój/moja/moje* ⓜ/ⓕ/ⓝ
  mooy/mo·ya/mo·ye

N

nail clippers *obcążki do paznokci* pl
  ob·tsonzh·kee do paz·nok·chee
name *imię* ⓝ ee·mye
napkin *serwetka* ⓕ ser·vet·ka
nappy *pieluszka* ⓕ pye·loosh·ka
nappy rash *pieluszkowe zapalenie
  skóry* ⓝ pye·loosh·ko·ve za·pa·le·nye
  skoo·ri
nationality *narodowość* ⓕ
  na·ro·do·voshch
national park *park narodowy* ⓜ
  park na·ro·do·vi
nature *natura* ⓕ na·too·ra
naturopathy *naturopatia* ⓕ
  na·too·ro·pa·tya
nausea *mdłości* pl mdwosh·chee
near *bliski* blees·kee
nearby *w pobliżu* v po·blee·zhoo
nearest *najbliższy* nai·bleezh·shi
necessary *konieczny* ko·nyech·ni
neck *szyja* ⓕ shi·ya
necklace *naszyjnik* ⓜ na·shiy·neek
need *potrzebować* po·tshe·bo·vach
needle (sewing) *igła* ⓕ ee·gwa
needle (syringe) *igła* ⓕ ee·gwa
negative *negatywny* ne·ga·tiv·ni
negatives (photos) *negatyw* ⓜ ne·ga·tif
neither *żaden* zha·den
net *siatka* ⓕ shyat·ka
Netherlands *Holandia* ⓕ ho·lan·dya
network (phone) *sieć* ⓕ shyech
never *nigdy* neeg·di
new *nowy* no·vi

news *wiadomości* pl vya·do·mosh·chee
newsagency *kiosk z prasą* ⓜ
  kyosk z pra·som
newspaper *gazeta* ⓕ ga·ze·ta
newsstand *kiosk z gazetami* ⓜ
  kyosk z ga·ze·ta·mee
New Year's Day *Nowy Rok* ⓜ no·vi rok
New Year's Eve *Sylwester* ⓜ sil·ves·ter
New Zealand *Nowa Zelandia* ⓕ
  no·va ze·lan·dya
next (following) *następny* nas·temp·ni
next to *obok* o·bok
nice *miły* mee·wi
nickname *przydomek* ⓜ pshi·do·mek
night *noc* ⓕ nots
nightclub *klub nocny* ⓜ kloob nots·ni
no *nie* nye
noisy *hałaśliwy* ha·wa·shlee·vi
none *żaden* zha·den
nonsmoking *niepalący* nye·pa·lon·tsi
noodles *makaron* ⓜ ma·ka·ron
noon *południe* ⓝ po·wood·nye
north *północ* ⓕ poow·nots
Norway *Norwegia* ⓕ nor·ve·gya
nose *nos* ⓜ nos
not *nie* nye
notebook *notes* ⓜ no·tes
nothing *nic* neets
November *listopad* ⓜ lees·to·pat
now *teraz* te·ras
nuclear energy *energia nuklearna* ⓕ
  e·ner·gya noo·kle·ar·na
nuclear waste *odpady nuklearne* pl
  od·pa·di noo·kle·ar·ne
number *numer* ⓜ noo·mer
numberplate *tablica rejestracyjna* ⓕ
  ta·blee·tsa re·ye·stra·tsiy·na
nun *zakonnica* ⓕ za·ko·nee·tsa
nurse *pielęgniarz/pielęgniarka* ⓜ/ⓕ
  pye·leng·nyash/pye·leng·nyar·ka
nut (food) *orzech* ⓜ o·zhekh

O

oak (tree) *dąb* ⓜ domb
oats *płatki owsiane* pl
  pwat·kee ov·shya·ne
ocean *ocean* ⓜ o·tse·an
October *październik* ⓜ pazh·jyer·neek
off (power) *wyłączone* vi·won·cho·ne
off (spoiled) *niezdatny* nyez·dat·ni
office *biuro* byoo·ro
office worker *pracownik biurowy* ⓜ
  pra·tsov·neek byoo·ro·vi

often *często* chen·sto
oil (cooking) *olej* ⓜ o·ley
oil (petrol) *ropa naftowa* ⓕ
ro·pa naf·to·va
old *stary* sta·ri
olive *oliwka* ⓕ o·leef·ka
olive oil *olej z oliwek* ⓜ o·ley z o·lee·vek
Olympic Games *olimpiada* ⓕ
o·leem·pya·da
on *na* na
on (power) *włączone* vwon·cho·ne
once *raz* ras
one *jeden* ye·den
one-way ticket *bilet w jedną stronę* ⓜ
bee·let v yed·nom stro·ne
onion *cebula* ⓕ tse·boo·la
only *tylko* til·ko
on time *na czas* na chas
open (business) *a otwarty* ot·far·ti
open v *otwierać* ot·fye·rach
opening hours *godziny otwarcia* pl
go·jee·ni ot·far·chya
opera *opera* ⓕ o·pe·ra
opera house *opera* ⓕ o·pe·ra
operation (medical) *operacja* ⓕ
o·pe·ra·tsya
opinion *opinia* ⓕ o·pee·nya
opposite *naprzeciwko* na·pshe·cheef·ko
optometrist *okulista* ⓜ o·koo·lees·ta
or *lub • albo* loob • al·bo
orange (fruit) *pomarańcza* ⓕ
po·ma·ran'·cha
orange (colour) *pomarańczowy*
po·ma·ran'·cho·vi
orange juice *sok pomarańczowy* ⓜ
sok po·ma·ran'·cho·vi
orchestra *orkiestra* ⓕ or·kyes·tra
order (command) *zamówienie* ⓝ
za·moo·vye·nye
order (tidiness) *porządek* ⓜ po·zhon·dek
order *zamawiać* za·ma·vyach
ordinary *zwyczajny* zvi·chai·ni
orgasm *orgazm* ⓜ or·gazm
original *oryginalny* o·ri·gee·nal·ni
Orthodox Church *kościół prawosławny* ⓜ
kosh·chyoow pra·vo·swav·ni
other *inny* ee·ni
our *nasz* nash
out of order *zepsuty* zep·soo·ti
outpatient clinic *ambulatorium* ⓝ
am·boo·la·tor·yoom
outside *na zewnątrz* na zev·nontsh

ovarian cyst *zapalenie jajników* ⓝ
za·pa·le·nye yai·nee·koof
ovary *jajnik* ⓜ yai·neek
oven *piekarnik* ⓜ pye·kar·neek
overcoat *płaszcz* ⓜ pwashch
overdose *przedawkowanie* ⓝ
pshe·daf·ko·va·nye
overnight *nocny* nots·ni
overseas *zagranica* ⓕ za·gra·nee·tsa
owe *być winnym* bich vee·nim
owner *właściciel/właścicielka* ⓜ/ⓕ
vwash·chee·chyel/vwash·chee·chyel·ka
oyster *ostryga* ⓕ os·tri·ga
ozone layer *warstwa ozonowa* ⓕ
varst·fa o·zo·no·va

P

pacemaker *rozrusznik* ⓜ roz·roosh·neek
pacifier (dummy) *smoczek* ⓜ smo·chek
package *paczka* ⓕ pach·ka
packet (general) *paczka* ⓕ pach·ka
padlock *kłódka* ⓕ kwood·ka
page *strona* ⓕ stro·na
pain *ból* ⓜ bool
painful *bolesny* bo·les·ni
painkiller *środek przeciwbólowy* ⓜ
shro·dek pshe·cheef·boo·lo·vi
painter (artist) *malarz* ⓜ ma·lash
painting (a work) *malarstwo* ⓝ
ma·lars·tfo
painting (the art) *obraz* ⓜ o·bras
pair (couple) *para* ⓕ pa·ra
Pakistan *Pakistan* pa·kees·tan
palace *pałac* ⓜ pa·wats
pan *rondel* ⓜ ron·del
pants (trousers) *spodnie* pl spod·nye
pantyhose *rajstopy* pl rai·sto·pi
paper *papier* ⓜ pa·pyer
paperwork *praca biurowa* ⓕ
pra·tsa byoo·ro·va
pap smear *wymaz z szyki macicy* ⓜ
vi·mas z shiy·ke ma·chee·tsi
paraplegic *osoba z niedowładem nóg* ⓕ
o·so·ba z nye·do·vwa·dem noog
parcel *paczka* ⓕ pach·ka
parents *rodzice* pl ro·jee·tse
park *park* ⓜ park
park (a car) *parkować* par·ko·vach
parliament *parlament* ⓜ par·la·ment
part (component) *część* ⓕ chenshch
part-time *na pół etatu* na poow e·ta·too
party (night out) *impreza* ⓕ eem·pre·za

party (politics) *partia* ① *par*·tya
pass (go by) *mijać* mee·yach
pass (kick/throw) *podać* po·dach
passenger *pasażer* ① pa·sa·zher
passport *paszport* ① *pash*·port
past *przeszłość* ① pshesh·woshch
pasta *makaron* ① ma·ka·ron
pastry *ciasta* pl chyas·ta
path *ścieżka* ① shchyesh·ka
pay *płacić* pwa·cheech
payment *zapłata* ① za·pwa·ta
peace *pokój* ① po·kooy
peach *brzoskwinia* ① bzhosk·fee·nya
peak (mountain) *szczyt* ① shchit
peanut *orzeszek ziemny* ①
  o·zhe·shek zhyem·ni
pear *gruszka* ① groosh·ka
pedal *pedał* ① pe·dow
pedestrian *pieszy* ① pye·shi
pen (ballpoint) *długopis* ① dwoo·go·pees
pencil *ołówek* ① o·woo·vek
penis *członek* ① chwo·nek
penknife *scyzoryk* ① stsi·zo·rik
pensioner *emeryt/emerytka* ①/①
  e·me·rit/e·me·rit·ka
people *ludzie* pl *loo*·jye
pepper (bell) *papryka* ① pa·*pri*·ka
pepper (condiment) *pieprz* ① pyepsh
per (day) *od • przez* od • pshes
per cent *procent* ① *pro*·tsent
perfect a *doskonały* dos·ko·na·wi
performance *przedstawienie* ①
  pshet·sta·*vye*·nye
perfume *perfumy* pl per·foo·mi
permit *zezwolenie* ① ze·zvo·le·nye
person *osoba* ① o·so·ba
petrol *benzyna* ① ben·zi·na
petrol station *stacja benzynowa* ①
  sta·tsya ben·zi·no·va
pharmacist *aptekarz* ① ap·*te*·kash
pharmacy *apteka* ① ap·te·ka
phone book *książka telefoniczna* ①
  kshyonzh·ka te·le·fo·*neech*·na
phone box *budka telefoniczna* ①
  bood·ka te·le·fo·*neech*·na
phonecard *karta telefoniczna* ①
  kar·ta te·le·fo·*neech*·na
photo *zdjęcie* ① *zdyen*·chye
photograph *fotografować*
  fo·to·gra·fo·vach
photographer *fotograf* ① fo·*to*·graf
photography *fotografika* ①
  fo·to·gra·*fee*·ka

phrasebook *minirozmówki* pl
  mee·nee·roz·*moof*·kee
piano *pianino* ① pya·*nee*·no
pickaxe *kilof* ① *kee*·lof
picnic *piknik* ① *peek*·neek
piece *kawałek* ① ka·*va*·wek
pig *świnia* ① *shfee*·nya
pill *pastylka* ① pas·*til*·ka
(the) pill *pigułka antykoncepcyjna* ①
  pee·*goow*·ka an·ti·kon·tsep·*tsiy*·na
pillow *poduszka* ① po·*doosh*·ka
pillowcase *poszewka* ① po·*shef*·ka
pine (tree) *sosna* ① *sos*·na
pink *różowy* roo·*zho*·vi
Pisces *Ryby* pl *ri*·bi
place *miejsce* ① *myeys*·tse
place of birth *miejsce urodzenia* ①
  myeys·tse oo·ro·*dze*·nya
plane *samolot* ① sa·*mo*·lot
planet *planeta* ① pla·*ne*·ta
plant *roślina* ① rosh·*lee*·na
plastic a *plastykowy* plas·ti·*ko*·vi
plate *talerz* ① *ta*·lesh
plateau *płaskowyż* ① pwas·*ko*·vish
platform *peron* ① *pe*·ron
play v *grać* grach
play (theatre) n *sztuka* *shtoo*·ka
plug (bath) n *korek* ① *ko*·rek
plug (electricity) n *wtyczka* ① *ftich*·ka
plum *śliwka* ① *shleef*·ka
plumber *hydraulik* ① hi·dra·*oo*·leek
pocket *kieszeń* ① *kye*·shen´
pocket knife *scyzoryk* ① stsi·*zo*·rik
poetry *poezja* ① po·*ez*·ya
point *wskazywać* vska·*zi*·vach
poisonous *trujący* troo·*yon*·tsi
Poland *Polska* ① *pol*·ska
police *policja* ① po·*lee*·tsya
police officer (in city) *policjant* ①
  po·*lee*·tsyant
police officer (in country)
  posterunkowy ① pos·te·roon·*ko*·vi
police station *komisariat policji* ①
  ko·mee·*sar*·yat po·*leets*·yee
policy *polisa* ① po·*lee*·sa
politician *polityk* ① po·*lee*·tik
politics *polityka* ① po·lee·*ti*·ka
pollution *zanieczyszczenie* ①
  za·nye·chish·*che*·nye
pool (game) *bilard* ① *bee*·lard
pool (swimming) *basen* ① *ba*·sen
poor (wealth) *biedny* *byed*·ni
popular *popularny* po·poo·*lar*·ni

pork *wieprzowina* ① vyep·sho·*vee*·na
pork sausage *kiełbasa wieprzowa* ①
   kyew·*ba*·sa vyep·*sho*·va
port (river/sea) *port* ⓜ port
positive *pozytywny* po·zi·*tiv*·ni
possible *możliwy* ⓜ mozh·*lee*·vi
post *poczta* ① poch·ta
post *posyłać* po·*si*·wach
postcard *pocztówka* ① poch·*toof*·ka
postcode *kod pocztowy* ⓜ kod poch·*to*·vi
poster *plakat* ⓜ *pla*·kat
post office *urząd pocztowy* ⓜ
   oo·zhond poch·*to*·vi
pot (cooking) *garnek* ⓜ *gar*·nek
potato *ziemniak* ⓜ *zhyem*·nyak
pottery *ceramika* ① tse·ra·*mee*·ka
pound (money/weight) *funt* ⓜ foont
poverty *ubóstwo* ⓝ oo·*boost*·fo
powder *proszek* ⓜ *pro*·shek
power *władza* ① *vwa*·dza
Prague *Praga* ① *pra*·ga
prawn *krewetka* ① kre·*vet*·ka
prayer *modlitwa* ① mod·*leet*·fa
prayer book *modlitewnik* ⓜ
   mod·lee·*tev*·neek
prefer *woleć* vo·lech
pregnant *w ciąży* v *chyon*·zhi
premenstrual tension *napięcie*
   przedmiesiączkowe ⓝ na·*pyen*·chye
   pshet·mye·shonch·*ko*·ve
prepare *przygotować* pshi·go·*to*·vach
prescription *recepta* ① re·*tse*·pta
present (gift) *prezent* ⓜ *pre*·zent
present (time) *teraźniejszość* ①
   te·razh·*nyey*·shoshch
president *prezydent* ⓜ pre·*zi*·dent
pretty *ładny* *wad*·ni
price *cena* ① *tse*·na
priest *kapłan* ⓜ *kap*·wan
prime minister *premier* ⓜ *prem*·yer
printer (computer) *drukarka* ①
   droo·*kar*·ka
prison *więzienie* ⓝ vyen·*zhye*·nye
prisoner *więzień* ⓜ *vyen*·zhyen´
private *prywatny* pri·*vat*·ni
produce *produkować* pro·doo·*ko*·vach
profit *zysk* ⓜ zisk
program *program* ⓜ *pro*·gram
projector *rzutnik* ⓜ *zhoot*·neek
promise *obiecywać* o·bye·*tsi*·vach
prostitute n *prostytutka* ① pros·ti·*toot*·ka
protect *chronić* *khro*·neech

protected *chroniony* khro·*nyo*·ni
protest *protest* ⓜ *pro*·test
protest *protestować* pro·tes·*to*·vach
provisions *zapasy* pl za·*pa*·si
pub (bar) *pub* ⓜ pab
public phone *telefon publiczny* ⓜ
   te·*le*·fon poob·*leech*·ni
public toilet *toaleta publiczna* ①
   to·a·*le*·ta poob·*leech*·na
publishing *wydawnictwo* ⓝ
   vi·dav·*neetst*·fo
pull *ciągnąć* chyong·nonch
pump *popma* ① *pom*·pa
puncture *przebicie* ① pshe·*bee*·chye
puppet *marionetka* ① ma·ryo·*net*·ka
puppet show *przedstawienie*
   kukiełkowe ⓝ pshet·sta·*vye*·nye
   koo·kyew·*ko*·ve
pure *czysty* *chis*·ti
purple *fioletowy* fyo·le·*to*·vi
purse *portmonetka* ① port·mo·*net*·ka
push *pchać* pkhach
put *kłaść* kwashch

Q

quadriplegic *osoba sparaliżowana* ①
   o·so·ba spa·ra·lee·zho·*va*·na
qualifications *kwalifikacje* pl
   kva·lee·fee·*ka*·tsye
quality *jakość* ① *ya*·koshch
quarantine *kwarantanna* ① kfa·ran·*ta*·na
quarter *ćwierć* ① chfyerch
queen *królowa* ① kroo·*lo*·va
question *pytanie* ⓝ pi·*ta*·nye
queue *kolejka* ① ko·*ley*·ka
quick *szybki* *shib*·kee
quiet *cichy* *chee*·khi

R

rabbit *królik* ⓜ *kroo*·leek
rabies *wścieklizna* ① fshchyek·*leez*·na
race (sport) *wyścigi* pl vish·*chee*·gee
racism *rasizm* ⓜ *ra*·sheezm
racquet *rakieta* ① ra·*kye*·ta
radiator *grzejnik* ⓜ *gzhey*·neek
radio *radio* ⓝ *ra*·dyo
radish *rzodkiewka* ① zhod·*kyef*·ka
railway station *stacja kolejowa* ①
   sta·tsya ko·le·*yo*·va

rain *deszcz* ⓜ deshch
raincoat *płaszcz nieprzemakalny* ⓜ
 pwashch nye-pshe-ma-*kal*-ni
rally (protest) *wiec* ⓜ viets
rape *gwałt* ⓜ gvowt
rape *gwałcić* gvow-cheech
rare (steak) *na pół surowy*
 na poow soo-*ro*-vi
rare (uncommon) *rzadki* zhad-kee
rash *wysypka* ① vi-*sip*-ka
raspberry *malina* ① ma-*lee*-na
rat *szczur* ⓜ shchoor
rave (party) n *impreza* ① eem-*pre*-za
raw *surowy* soo-*ro*-vi
razor *brzytwa* ① *bzhit*-fa
razor blade *żyletka* ① zhi-*let*-ka
read *czytać* chi-*tach*
reading *czytanie* ① chi-*ta*-nye
ready *gotowy* go-*to*-vi
real-estate agent *agent nieruchomości* ⓜ
 a-gent nye-roo-kho-*mosh*-chee
realistic *realistyczny* re-a-lees-*tich*-ni
rear (location) a *tylny* *til*-ni
reason *powód* ⓜ *po*-vood
receipt *rachunek* ⓜ ra-*khoo*-nek
recently *ostatnio* os-*tat*-nyo
recommend *polecać* po-*le*-tsach
recyclable *do wtórnego przerobu*
 do vtoor-*ne*-go pshe-*ro*-boo
recycle *przetwarzać* pshet-*fa*-zhach
red *czerwony* cher-*vo*-ni
red wine *wino czerwone* ⓝ
 vee-no cher-*vo*-ne
referee *sędzia* ⓜ *sen*-jya
reference *wzmianka* ① *vzmyan*-ka
refrigerator *lodówka* ① lo-*doof*-ka
refugee *uchodźca* ⓜ oo-*khoj*-tsa
refund *zwrot pieniędzy* ⓜ
 zvrot pye-*nyen*-dzi
refuse *odmawiać* od-*ma*-vyach
regional *regionalny* re-gyo-*nal*-ni
registered mail *list polecony* ⓜ
 leest po-le-*tso*-ni
reiki *reiki* ⓝ *rey*-kee
relax *odpoczywać* od-po-*chi*-vach
religion *religia* ① re-*lee*-gya
religious *religijny* re-lee-*geey*-ni
remote *daleki* da-*le*-kee
remote control *pilot* ⓜ *pee*-lot
rent *czynsz* ⓜ chinsh
rent *wynająć* vi-*na*-yonch
repair *naprawić* na-*pra*-veech

reservation (booking) *rezerwacja* ①
 re-zer-*va*-tsya
rest *odpoczywać* od-po-*chi*-vach
restaurant *restauracja* ① res-tow-*ra*-tsya
retired *emerytowany* e-me-ri-to-*va*-ni
return *wracać* *vra*-tsach
return ticket *bilet powrotny* ⓜ
 bee-let po-*vro*-tni
rhythm *rytm* ⓜ ritm
rib (body) *żebro* ⓝ *zhe*-bro
rice *ryż* ⓜ rizh
rich (wealthy) *bogaty* bo-*ga*-ti
ride (bike, horse) v *jeździć* yezh-jeech
right (correct) *prawidłowy* pra-vee-*dwo*-vi
right (direction) *prawoskrętny*
 pra-vo-*skrent*-ni
ring (jewellery) *pierścionek* ⓜ
 pyersh-*chyo*-nek
ring (phone) *dzwonić* dzvo-neech
rip-off *zdzierstwo* ⓝ *zjyerst*-fo
river *rzeka* ① *zhe*-ka
road *droga* ① *dro*-ga
road map *mapa drogowa* ①
 ma-pa dro-*go*-va
rob *okraść* o-*krashch*
rock (music) *rock* ⓜ rok
rock climbing *wspinaczka skałkowa* ①
 fspee-*nach*-ka skow-*ko*-va
roll (bread) *bułka* ① *boow*-ka
romantic *romantyczny* ro-man-*tich*-ni
room *pokój* ⓜ *po*-kooy
room number *numer pokoju* ⓜ
 noo-mer po-*ko*-yoo
rope *lina* ① *lee*-na
round (drinks) *kolejka* ① ko-*ley*-ka
round a *okrągły* o-*krong*-wi
route *trasa* ① *tra*-sa
rowing *wioślarstwo* ⓝ vyo-*shlarst*-fo
rubbish *śmieci* pl *shmye*-chee
rubella *różyczka* ① roo-*zhich*-ka
rug *dywan* ⓜ *di*-van
rugby *rugby* ⓜ *rag*-bi
ruins *ruiny* pl roo-ee-ni
rule *reguła* ① re-*goo*-wa
rum *rum* ⓜ room
run *biegać* bye-*gach*
running *bieganie* ⓝ bye-*ga*-nye
Russia *Rosja* ① *ro*-sya

S

sad *smutny* smoo·tni
saddle *siodło* ⓝ shyo·dwo
safe *sejf* ⓜ seyf
safe *bezpieczny* bes·pyech·ni
safe sex *bezpieczny seks* ⓜ
    bes·pyech·ni seks
Sagittarius *Strzelec* ⓜ stshe·lets
saint *święty* ⓜ shvyen·ti
salad *sałatka* ⓕ sa·wat·ka
salary *pensja* ⓕ pen·sya
sale *sprzedaż* ⓕ spshe·dash
sales assistant
    sprzedawca/sprzedawczyni ⓜ/ⓕ
    spshe·daf·tsa/spshe·daf·chi·nee
sales tax *podatek obrotowy* ⓜ
    po·da·tek o·bro·to·vi
salt *sól* ⓕ sool
same *taki sam* ⓜ ta·kee sam
sand *piasek* ⓜ pya·sek
sandals *sandały* pl san·da·wi
sandwich *kanapka* ⓕ ka·nap·ka
sanitary napkin *podpaski higieniczne* pl
    pod·pas·kee hee·gye·neech·ne
Saturday *sobota* ⓕ so·bo·ta
sauce *sos* ⓜ sos
saucepan *rondel* ⓜ ron·del
sausage *kiełbasa* ⓕ kyew·ba·sa
say *mówić* moo·veech
scalp *skóra głowy* ⓕ skoo·ra gwo·vi
scarf *szal* ⓜ shal
school *szkoła* ⓕ shko·wa
science *nauka* ⓕ na·oo·ka
scientist *naukowiec* ⓜ now·ko·vyets
scissors *nożyczki* pl no·zhich·kee
score *zdobyć* zdo·bich
scoreboard *tablica wyników* ⓕ
    ta·blee·tsa vi·nee·koof
Scorpio *Skorpion* ⓜ skor·pyon
Scotland *Szkocja* ⓕ shko·tsya
sculpture *rzeźba* ⓕ zhezh·ba
sea *morze* ⓝ mo·zhe
seasick *choroba morska* ⓕ
    kho·ro·ba mor·ska
seaside *wybrzeże* ⓝ vib·zhe·zhe
season *sezon* ⓜ se·zon
seat (place) *miejsce* ⓝ myeys·tse
seatbelt *pasy bezpieczeństwa* pl
    pa·si bes·pye·chen'st·fa
second *sekunda* ⓕ se·koon·da
second *drugi* droo·gee

second class *druga klasa* ⓕ
    droo·ga kla·sa
secondhand *używany* oo·zhi·va·ni
secretary *sekretarz/sekretarka* ⓜ/ⓕ
    se·kre·tash/se·kre·tar·ka
see *widzieć* vee·jyech
selfish *samolubny* sa·mo·loob·ni
self-service *samoobsługowy*
    sa·mo·ob·swoo·go·vi
sell *sprzedawać* spshe·da·vach
send *wysyłać* vi·si·wach
sensible *sensowny* ⓜ sen·sov·ni
separate *osobny* o·so·bni
September *wrzesień* ⓜ vzhe·shyen'
serious *poważny* po·vazh·ni
service *obsługa* ⓕ ob·swoo·ga
service charge *dodatek za obsługę*
    do·da·tek za ob·swoo·ge
service station *stacja obsługi* ⓕ
    sta·tsya ob·swoo·gee
serviette *serwetka* ⓕ ser·vet·ka
several *kilka* keel·ka
sew *szyć* shich
sex *seks* ⓜ seks
sexism *seksizm* ⓜ sek·sheezm
sexy *seksowny* sek·sov·ni
shade *cień* ⓜ chyen'
shadow *cień* ⓜ chyen'
shampoo *szampon* ⓜ sham·pon
shape *kształt* ⓜ kshtowt
share (accommodation) v *mieszkać z kimś*
    myesh·kach z keemsh
share (with) *dzielić się* jye·leech shye
shave *golić się* go·leech shye
shaving cream *krem do golenia* ⓜ
    krem do go·le·nya
she *ona* o·na
sheep *owca* ⓕ ov·tsa
sheet (bed) *prześcieradło* ⓝ
    pshesh·chye·ra·dwo
shelf *półka* ⓕ poow·ka
shiatsu *shiatsu* ⓜ shya·tsoo
shingles (illness) *półpasiec* ⓜ
    poow·pa·shyets
ship *statek* ⓜ sta·tek
shirt *koszula* ⓕ ko·shoo·la
shoes *buty* pl boo·ti
shoe shop *sklep obuwniczy* ⓜ
    sklep o·boov·nee·chi
shoot *strzelać* stshe·lach
shop *sklep* ⓜ sklep
shop *robić zakupy* ro·beech za·koo·pi
shopping *zakupy* pl za·koo·pi

shopping centre *centrum zakupowe* ⓜ *tsen*-troom za-*koo*-po-ve
short (height) *niski* nees-kee
short (length) *krótki* kroot-kee
shorts *szorty* pl *shor*-ti
shoulder *ramię* ⓝ *ra*-mye
shout *krzyczeć* kshi-chech
show *pokaz* ⓜ *po*-kas
show *pokazać* po-*ka*-zach
shower *prysznic* ⓜ *prish*-neets
shut *zamknięty* zam-*knyen*-ti
shy *nieśmiały* nyesh-*mya*-wi
sick *chory* kho-ri
side *strona* ① *stro*-na
sign *znak* ⓜ znak
sign *podpisać się* pod-*pee*-sach shye
signature *podpis* ⓜ *pod*-pees
silk *jedwab* ⓜ *yed*-vab
silver *srebro* ① *sre*-bro
SIM card *karta SIM* ① *kar*-ta seem
simple *prosty* pros-ti
since (time) *od* od
sing *śpiewać* shpye-vach
Singapore *Singapur* ⓜ seen-*ga*-poor
singer *śpiewak* ⓜ shpye-vak
single (person) *nieżonaty/ niezamężna* ⓜ/① nye-zho-*na*-ti/ nye-za-*menzh*-na
single room *pokój jednoosobowy* ⓜ *po*-kooy ye-dno-o-so-*bo*-vi
sister *siostra* ① *shyos*-tra
sit *siedzieć* shye-jyech
size (general) *rozmiar* ⓜ *roz*-myar
skate *jeździć na łyżwach* yezh-jyeech na *wizh*-vakh
skateboarding *jazda na deskorolce* ① *yaz*-da na des-ko-*rol*-tse
skis *narty* pl *nar*-ti
ski *jeździć na nartach* yezh-jyeech na *nar*-takh
skiing *narciarstwo* ① nar-*chyarst*-fo
skin *skóra* ① *skoo*-ra
skirt *spódnica* ① spood-*nee*-tsa
sky *niebo* ⓝ *nye*-bo
sleep *sen* ⓜ sen
sleep *spać* spach
sleeping bag *śpiwór* ⓜ shpee-voor
sleeping berth *miejsce sypialne* ⓝ *myeys*-tse si-*pyal*-ne
sleeping car *wagon sypialny* ⓜ *va*-gon si-*pyal*-ni
sleeping pills *pigułki nasenne* pl pee-*goow*-kee na-*se*-ne

sleepy *śpiący* shpyon-tsi
slice *plasterek* ⓜ plas-*te*-rek
slide film *film do slajdów* ⓜ feelm do *slai*-doof
Slovakia *Słowacja* ① swo-*va*-tsya
slow *wolny* vol-ni
slowly *powoli* po-*vo*-lee
small *mały* ma-wi
smaller *mniejszy* mnyey-shi
smallest *najmniejszy* nai-*mnyey*-shi
smell *zapach* ⓜ *za*-pakh
smile *uśmiechać się* oosh-*mye*-khach shye
smoke *palić* pa-leech
snack *przekąska* ① pshe-*kons*-ka
snail *ślimak* ⓜ shlee-mak
snake *wąż* ⓜ vonzh
snow *śnieg* ⓜ shnyeg
snowboarding *jazda na snowboardzie* ① *yaz*-da na snow-*bor*-jye
snow pea *groszek zielony* ⓜ *gro*-shek zhye-*lo*-ni
soap *mydło* ⓝ *mid*-wo
soccer *piłka nożna* ① *peew*-ka *nozh*-na
socialist *socjalista* ① so-tsya-*lees*-ta
social welfare *opieka społeczna* ① o-*pye*-ka spo-*wech*-na
socks *skarpetki* pl skar-*pet*-kee
soft drink *napój bezalkoholowy* ⓜ *na*-pooy bes-al-ko-kho-*lo*-vi
soldier *żołnierz* ⓜ zhow-nyezh
Solidarity (union) *Solidarność* ① so-lee-*dar*-noshch
some *kilka* keel-ka
someone *ktoś* ktosh
something *coś* tsosh
sometimes *czasem* cha-sem
son *syn* ⓜ sin
song *piosenka* ① pyo-*sen*-ka
soon *wkrótce* fkroot-tse
sore *obolały* o-bo-*la*-wi
sour cream *śmietana* ① shmye-*ta*-na
south *południe* ⓜ po-*wood*-nye
souvenir *pamiątka* ① pa-*myont*-ka
soy milk *mleko sojowe* ⓝ *mle*-ko so-*yo*-ve
soy sauce *sos sojowy* ⓜ sos so-*yo*-vi
space (room) *przestrzeń* ① pshes-tshen'
Spain *Hiszpania* ① kheesh-*pa*-nya
sparkling wine *wino musujące* ⓝ *vee*-no moo-soo-*yon*-tse
speak *mówić* moo-veech
special *specjalny* spets-*yal*-ni
specialist *specjalista* ① spets-ya-*lees*-ta
speed (drug) *speed* ⓜ speed

S

speed (travel) *prędkość* ① prend-koshch
speed limit *ograniczenie prędkości* ⑩
  o-gra-nee-*che*-nye prend-*kosh*-chee
speedometer *szybkościomierz* ⑩
  shib-kosh-*chyo*-myesh
spider *pająk* ⑩ *pa*-yonk
spoilt (food) *zepsuty* zep-*soo*-ti
spoke *szprycha* ① *shpri*-kha
spoon *łyżka* ① wish-ka
sport *sport* ⑩ sport
sportsperson *sportowiec* ⑩ spor-*to*-vyets
sprain *zwichnięcie* ① zveekh-*nyen*-chye
spring (coil) *sprężyna* ① spren-*zhi*-na
spring (season) *wiosna* ① *vyos*-na
square (town) *rynek* ⑩ *ri*-nek
stadium *stadion* ⑩ *sta*-dyon
stairway *klatka schodowa* ①
  klat-ka skho-*do*-va
stale *stęchły* stenkh-wi
stamp (postage) *znaczek* ⑩ *zna*-chek
stand-by ticket *bilet z listy rezerwowej* ⑩
  bee-let z *lees*-ti re-zer-*vo*-vey
star *gwiazda* ① *gvyaz*-da
(four-)star *(cztero-)gwiazdkowy* ⑩
  (chte-ro-)gvyazt-*ko*-vi
start *start* ⑩ start
start *zaczynać* za-*chi*-nach
station *stacja* ① *sta*-tsya
statue *pomnik* ⑩ *pom*-neek
stay (at a hotel) *przenocować*
  pshe-no-*tso*-vach
stay (in one place) *pozostać* po-zo-stach
steak (beef) *stek* ⑩ stek
steal *kraść* krashch
steep *stromy* stro-mi
step *krok* ⑩ krok
stereo *stereo* ⑩ ste-*re*-o
Stockholm *Sztokholm* ⑩ shtok-kholm
stockings *pończochy* pl pon'-*cho*-khi
stolen *kradziony* kra-*jyo*-ni
stomach *żołądek* ⑩ zho-*won*-dek
stomachache *ból żołądka* ⑩
  bool zho-*wont*-ka
stone *kamień* ⑩ *ka*-myen'
stoned (drugged) *urżnięty* oorzh-*nyen*-ti
stop (bus, tram) *przystanek* ⑩
  pshis-*ta*-nek
stop (cease) *przestać* pshes-tach
stop (prevent) *zatrzymać* za-*tshi*-mach
storm *burza* ① boo-zha
story *opowiadanie* ① o-po-vya-*da*-nye
stove *piec* ⑩ pyets

straight *prosty* pros-ti
strange *dziwny* jeev-ni
stranger *nieznajomy* ⑩ nye-zna-*yo*-mi
strawberry *truskawka* ① troos-*kaf*-ka
stream *strumień* ⑩ stroo-myen'
street *ulica* ① oo-*lee*-tsa
street market *handel uliczny* ⑩
  han-del oo-*leech*-ni
strike *strajk* ⑩ straik
string *sznurek* ⑩ shnoo-rek
stroke (health) *wylew* ⑩ *vi*-lef
stroller *wózek spacerowy* ⑩
  voo-zek spa-tse-*ro*-vi
strong *silny* sheel-ni
student *student* ⑩ *stoo*-dent
stupid *głupi* gwoo-pee
style *styl* ⑩ stil
subtitles *napisy* pl na-*pee*-si
suburb *dzielnica* ① jyel-*nee*-tsa
subway (train) *metro* ⑩ *met*-ro
Sudeten mountains *Sudety* pl soo-*de*-ti
sugar *cukier* ⑩ *tsoo*-kyer
suitcase *walizka* ① va-*lees*-ka
summer *lato* ⑩ *la*-to
sun *słońce* ⑩ *swon'*-tse
sunblock *krem przeciwsłoneczny* ⑩
  krem pshe-cheef-swo-*nech*-ni
sunburn *oparzenie słoneczne* ①
  o-pa-zhe-nye swo-*nech*-ne
Sunday *niedziela* ① nye-*jye*-la
sunglasses *okulary słoneczne* pl
  o-koo-*la*-ri swo-*nech*-ne
sunny *słoneczny* swo-*nech*-ni
sunrise *wschód słońca* ⑩
  fskhood *swon'*-tsa
sunset *zachód słońca* ⑩
  za-khood *swon'*-tsa
sunstroke *udar słoneczny* ⑩
  oo-dar swo-*nech*-ni
supermarket *supermarket* ⑩
  soo-per-*mar*-ket
superstition *zabobon* ⑩ za-*bo*-bon
surf *fale przybrzeżne* pl
  fa-le pshi-*bzhezh*-ne
surf *surfować* ser-*fo*-vach
surface mail (land) *poczta zwykła
  (lądowa)* ① *poch*-ta zvik-wa (lon-*do*-va)
surface mail (sea) *poczta zwykła (morsk*
  ① *poch*-ta zvik-wa (mor-ska)
surfboard *deska surfingowa* ①
  des-ka ser-feen-*go*-va
surfing *surfing* ⑩ *ser*-feeng
surname *nazwisko* ⑩ naz-*vees*-ko

DICTIONARY

surprise *niespodzianka* ① nye·spo·*jyan*·ka
sweater *sweter* ⓜ *sve*·ter
Sweden *Szwecja* ① *shve*·tsya
sweet *słodki* *swod*·kee
swelling *opuchlizna* ① o·pookh·*leez*·na
swim *pływać* *pwi*·vach
swimming *pływanie* ⓝ pwi·*va*·nye
swimming pool *basen* ⓜ *ba*·sen
swimsuit *kostium kąpielowy* ⓜ
  kos·tyoom kom·pye·*lo*·vi
Switzerland *Szwajcaria* ① shvai·*tsar*·ya
synagogue *synagoga* ① si·na·*go*·ga
syringe *strzykawka* ① stshi·*kaf*·ka

T

table *stół* ⓜ stoow
tablecloth *obrus* ⓜ o·broos
table tennis *tenis stołowy* ①
  te·nees sto·*wo*·vi
tailor *krawiec* ⓜ *kra*·vyets
take *brać* brach
talk *rozmawiać* roz·*ma*·vyach
tall *wysoki* vi·so·kee
tampon *tampon* ⓜ *tam*·pon
tanning lotion *olejek do opalnia* ⓜ
  o·*le*·yek do o·pa·*la*·nya
tap *kran* ⓜ kran
tasty *smaczny* *smach*·ni
Taurus *Byk* ⓜ bik
tax *podatek* ⓜ po·*da*·tek
taxi *taksówka* ① tak·*soof*·ka
taxi stand *postój taksówek* ⓜ
  pos·tooy tak·*soo*·vek
tea *herbata* ① her·*ba*·ta
teacher *nauczyciel* ⓜ na·oo·*chi*·chyel
team *drużyna* ① droo·*zhi*·na
teaspoon *łyżeczka* ① wi·*zhech*·ka
teeth *zęby* pl *zem*·bi
telegram *telegram* ⓜ te·*le*·gram
telephone *telefon* ⓜ te·*le*·fon
telephone *telefonować* te·le·fo·no·*vach*
telescope *teleskop* ⓜ te·*les*·kop
television *telewizja* ① te·le·*veez*·ya
tell *powiedzieć* po·*vye*·jyech
temperature (fever) *gorączka* ①
  go·*ronch*·ka
temperature (weather) *temperatura* ①
  tem·pe·ra·*too*·ra
temple (body) *skroń* ① skron'
tennis *tenis* ⓜ *te*·nees
tennis court *kort tenisowy* ⓜ
  kort te·nee·*so*·vi

tent *namiot* ⓜ *na*·myot
tent peg *śledź namiotowy* ⓜ
  shlej na·myo·*to*·vi
terrorism *terroryzm* ⓜ te·ro·*rizm*
test *próba* ① *proo*·ba
thank *dziękować* jyen·*ko*·vach
that *który* ktoo·ri
theatre *teatr* ⓜ *te*·atr
their *ich* eekh
there *tam* tam
they *oni* *o*·nee
thick *gruby* *groo*·bi
thief *złodziej* ⓜ *zwo*·jyey
thin *cienki* *chyen*·kee
think *myśleć* *mish*·lech
thirsty *spragniony* sprag·*nyo*·ni
this *to* ⓝ to
this (one) *ten* ⓜ ten
throat *gardło* *gard*·wo
thrush (health) *pleśniawka* ①
  plesh·*nyaf*·ka
thunderstorm *burza z piorunami* ①
  boo·zha z pyo·roo·*na*·mee
Thursday *czwartek* ⓜ *chfar*·tek
ticket *bilet* ⓜ *bee*·let
ticket collector *kontroler biletowy* ⓜ
  kon·*tro*·ler bee·le·*to*·vi
ticket machine *automat biletowy* ⓜ
  ow·*to*·mat bee·le·*to*·vi
ticket office *kasa biletowa* ①
  ka·sa bee·le·*to*·va
tide *przypływ* ⓜ *pshi*·pwif
tight *ciasny* *chyas*·ni
time *czas* ⓜ chas
timetable *rozkład jazdy* ⓜ
  ros·kwad *yaz*·di
tin (can) *puszka* ① *poosh*·ka
tin opener *otwieracz do konserw* ⓜ
  ot·*fye*·rach do kon·*serf*
tiny *drobny* *drob*·ni
tip (gratuity) *napiwek* ⓜ na·*pee*·vek
tire *opona* ① o·*po*·na
tired *zmęczony* zmen·*cho*·ni
tissues *chusteczki* pl khoos·*tech*·kee
to *do* do
toast (food) *grzanka* ① *gzhan*·ka
toaster *opiekacz* ⓜ o·*pye*·kach
tobacco *tytoń* ⓜ *ti*·ton'
today *dzisiaj* *jee*·shyai
toe *palec u nogi* ⓜ *pa*·lets *no* *no*·gee
tofu *tofu* ⓝ *to*·foo
together *razem* *ra*·zem
toilet *toaleta* ① to·a·*le*·ta

toilet paper *papier toaletowy* ⓜ
pa·pyer to·a·le·to·vi
tomato *pomidor* ⓜ po·mee·dor
tomato sauce *keczup* ⓜ ke·choop
tomorrow *jutro* yoo·tro
tonight *dzisiaj wieczorem* ⓜ
jee·shai vye·cho·rem
too (also) *też* tesh
too (much) *za* za
tooth *ząb* ⓜ zomb
toothache *ból zęba* ⓜ bool zem·ba
toothbrush *szczotka do zębów* ①
shchot·ka do zem·boof
toothpaste *pasta do zębów* ①
pas·ta do zem·boof
torch (flashlight) *latarka* ① la·tar·ka
touch *dotykać* do·ti·kach
tour *wycieczka* ① vi·chyech·ka
tourist *turysta* ⓜ too·ris·ta
tourist office *biuro turystyczne* ⓝ
byoo·ro too·ris·tich·ne
towards *w kierunku* v kye·roon·koo
towel *ręcznik* ⓜ rench·neek
tower *wieża* ① vye·zha
track (path) *ścieżka* ① shchyesh·ka
track (sport) *bieżnia* ① byezh·nya
trade *handel* ⓜ han·del
traffic *ruch* ⓜ rookh
trail *szlak* ⓜ shlak
train *pociąg* ⓜ po·chyonk
train station *stacja kolejowa* ①
sta·tsya ko·le·yo·va
tram *tramwaj* ⓜ tram·vai
translate *przetłumaczyć*
pshe·twoo·ma·chich
translator *tłumacz* ⓜ twoo·mach
transport *transport* ⓜ trans·port
travel *podróżować* po·droo·zho·vach
travel agency *biuro podróży* ①
byoo·ro po·droo·zhi
travellers cheque *czeki podróżne* pl
che·kee po·droozh·ne
travel sickness *choroba lokomocyjna* ①
kho·ro·ba lo·ko·mo·tsiy·na
tree *drzewo* ⓝ dzhe·vo
trip (journey) *podróż* ① po·droozh
trolley-bus *trolejbus* ⓜ tro·ley·boos
trousers *spodnie* pl spo·dnye
truck *ciężarówka* ① chyen·zha·roof·ka
trust *ufać* oo·fach
try (attempt) *próbować* proo·bo·vach
T-shirt *koszulka* ① ko·shool·ka
tube (tyre) *dętka* ① dent·ka

Tuesday *wtorek* ⓜ fto·rek
tuna *tuńczyk* ⓜ toon'·chik
tune *melodia* ① me·lo·dya
turkey *indyk* ⓜ een·dik
turn *skręcić* skren·cheech
TV *telewizor* ⓜ te·le·vee·zor
tweezers *pinceta* ① peen·tse·ta
twin beds *dwa łóżka* pl dva woosh·ka
twins *bliźnięta* pl bleezh·nyen·ta
two *dwa* dva
type *typ* ⓜ tip
tyre *opona* ① o·po·na

U

Ukraine *Ukraina* ① oo·kra·ee·na
umbrella *parasol* ⓜ pa·ra·sol
uncomfortable *niewygodny* nye·vi·go·dni
understand *rozumieć* ro·zoo·myech
underwear *bielizna* ① bye·leez·na
unemployed *bezrobotny* bez·ro·bot·ni
uniform *mundur* ⓜ moon·door
universe *wszechświat* ⓜ fshekh·shfyat
university *uniwersytet* ① oo·nee·ver·si·t
unleaded petrol *benzyna bezołowiowa* ①
ben·zi·na bes·o·wo·vyo·va
unsafe *niebezpieczny* nye·bes·pyech·ni
until *do* do
unusual *niezwykły* nye·zvi·kwi
up *do góry* do goo·ri
urgent *pilny* peel·ni
USA *USA* pl oo·es·a
useful *użyteczny* oo·zhi·tech·ni

V

vacancy *wolne miejsca* pl vol·ne myes·tsa
vacant *wolny* vol·ni
vacation *wakacje* pl va·ka·tsye
vaccination *szczepienie* ⓝ shche·pye·nye
validate *uprawomocniać*
oo·pra·vo·mots·nyach
valley *dolina* ① do·lee·na
valuable *cenny* tse·ni
value (price) *wartość* ① var·toshch
van *furgonetka* ① foor·go·net·ka
veal *cielęcina* ① chye·len·chee·na
vegetable *warzywo* ⓝ va·zhi·vo
vegetarian *wegetarianin* ⓜ
ve·ge·tar·ya·neen
vegetarian *wegetariański*
ve·ge·tar·yan'·skee

venereal disease *choroba weneryczna* ①
kho·ro·ba ve·ne·*rich*·na
venue *miejsce* ⓝ *myes*·tse
very *bardzo* *bar*·dzo
video camera *kamera wideo* ①
ka·*me*·ra vee·*de*·o
video recorder *magnetowid* ⓜ
mag·ne·to·veed
video tape *taśma wideo* ① *tash*·ma
vee·*de*·o
view *widok* ⓜ vee·dok
village *wieś* ① vyesh
Vilnius *Wilno* ⓝ veel·no
vine *winorośl* ① vee·no·roshl
vinegar *ocet* ⓜ o·tset
vineyard *winnica* ① vee·*nee*·tsa
violin *skrzypce* pl *skship*·tse
Virgo *Panna* ① *pa*·na
virus *wirus* ⓜ vee·roos
visa *wiza* ① *vee*·za
visit *odwiedzać* od·*vye*·dzach
vitamins *witaminy* pl vee·ta·*mee*·ni
vodka *wódka* ① *vood*·ka
voice *głos* ⓜ gwos
volleyball (sport) *siatkówka* ①
shyat·*koof*·ka
volume *księga* ① *kshyen*·ga
vote *głosować* gwo·so·vach

W

wage *zarobki* pl za·*rob*·kee
wait *czekać* che·kach
waiter *kelner* ⓜ *kel*·ner
waiting room *poczekalnia* ①
po·che·*kal*·nya
wake (someone) up *budzić* boo·jeech
walk *spacerować* spa·tse·ro·vach
want *chcieć* khchyech
war *wojna* ① *voy*·na
warm *ciepły* chyep·wi
Warsaw *Warszawa* ① var·*sha*·va
wash (oneself) *myć się* mich shye
wash (something) *prać* prach
washing machine *pralka* ① *pral*·ka
wasp *osa* ① o·sa
watch *zegarek* ⓜ ze·*ga*·rek
watch *oglądać* o·*glon*·dach
water *woda* ① *vo*·da
water bottle *manierka* ① ma·*nyer*·ka
(hot) water bottle *termofor* ⓜ ter·mo·for
waterfall *wodospad* ⓜ vo·do·spad
watermelon *arbuz* ⓜ *ar*·boos

waterproof *wodoodporny* vo·do·od·*por*·ni
water-skiing *narty wodne* pl *nar*·ti *vod*·ne
way *droga* ① *dro*·ga
we *my* mi
weak *słaby* swa·bi
wealthy *bogaty* bo·*ga*·ti
wear *nosić* no·sheech
weather *pogoda* ① po·*go*·da
wedding *ślub* ⓜ shloob
Wednesday *środa* ① *shro*·da
week *tydzień* ⓜ *ti*·jyen'
weekend *weekend* ⓜ *wee*·kend
weigh *ważyć* va·zhich
weight *waga* ① *va*·ga
welcome *witać* vee·tach
well adv *dobrze* dob·zhe
west *zachód* ⓜ za·khood
wet *mokry* mo·kri
what *co* tso
wheel *koło* ⓝ *ko*·wo
wheelchair *wózek inwalidzki* ⓜ
voo·zek een·va·*leets*·kee
when *kiedy* kye·di
where *gdzie* gjye
which *który* ktoo·ri
whisky *whisky* ⓝ *wis*·kee
white *biały* bya·wi
white wine *białe wino* ① *bya*·we *vee*·no
who *kto* kto
why *dlaczego* dla·*che*·go
wide *szeroki* she·ro·ki
wife *żona* ① *zho*·na
win *wygrać* *vi*·grach
wind *wiatr* ⓜ vyatr
window *okno* ⓝ *ok*·no
windscreen *przednia szyba* ①
pshed·nya *shi*·ba
wine *wino* ① *vee*·no
winner *zwycięzca* ⓜ zvi·*chyens*·tsa
winter *zima* ① *zhee*·ma
wire *drut* ⓜ droot
wish *życzyć* zhi·chich
with *z* z
within (time) *w* v
without *bez* bes
woman *kobieta* ① ko·*bye*·ta
wood *drewno* ⓝ *drev*·no
wool *wełna* ① *vew*·na
work *praca* ① *pra*·tsa
work *pracować* pra·*tso*·vach
workout *trening* ⓜ *tre*·neeng
work permit *zezwolenie na pracę* ⓜ
zez·vo·*le*·nye na *pra*·tse

world *świat* ⓜ shfyat
World Cup *Puchar Świata* ⓜ
poo-khar shfya-ta
World War I/II *pierwsza/druga wojna
światowa* ⓕ pyerf-sha/droo-ga voy-na
shfya-to-va
worms (intestinal) *robaki* pl ro-ba-kee
worried *zmartwiony* zmart-fyo-ni
wrist *nadgarstek* ⓜ nad-gars-tek
write *pisać* pee-sach
writer *pisarz* ⓜ pee-sash
wrong *zły* zwi

Y

year *rok* ⓜ rok
yellow *żółty* zhoow-ti
yes *tak* tak
yesterday *wczoraj* fcho-rai
yet *już* yoosh
yoga *joga* ⓕ yo-ga
yogurt *jogurt* ⓜ yo-goort

you inf sg *ty* ti
you pol sg *pan/pani* ⓜ/ⓕ pan/pa-nee
you inf pl *wy* vi
you pol pl *panowie* ⓜ pa-no-vye
you pol pl *panie* ⓕ pa-nye
you pol pl *państwo* ⓜ&ⓕ pan'-stfo
young *młody* mwo-di
your inf sg *twój* tfooy
your pol sg *pana/pani* ⓜ/ⓕ
pa-na/pa-nee
your inf pl *wasz* vash
your pol pl *państwa* ⓜ&ⓕ pl pan'-stfa
youth hostel *schronisko młodzieżowe* ⓝ
skhro-nees-ko mwo-jye-zho-ve

Z

zip/zipper *zamek błyskawiczny* ⓜ
za-mek bwis-ka-veech-ni
zodiac *zodiak* ⓜ zo-dyak
zoo *zoo* ⓝ zoo
zoom lens *teleobiektyw* ⓜ te-le-o-byek-tif

This dictionary is arranged according to Polish alphabetical order (shown below). Polish nouns in the **dictionary** have their gender indicated by ⓜ (masculine), ⓕ (feminine) or ⓝ (neuter). If it's a plural noun, you'll also see pl, but you won't see a gender marker as all plural nouns in this dictionary belong to the general (genderless) plural category (refer to the **a–z phrasebuilder** for more on this). When a word that could be either a noun or a verb has no gender indicated, it's a verb. For added clarity, certain words are marked as adjectives a or verbs v. Adjectives, however, are given in the masculine form only. Both nouns and adjectives are provided in the nominative case only. For information on case and gender, refer to the **a–z phrasebuilder**. For any food terms, refer to the **menu decoder**.

A a	Ą ą	B b	C c	Ć ć	D d	E e	Ę ę
F f	G g	H h	I i	J j	K k	L l	Ł ł
M m	N n	Ń ń	O o	Ó ó	P p	R r	S s
Ś ś	T t	U u	W w	Y y	Z z	Ż ż	Ż ż

A

adres ⓜ *a·*dres *address*
aleja ⓕ a·*le·*ya *avenue*
alergia ⓕ a·*ler·*gya *allergy*
alkohol ⓜ al·*ko·*khol *alcohol*
ambasada ⓕ am·ba·*sa·*da *embassy*
angielski ⓜ an·*gyel·*skee
  English (language/nationality)
Anglia ⓕ *an·*glya *England*
antyk ⓜ *an·*tik *antique*
aparat ⓜ a·*pa·*rat *camera*
apteka ⓕ ap·*te·*ka *chemist • pharmacy*
aptekarz ⓜ ap·*te·*kash *pharmacist*
autobus ⓜ ow·*to·*boos *bus (city)*
autokar ⓜ ow·*to·*kar *bus (intercity)*
automat biletowy ⓜ
  ow·*to·*mat bee·le·*to·*vi *ticket machine*
autostop ⓜ ow·*to·*stop *hitchhike*
autostrada ⓕ ow·to·*stra·*da *motorway*

B

babcia ⓕ *bab·*chya *grandmother*
bagaż ⓜ *ba·*gash *luggage*
balet ⓜ *ba·*let *ballet*

balkon ⓜ *bal·*kon *balcony*
bandaż ⓜ *ban·*dash *bandage*
bank ⓜ bank *bank*
bankomat ⓜ ban·*ko·*mat
  automated teller machine (ATM)
bar ⓜ bar *bar*
  — mleczny *mlech·*ni
  self-service cafeteria
bardzo *bar·*dzo *very*
basen ⓜ *ba·*sen *swimming pool*
benzyna ⓕ ben·*zi·*na *gas • petrol*
bez bes *without*
bezpieczny bes·*pyech·*ni *safe* a
bezpłatny ⓜ bes·*pwat·*ni *free (gratis)*
bezpośredni bes·po·*shred·*nee *direct*
bęben ⓜ *bem·*ben *drum*
Białoruś ⓕ bya·wo·roosh *Belarus*
biały *bya·*wi *white*
biblioteka ⓕ beeb·lyo·*te·*ka *library*
biedny *byed·*ni *poor (not wealthy)*
biegać *bye·*gach *run*
bilet ⓜ *bee·*let *ticket*
  — powrotny po·*vro·*tni *return ticket*
  — w jedną stronę v yed·nom stro·ne
  one-way ticket
  — z listy rezerwowej
  z lees·ti re·zer·vo·vey *stand-by ticket*

biuro ⓝ *byoo*-ro *office*
— **podróży** po-*droo*-zhi *travel agency*
— **turystyczne** too-ris-*tich*-ne *tourist office*
biżuteria ⓕ bee-zhoo-*ter*-ya *jewellery*
bliski *blees*-kee *close* a
bocian (biały) ⓜ *bo*-chyan (*bya*-wi) *(white) stork*
boczek ⓜ *bo*-chek *bacon*
bogaty bo-*ga*-ti *wealthy*
bolesny bo-*les*-ni *painful*
ból ⓜ bool *pain*
— **głowy** *gwo*-vi *headache*
— **okresowy** o-kre-*so*-vi *period pain*
— **zęba** *zem*-ba *toothache*
— **żołądka** zho-*wont*-ka *stomachache*
Boże Narodzenie ⓝ *bo*-zhe na-ro-*dze*-nye *Christmas*
brać brach *take*
brat ⓜ brat *brother*
Bratysława ⓕ bra-ti-*swa*-va *Bratislava*
brązowy bron-*zo*-vi *brown*
brzytwa ⓕ *bzhit*-fa *razor*
budynek ⓜ boo-*di*-nek *building*
budzić *boo*-jeech *wake (someone) up*
budzik ⓜ *boo*-jeek *alarm clock*
bursztyn ⓜ *boorsh*-tin *amber*
burza ⓕ *boo*-zha *storm*
butelka ⓕ boo-*tel*-ka *bottle*
buty pl *boo*-ti *boots · shoes*
być bich *be*

C

całować tsa-*wo*-vach *kiss*
cały *tsa*-wi *all*
cena ⓕ *tse*-na *price*
centrum ⓝ *tsen*-troom *city centre*
— **zakupowe** za-koo-*po*-ve *shopping centre*
chcieć khchyech *want*
chleb ⓜ khlep *bread*
chłodny *khwo*-dni *cool (temperature)*
chłopak ⓜ *khwo*-pak *boyfriend*
chłopiec ⓜ *khwo*-pyets *boy*
chmura ⓕ *khmoo*-ra *cloud*
chodzić *kho*-jeech *go*
choroba ⓕ kho-*ro*-ba *disease · illness*
— **lokomocyjna** lo-ko-mo-*tsiy*-na *travel sickness*
chory *kho*-ri *sick*

chrześcijanin ⓜ khshesh-chee-*ya*-neen *Christian*
chusteczki pl khoos-*tech*-kee *tissues*
ciało ⓝ *chya*-wo *body*
ciasta pl *chyas*-ta *pastry*
ciasto ⓝ *chyas*-to *cake*
ciąć chyonch *cut*
ciągnąć *chyong*-nonch *pull*
cichy *chee*-khi *quiet*
ciemny *chyem*-ni *dark*
cienki *chyen*-kee *thin*
ciepły *chyep*-wi *warm*
ciężki *chyensh*-kee *heavy (weight)*
ciotka ⓕ *chyot*-ka *aunt*
ciśnienie ⓝ cheesh-*nye*-nye *pressure (tyre)*
co tso *what*
codzienny tso-*jye*-ni *daily*
coś tsosh *something*
córka ⓕ *tsoor*-ka *daughter*
cukier ⓜ *tsoo*-kyer *sugar*
cukiernia ⓕ tsoo-*kyer*-nya *cake shop*
cukrzyca ⓕ tsook-*shi*-tsa *diabetes*
cyfrowy tsi-*fro*-vi *digital*
cyrk ⓜ tsirk *circus*
czarny *char*-ni *black*
czas ⓜ chas *time*
Czechy pl *che*-khi *Czech Republic*
czek ⓜ chek *check (banking) · cheque (banking)*
czekać *che*-kach *wait*
czeki podróżne pl *che*-kee po-*droozh*-ne *travellers cheque*
czekolada ⓕ che-ko-*la*-da *chocolate*
czerwiec ⓜ *cher*-vyets *June*
czerwony cher-*vo*-ni *red*
często *chen*-sto *often*
czuć chooch *feel (touch)*
czwartek ⓜ *chfar*-tek *Thursday*
czynsz ⓜ chinsh *rent*
czysty *chi*-sti *clean · pure*
czytać *chi*-tach *read*

D

dać dach *give*
daktyl ⓜ *dak*-til *date (fruit)*
daleki da-*le*-kee *far*
Dania ⓕ *da*-nya *Denmark*
data ⓕ *da*-ta *date (day)*
— **urodzenia** oo-ro-*dze*-nya *date of birth*

dąb ⓜ domb *oak (tree)*
delikatesy pl de-lee-ka-te-si *delicatessen*
dentysta ⓜ den-*tis*-ta *dentist*
depozyt ⓜ de-*po*-zit *deposit*
deser ⓜ *de*-ser *dessert*
deszcz ⓜ deshch *rain*
dętka ① *dent*-ka *tube (tyre)*
dieta ① *dye*-ta *diet*
dlaczego dla-*che*-go *why*
długi dwoo-gee *long*
dno ⓝ dno *bottom (position)*
do to • *until*
dobry *do*-bri *good*
dobrze *dob*-zhe *well*
dolar ⓜ *do*-lar *dollar*
dolina ① do-*lee*-na *valley*
dom ⓜ dom *home • house*
— **towarowy** to-va-*ro*-vi
   department store
dorosły ⓜ do-*ro*-swi *adult* n
dostać *dos*-tach *get*
dowód tożsamości ⓜ
   do-vood tozh-sa-*mosh*-chee
   identification card (ID)
drewno ⓝ *drev*-no *wood* n
drobny *drob*-ni *tiny*
droga ① *dro*-ga *road • way*
drogi *dro*-gee *expensive*
druga klasa ① *droo*-ga *kla*-sa
   second class
drugi *droo*-gee *second* a
drukarka ① droo-*kar*-ka *printer (computer)*
drużyna ① droo-*zhi*-na *team*
drzewo ⓝ *dzhe*-vo *tree*
drzwi dzhvee *door*
dużo *doo*-zho *(a) lot • many*
duży *doo*-zhi *big*
dwa dva *two*
dworzec autobusowy ⓜ
   dvo-zhets ow-to-boo-*so*-vi *bus station*
dyplom ⓜ *dip*-lom *certificate (education)*
dyskietka ① dis-*kyet*-ka *disk (floppy)*
dziadek ⓜ *jya*-dek *grandfather*
dzieci pl *jye*-chee *children*
dziecko ⓝ *jye*-tsko *child*
dzielić się *jye*-leech shye *share (with)*
dzielnica ① jyel-*nee*-tsa *suburb*
dzień ⓜ jyen' *day*
Dzień Bożego Narodzenia ⓜ
   jyen' bo-*zhe*-go na-ro-*dze*-nya
   Christmas Day

dziennikarz ⓜ jye-*nee*-kash *journalist*
dziewczyna ① jyev-*chi*-na *girl • girlfriend*
dzisiaj jee-*shyai* *today*
dziwny *jeev*-ni *strange*
dzwonić *dzvo*-neech *call (phone)*
dżin ⓜ jeen *gin*
dżinsy pl *jeen*-si *jeans*
dżip ⓜ jeep *jeep*

E

egzema ① eg-*ze*-ma *eczema*
ekspresowy eks-pre-*so*-vi *express* a
elektryczność ① e-lek-*trich*-noshch
   electricity
email ⓜ e-*mail* *email*
emeryt/emerytka ⓜ/①
   e-*me*-rit/e-me-*rit*-ka *pensioner*

F

fabryka ① fa-*bri*-ka *factory*
faks ⓜ faks *fax machine*
fala ① *fa*-la *wave (beach)*
farmaceuta ⓜ far-ma-*tsew*-ta
   chemist (pharmacist)
filiżanka ① fee-lee-*zhan*-ka *cup*
film ⓜ feelm *film (camera/cinema)*
Finlandia ① feen-*lan*-dya *Finland*
fioletowy fyo-le-*to*-vi *purple*
firma ① *feer*-ma *business*
flesz ⓜ flesh *flash (camera)*
flet ⓜ flet *flute*
fotograf ⓜ fo-*to*-graf *photographer*
fotografika ① fo-to-gra-*fee*-ka
   photography
fotografować fo-to-gra-*fo*-vach
   photograph
Francja ① *fran*-tsya *France*
fryzjer ⓜ *fri*-zyer *hairdresser*
funt ⓜ foont *pound (money/weight)*

G

galeria sztuki ① ga-*ler*-ya *shtoo*-kee
   art gallery
garaż ⓜ *ga*-razh *garage*
gaz ⓜ gaz *gas (for cooking)*
gazeta ① ga-*ze*-ta *newspaper*
gdzie gjye *where*

gej ⓜ gey *gay (homosexual)*
gimnastyka ⓕ geem-*nas*-ti-ka *gymnastics*
gimnazjum ⓝ geem-*na*-zyoom
  high school
głęboki gwem-*bo*-kee *deep*
głodny *gwo*-dni *hungry*
głowa ⓕ *gwo*-va *head*
główny gwoov-ni *main*
głuchy *gwoo*-khi *deaf*
godzina ⓕ go-*jee*-na *hour*
godziny otwarcia pl go-*jee*-ni ot-*far*-chya
  opening hours
gol ⓜ gol *goal (sport)*
gorący go-*ron*-tsi *hot*
gorączka ⓕ go-*ronch*-ka *fever*
gospodarstwo agroturystyczne ⓝ
  gos-po-*darst*-fo a-gro-too-ris-*tich*-ne
  agritourist farm
gospodarstwo rolne ⓝ
  gos-po-*darst*-fo *rol*-ne *farm*
gościnność ⓕ gosh-*chee*-noshch
  hospitality
gotować go-*to*-vach *cook*
gotowanie ⓝ go-to-*va*-nye *cooking*
gotowy go-*to*-vi *ready*
gotówka ⓕ go-*toof*-ka *cash*
góra ⓕ *goo*-ra *mountain*
granat ⓜ *gra*-nat *garnet*
granica ⓕ gra-*nee*-tsa *border*
grób ⓜ groob *grave*
grudzień ⓜ groo-*jyen'* *December*
grypa ⓕ *gri*-pa *influenza*
grzejnik ⓜ *gzhey*-neek *heater*
guma ⓕ *goo*-ma *gum*
  — do żucia do *zhoo*-chya *chewing gum*
gwałt ⓜ gvowt *rape*
gwarancja ⓕ gva-*ran*-tsya *guarantee*

H

hałaśliwy kha-*wash*-lee-vi *noisy*
herbata ⓕ kher-*ba*-ta *tea*
heroina ⓕ khe-ro-*ee*-na *heroin*
historia ⓕ khees-*to*-rya *history*
historyczny khees-to-*rich*-ni *historical*
Hiszpania ⓕ kheesh-*pa*-nya *Spain*
Holandia ⓕ kho-*lan*-dya *Netherlands*
homoseksualista ⓜ
  kho-mo-sek-soo-a-*lees*-ta *homosexual*

I

i ee *and*
ich eekh *their*
identyfikacja ⓕ ee-den-ti-fee-*ka*-tsya
  identification
ile *ee*-le *how much*
imię ⓝ *ee*-mye *given name*
imigracja ⓕ ee-mee-*gra*-tsya
  immigration
infekcja ⓕ een-*fek*-tsya *infection*
informacja ⓕ een-for-*mats*-ya *information*
informatyka ⓕ een-for-ma-*ti*-ka *IT*
inny *ee*-ni *another (a different one)*
interesujący ⓜ een-te-re-soo-*yon*-tsi
  interesting
internet ⓜ een-*ter*-net *Internet*
inżynier ⓜ een-*zhi*-nyer *engineer*
Irlandia ⓕ eer-*lan*-dya *Ireland*
iść eeshch *go (on foot)*

J

Ja ya *I*
jadłospis ⓜ ya-*dwo*-spees *menu*
jak yak *how*
jakiś *ya*-keesh *any (some)*
jakość ⓕ *ya*-koshch *quality*
Japonia ⓕ ya-*po*-nya *Japan*
jaskinia ⓕ yas-*kee*-nya *cave*
jasny *yas*-ni *light (colour)*
jaszczurka ⓕ yash-*choor*-ka *lizard*
jazda ⓕ *yaz*-da *ride* n
jechać ye-khach *go (by mechanised means)*
jeden *ye*-den *one*
jesień ⓕ *ye*-shyen' *autumn • fall*
jeszcze (nie) *yesh*-che (nye) *(not) yet*
jeść yeshch *eat* v
jeśli *yesh*-lee *if*
jetlag ⓜ *jet*-lag *jet lag*
jezioro ⓝ ye-*zhyo*-ro *lake*
jeździć *yezh*-jeech *ride (bike, horse)*
język ⓜ *yen*-zik *language*
jutro *yoo*-tro *tomorrow*
już yoosh *already • yet*

K

kamień ⓜ *ka*-myen' *stone*
kamping ⓜ *kam*-peeng *camping ground*

kanapka ① ka-*nap*-ka *sandwich*
kantor ⓜ *kan*-tor *currency exchange*
kapelusz ⓜ ka-*pe*-loosh *hat*
kapłan ⓜ *kap*-wan *priest*
kara ① *ka*-ra *fine* n
karetka pogotowia ①
  ka-*ret*-ka po-go-*to*-vya *ambulance*
Karpaty kar-*pa*-ti *Carpathian mountains*
karton ⓜ *kar*-ton *carton*
karty *kar*-ti *cards (playing)*
kasa biletowa ① *ka*-sa bee-le-*to*-va
  ticket office
kasjer/kasjerka ⓜ/① kas-yer/kas-*yer*-ka
  cashier
kask ⓜ kask *helmet*
kaszel ⓜ *ka*-shel *cough*
katar ⓜ *ka*-tar *cold (illness)*
katedra ① ka-*te*-dra *cathedral*
katolik ⓜ ka-*to*-leek *Catholic* n
kawa ① *ka*-va *coffee*
kawałek ⓜ ka-*va*-wek *piece*
kawiarnia ① ka-*vyar*-nya *café*
każdy *kazh*-di *each • everyone • every*
kąpiel ① *kom*-pyel *bath*
kelner ⓜ *kel*-ner *waiter*
kibic ⓜ *kee*-beets *fan (sport, politics)*
kiedy *kye*-di *when*
kierować kye-*ro*-vach *drive*
kierownik ⓜ kye-*rov*-neek
  manager (of a business)
kierunek ⓜ kye-*roo*-nek *direction*
Kijów ⓜ *kee*-yoof *Kievy*
kilka *keel*-ka *few • several • some*
kino ⓝ *kee*-no *cinema*
kiosk ⓜ kyosk *kiosk*
klasyczny kla-*sich*-ni *classical*
klasztor ⓜ *klash*-tor *convent • monastery*
klej ⓜ kley *glue*
klient ⓜ *klee*-yent *client*
klimatyzacja ① klee-ma-ti-*za*-tsya
  air conditioning
klimatyzowany ⓜ klee-ma-ti-zo-*va*-ni
  air-conditioned
klucz ⓜ klooch *key (door etc)*
kłaść kwashch *put*
kłódka ① *kwood*-ka *padlock*
kobieta ① ko-*bye*-ta *woman*
koc ⓜ kots *blanket*
kochać ko-*khach* *love*
kolacja ① ko-*la*-tsya *dinner • supper*
kolano ⓝ ko-*la*-no *knee*

kolczyki kol-*chi*-kee *earrings*
kolejka ① ko-*ley*-ka *queue • round (drinks)*
kolor ⓜ *ko*-lor *colour*
kołdry i pościel ① *kow*-dri ee *posh*-chyel
  bedding
koło ⓝ *ko*-wo *wheel* n
komar ⓜ *ko*-mar *mosquito*
komis ⓜ *ko*-mees *secondhand shop*
komisariat policji ⓜ
  ko-mee-*sar*-yat po-*leets*-yee
  police station
komunia ① ko-*moo*-nya *communion*
komunista ⓜ ko-moo-*nees*-ta *communist*
koncert ⓜ *kon*-tsert *concert*
konferencja ① kon-fe-*ren*-tsya
  conference (big)
koniec ⓜ *ko*-nyets *end*
konsulat ⓜ kon-*soo*-lat *consulate*
konto ⓝ *kon*-to *account (bill)*
  — **bankowe** ban-*ko*-ve *bank account*
kontrakt ⓜ *kon*-trakt *contract*
koń ⓜ kon' *horse*
kończyć *kon'*-chich *finish*
kopać ko-*pach* *kick*
korek ⓜ *ko*-rek *plug (bath)*
koronka ① ko-*ron*-ka *lace (fabric)*
kort ⓜ kort *court (tennis)*
  — **tenisowy** te-nee-*so*-vi *tennis court*
korupcja ① ko-*roop*-tsya *corruption*
kościół ⓜ *kosh*-chyoow *church*
  — **prawosławny** pra-vo-*swav*-ni
  Orthodox Church
kość ① koshch *bone*
kosmetyczka ① kos-me-*tich*-ka
  beautician
kostium kąpielowy ⓜ
  kos-tyoom kom-pye-*lo*-vi *swimsuit*
kostka ① *kos*-tka *ankle*
koszt ⓜ kosht *cost*
koszula ① ko-*shoo*-la *shirt*
koszykówka ① ko-shi-*koof*-ka *basketball*
kot ⓜ kot *cat*
koza ① *ko*-za *goat*
kradziony kra-*jyo*-ni *stolen*
kraj ⓜ krai *country*
kran ⓜ kran *faucet • tap*
kraść krashch *steal*
krawiec ⓜ *kra*-vyets *tailor*
kredyt ⓜ *kre*-dit *credit*
krem ⓜ krem *cream (lotion)*
krew ① kref *blood*

krewetka ① kre-*vet*-ka *prawn*
krok ⓜ krok *step*
krople do oczu *kro*-ple do o-*choo* *eye drops*
krowa ① *kro*-va *cow*
król ⓜ krool *king*
królowa ① kroo-*lo*-va *queen*
krótki *kroot*-kee *short (length)*
kryształ ⓜ *krish*-tow *crystal*
książka ① *ksyonsh*-ka *book* n
— **telefoniczna** te-le-fo-*neech*-na *phone book*
księgarnia ① kshyen-*gar*-nya *book shop*
kto kto *who*
ktoś ktosh *someone*
który *ktoo*-ri *that · which*
kucharz ⓜ *koo*-khash *cook*
kuchnia ① *kookh*-nya *kitchen*
kupować koo-*po*-vach *buy*
kurs wymiany ⓜ koors vi-*mya*-ni *exchange rate*
kurtka ① *koort*-ka *jacket*
kuszetka ① koo-*shet*-ka *couchette*
kwiaciarnia ① kvya-*chyar*-nya *florist*
kwiat ⓜ kvyat *flower*
kwiecień ⓜ *kfye*-chen' *April*

L

las ⓜ las *forest*
latać *la*-tach *fly* v
latarka ① la-*tar*-ka *flashlight · torch*
lato ⓜ *la*-to *summer*
lek ⓜ lek *drug (medicinal)*
lekarstwo ⓜ le-*karst*-fo *medicine (medication)*
— **na kaszel** na *ka*-shel *cough medicine*
lekarz ⓜ *le*-kash *doctor*
lekki *le*-kee *light (weight)*
len ⓜ len *linen (material)*
lepszy *lep*-shi *better*
lesbijka ① les-*beey*-ka *lesbian*
lewy *le*-vi *left (direction)*
leżeć *le*-zhech *lie (not stand)* v
licencja ① lee-*tsen*-tsya *licence*
lipiec ⓜ *lee*-pyets *July*
list ⓜ leest *letter (mail)*
listopad ⓜ lees-to-pat *November*
Litwa ① *lee*-tfa *Lithuania*
lodówka ① lo-*doof*-ka *refrigerator*
lody pl *lo*-di *ice cream*
lodziarnia ① lo-*jyar*-nya *ice-cream parlour*
lot ⓜ lot *flight*
lotnisko ⓜ lot-*nees*-ko *airport*
lubić *loo*-beech *like* v
ludzie pl *loo*-jye *people*
luksusowy ⓜ look-soo-*so*-vi *luxury*
luty ⓜ *loo*-ti *February*
luźny *loozh*-ni *loose*

Ł

ładny *wad*-ni *fine · pretty*
łapówka ① wa-*poof*-ka *bribe*
łatwy ⓜ *wa*-tfi *easy*
łazienka ① wa-*zhyen*-ka *bathroom*
lód ⓜ lood *ice*
łódź ① wooj *boat*
łóżko ⓜ *woozh*-ko *bed*
— **małżeńskie** mow-*zhen'*-skye *double bed*
łyżeczka ① wi-*zhech*-ka *teaspoon*
łyżka ① *wish*-ka *spoon*

M

magnetowid ⓜ mag-ne-*to*-veed *video recorder*
maj ⓜ mai *May*
makijaż ① ma-*kee*-yash *make-up*
malarstwo ⓜ ma-*lars*-tfo *painting (a work)*
mały *ma*-wi *small*
małżeństwo ⓜ mow-*zhen'st*-fo *marriage*
manierka ① ma-*nyer*-ka *water bottle*
mapa ① *ma*-pa *map (of country)*
— **drogowa** dro-*go*-va *road map*
marihuana ① ma-ree-khoo-*a*-na *marijuana*
marionetka ① ma-ryo-*net*-ka *puppet*
martwy ⓜ *mart*-fi *dead*
marzec ⓜ *ma*-zhets *March*
masaż ⓜ *ma*-sash *massage*
masło ⓜ *mas*-wo *butter*
maszyna ① ma-*shi*-na *machine*
materac ⓜ ma-*te*-rats *mattress*
materiał ⓜ ma-*ter*-yow *fabric*
matka ① *mat*-ka *mother*
mąż ⓜ monzh *husband*
mdłości pl *mdwosh*-chee *nausea*
meble pl *me*-ble *furniture*

mecz ⓜ mech *match (sports)*
meczet ⓜ me-chet *mosque*
medycyna ⓕ me-di-tsi-na
  medicine (study/profession)
menedżer ⓜ me-ne-jer *manager (sport)*
metro ⓝ me-tro *metro • subway*
mężczyzna ⓜ menzh-chiz-na *man*
mi mee *me*
miasto ⓝ myas-to *city*
mieć myech *have*
miejsce ⓝ myeys-tse *place • seat*
  — urodzenia oo-ro-dze-nya
  place of birth
miejscowy ⓜ myeys-tso-vi *local*
miesiąc ⓜ mye-shonts *month*
  — miodowy myo-do-vi *honeymoon*
mieszać mye-shach *mix*
mieszkać myesh-kach *live (somewhere)*
mieszkanie ⓝ myesh-ka-nye
  apartment • flat
między myen-dzi *between*
międzynarodowy myen-dzi-na-ro-do-vi
  international
mięso ⓝ myen-so *meat*
mijać mee-yach *pass (go by)*
miłość ⓕ mee-woshch *love*
miły mee-wi *kind • nice*
minuta ⓕ mee-noo-ta *minute*
Mińsk ⓜ meen'sk *Minsk*
miska ⓕ mee-ska *bowl (plate)* n
mleko ⓝ mle-ko *milk*
młody mwo-di *young* a
mnich ⓜ mneekh *monk*
mniej mnyey *less*
mniejszy mnyey-shi *smaller*
moda ⓕ mo-da *fashion* n
mokry mo-kri *wet* a
monety pl mo-ne-ti *coins*
morze ⓝ mo-zhe *sea*
Morze Bałtyckie ⓝ mo-zhe bow-tits-kye
  Baltic Sea
Moskwa ⓕ mosk-fa *Moscow*
most ⓜ most *bridge (structure)*
motel ⓜ mo-tel *motel*
motor ⓜ mo-tor *motorbike*
motorówka ⓕ mo-to-roof-ka *motorboat*
możliwy ⓜ mozh-lee-vi *possible*
mówić moo-veech *say • speak*
mrożony mro-zho-ni *frozen*
mróz ⓜ mrooz *frost*
msza ⓕ msha *mass (Catholic)*
mucha ⓕ moo-kha *fly*

muzeum ⓝ moo-ze-oom *museum*
muzyka ⓕ moo-zi-ka *music*
my mi *we*
mydło ⓝ mid-wo *soap*

N

na na *on*
nad nad *above*
nagły przypadek ⓜ na-gwi pshi-pa-dek
  emergency
najbliższy nai-bleezh-shi *nearest*
najlepszy nai-lep-shi *best*
najmniejszy nai-mnyey-shi *smallest*
największy nai-vyenk-shi *biggest*
namiot ⓜ na-myot *tent*
napiwek ⓜ na-pee-vek *tip (gratuity)*
napój ⓜ na-pooy *drink* n
naprawić na-pra-veech *repair*
naprzeciwko na-pshe-cheef-ko *opposite*
naprzód na-pshoot *ahead*
narciarstwo ⓝ nar-chyarst-fo *skiing*
narkotyki nar-ko-ti-kee *drugs (illicit)*
narodowość ⓕ na-ro-do-voshch
  nationality
narty pl nar-ti *skis*
następny nas-temp-ni *next (following)*
nasz nash *our*
nauczyciel ⓜ na-oo-chi-chyel *teacher*
nauka ⓕ na-oo-ka *science*
nauki humanistyczne pl na-oo-kee
  khoo-ma-nees-tich-ne *humanities*
nazwisko ⓝ naz-vees-ko *surname*
negatyw ⓜ ne-ga-tif *negatives (photos)*
nic neets *nothing*
nić ⓕ neech *thread*
nie nye *no • not*
niebieski ⓜ nye-byes-kee *blue*
niebo ⓝ nye-bo *sky*
niedziela ⓕ nye-jye-la *Sunday*
Niemcy pl nyem-tsi *Germany*
niemowlę ⓝ nye-mov-le *baby*
niemożliwy ⓜ nye-mozh-lee-vi *impossible*
niemy ⓜ nye-mi *mute*
niepalący ⓜ nye-pa-lon-tsi *nonsmoking*
niepełnosprawny ⓜ nye-pew-no-sprav-ni
  disabled
niestrawność ⓕ nye-strav-noshch
  indigestion
niewygodny ⓜ nye-vi-go-dni
  uncomfortable

nieznajomy ⓜ nye-zna-yo-mi *stranger*
nigdy neeg-di *never*
niski nees-kee *low • short (height)*
noc ① nots *night*
nocleg ⓜ nots-leg *accommodation*
nocny nots-ni *overnight*
noga ① no-ga *leg (body)*
nosić no-sheech *carry • wear*
notatnik ⓜ no-tat-neek *diary*
notes ⓜ no-tes *notebook*
Nowa Zelandia ① no-va ze-lan-dya *New Zealand*
nowoczesny m no-vo-ches-ni *modern*
nowy no-vi *new*
Nowy Rok ⓜ no-vi rok *New Year's Day*
nożyczki pl no-zhich-kee *scissors*
nóż ⓜ noosh *knife*
nudny noo-dni *boring*
numer ⓜ noo-mer *number*

O

obaj/obie/oboje ⓜ/①/ⓝ o-bai/o-bye/o-bo-ye *both*
obiektyw ⓜ o-byek-tif *lens (camera)*
obok o-bok *beside*
obsługa ① ob-swoo-ga *service* n
obywatelstwo ⓝ o-bi-va-telst-fo *citizenship*
od od *from • per (day) • since (time)*
oddychać o-di-khach *breathe*
odjazd ⓜ od-yazd *departure (by land)*
odjeżdżać od-yezh-jach *depart*
odlot ⓜ od-lot *departure (by air)*
odpoczywać od-po-chi-vach *relax • rest*
odpowiedź ① od-po-vyej *answer*
odwiedzać od-vye-dzach *visit*
oglądać o-glon-dach *watch*
ogród ⓜ o-grood *garden*
ogrzewanie ⓝ o-gzhe-va-nye *heating*
ojciec ⓜ oy-chyets *father*
okno ⓝ ok-no *window*
oko ⓝ o-ko *eye*
okolica ① o-ko-lee-tsa *countryside*
okraść o-krashch *rob*
okulary pl o-koo-la-ri *glasses (spectacles)*
— słoneczne swo-nech-ne *sunglasses*
okulista ⓜ o-koo-lees-ta *optometrist*
ołówek ⓜ o-woo-vek *pencil*
ołtarz ⓜ ow-tazh *altar*
on on *he*

ona o-na *she*
oni o-nee *they*
operacja ① o-pe-ra-tsya *operation (medical)*
opona ① o-po-na *tyre*
opóźnienie ⓝ o-poozh-nye-nye *delay*
orzech ⓜ o-zhekh *nut (food)*
orzeszek ziemny o-zhe-shek zhyem-ni *groundnut • peanut*
osoba ① o-so-ba *person*
osobny o-so-bni *separate*
ostatni os-tat-nee *last (final)*
ostatnio os-tat-nyo *recently*
otwarty ot-far-ti *open (business)*
owoc ⓜ o-vots *fruit*

P

paczka ① pach-ka *package • packet • parcel*
palec ⓜ pa-lets *finger*
— u nogi oo no-gee *toe*
pamiątka ① pa-myont-ka *souvenir*
pan ⓜ pan *Mr*
pan/pani ⓜ/① pan/pa-nee *you* pol sg
pana/pani ⓜ/① pa-na/pa-nee *your* pol sg
pani ① pa-nee *Mrs • Ms*
panie pa-nye *you* pol ① pl
panna ① pa-na *Miss*
panowie pa-no-vye *you* pol ⓜ pl
państwa pan'-stfa *your* pol ⓜ&① pl
państwo pan'-stfo *you* pol ⓜ&① pl
papieros ⓜ pa-pye-ros *cigarette*
para ① pa-ra *pair (couple)*
parasol ⓜ pa-ra-sol *umbrella*
park ⓜ park *park*
— narodowy na-ro-do-vi *national park*
pasażer ⓜ pa-sa-zher *passenger*
pastylka ① pas-til-ka *pill*
patrzeć pat-shech *look*
październik ⓜ pazh-jyer-neek *October*
pchli targ ⓜ pkhlee tark *fleamarket*
pełny pew-ni *full*
pensja ① pen-sya *salary*
pensjonat ⓜ pen-syo-nat *guesthouse*
perkusja ① per-koo-sya *drums (kit)*
peron ⓜ pe-ron *platform*
piątek ⓜ pyon-tek *Friday*
pić peech *drink*
piekarnia ① pye-kar-nya *bakery*
pieniądze pl pye-nyon-dze *money*

pierwsza klasa ① *pyerf*-sha *kla*-sa *first class*
pierwszy *pyerf*-shi *first* a
pies ⓜ pyes *dog*
pieszy *pye*-shi *pedestrian* n
piękny *pyen*-kni *beautiful*
piętro ⓝ *pyen*-tro *floor (storey)*
pijany pee-*ya*-ni *drunk*
pilny *peel*-ni *urgent*
piłka ① *peew*-ka *ball (sport)*
— **nożna** *nozh*-na *football (soccer)*
— **ręczna** *rench*-na *handball*
piosenka ① pyo-*sen*-ka *song*
pisać *pee*-sach *write*
piwo ⓝ *pee*-vo *beer*
plakat ⓜ *pla*-kat *poster*
plan ⓜ plan *map (of town)*
plastykowy plas-ti-*ko*-vi *plastic* a
plaża ① *pla*-zha *beach*
plecak ⓜ *ple*-tsak *backpack*
płacić pwa-cheech *pay*
płaski ⓜ *pwas*-kee *flat* a
płaskowyż ⓜ pwas-*ko*-vish *plateau*
płaszcz ⓜ pwashch *coat*
— **nieprzemakalny** nye-pshe-ma-*kal*-ni *raincoat*
pływać *pwi*-vach *swim*
pływanie ⓝ pwi-*va*-nye *swimming*
po po • za *after*
pochmurny pokh-*moor*-ni *cloudy*
pociąg ⓜ *po*-chyonk *train*
poczekalnia ① po-che-*kal*-nya *waiting room*
poczta ① *poch*-ta *mail (postal system)*
pod pod *below*
podatek ⓜ po-*da*-tek *tax*
podgrzewany pod-gzhe-*va*-ni *heated*
podłoga ① pod-*wo*-ga *floor*
podobny po-*do*-bni *similar*
podpis ⓜ *pod*-pees *signature*
podpisać się pod-*pee*-sach shye *sign*
podróż ① *po*-droozh *trip (journey)*
— **służbowa** swoozh-*bo*-va *business trip*
podróżować po-droo-*zho*-vach *travel*
poduszka ① po-*doosh*-ka *pillow*
podwójny pod-*vooy*-ni *double*
pogoda ① po-*go*-da *weather*
pokaz ⓜ *po*-kas *demonstration • show*
pokój ⓜ *po*-kooy *peace • room*
— **dwuosobowy** dvoo-o-so-*bo*-vi *double room*
— **jednoosobowy** ye-dno-o-so-*bo*-vi *single room*

polecać po-*le*-tsach *recommend*
policja ① po-*lee*-tsya *police*
policjant ⓜ po-*lee*-tsyant *police officer (in city)*
Polska ① *pol*-ska *Poland*
połamany po-wa-*ma*-ni *broken*
połączenie ⓝ po-won-*che*-nye *connection (transport)*
połówka ① po-*woof*-ka *half*
południe ⓝ po-*wood*-nye *midday • south*
pomagać po-*ma*-gach *help* v
pomnik ⓜ *pom*-neek *monument*
pomoc ① *po*-mots *help*
pomyłka ① po-*miw*-ka *mistake*
poniedziałek ⓜ po-nye-*jya*-wek *Monday*
poparzenie ⓝ po-pa-*zhe*-nye *burn*
popołudnie ⓝ po-po-*wood*-nye *afternoon*
poprzedni po-*pshed*-nee *last (previous)*
poprzez po-phes *across*
popularny po-poo-*lar*-ni *popular*
portmonetka ① port-mo-*net*-ka *purse*
posiłek ⓜ po-*shee*-wek *meal*
posterunkowy ⓜ pos-te-roon-*ko*-vi *police officer (in country)*
posyłać po-*si*-wach *post*
poszewka ① po-*shef*-ka *pillowcase*
pościel ① *posh*-chyel *bed linen*
potrawa ① po-*tra*-va *dish (food)*
potwierdzać pot-*fyer*-dzach *confirm (a booking)*
poważny po-*vazh*-ni *serious*
powódź ① *po*-vooj *flood*
pozwolenie ⓝ poz-vo-*le*-nye *permission*
pożar ⓜ *po*-zhar *fire (inferno)*
pożyczać po-*zhi*-chach *borrow*
pójść pooyshch *go (on foot)*
półka ① *poow*-ka *shelf*
północ ① *poow*-nots *midnight • north*
później *poozh*-nyey *later*
późno *poozh*-no *late*
praca ① *pra*-tsa *job • work*
pracodawca ⓜ pra-tso-*daf*-tsa *employer*
pracować pra-*tso*-vach *work*
pracownik ⓜ pra-*tsov*-neek *employee*
Praga ① *pra*-ga *Prague*
pralka ① *pral*-ka *washing machine*
pralnia ① *pral*-nya *laundry (place)*
prawie *pra*-vye *almost*
prawnik ⓜ *prav*-neek *lawyer*

prawo ⓝ *pra*-vo law
— **jazdy** *yaz*-di drivers licence
prędkość ⓕ *prend*-koshch speed (travel)
przez pshes per (day)
prom ⓜ prom ferry
prosić *pro*-sheech ask (for something)
prosty *pros*-ti simple • straight
prowizja ⓕ pro-*vee*-zya commission
prysznic ⓜ *prish*-neets shower
prywatny pri-*vat*-ni private
przed pshet before • in front of
przedstawienie ⓝ pshet-sta-*vye*-nye
performance
przedszkole ⓝ pshet-*shko*-le
crèche • kindergarten
przedwczoraj ⓜ pshet-*fcho*-rai
day before yesterday
przekąska ⓕ pshe-*kons*-ka snack
przenocować pshe-no-*tso*-vach
stay (at a hotel)
przestać *pshes*-tach stop (cease)
przetłumaczyć pshe-twoo-*ma*-chich
translate
przetwarzać pshet-*fa*-zhach recycle
przewodnik ⓜ pshe-*vod*-neek
guide (person) • guidebook
przez pshes across
przy pshi at
przydomek ⓜ pshi-*do*-mek nickname
przygotować pshi-go-*to*-vach prepare
przyjaciel/przyjaciółka ⓜ/ⓕ
pshi-*ya*-chyel/pshi-ya-*choow*-ka friend
przyjazdy pl pshi-*yaz*-di arrivals (general)
przyjechać pshi-*ye*-khach arrive
przyjść pshiyshch
come (by mechanised means)
przyloty pl pshi-*lo*-ti arrivals (plane)
przynosić pshi-*no*-sheech bring
przystanek ⓜ pshis-*ta*-nek stop (bus, tram)
ptak ⓜ ptak bird
pusty *poos*-ti empty a

R

rachunek ⓜ ra-*khoo*-nek
bill (restaurant) • receipt
rak ⓜ rak cancer
randka ⓕ *rand*-ka date (appointment)
rano ⓝ *ra*-no morning
raz ras once

recepta ⓕ re-*tse*-pta prescription
religia ⓕ re-*lee*-gya religion
relikt ⓜ *re*-leekt relic
restauracja ⓕ res-tow-*ra*-tsya restaurant
rezerwacja ⓕ re-zer-*va*-tsya
reservation (booking)
rezerwować re-zer-*vo*-vach
book (make a booking)
ręka ⓕ *ren*-ka arm (body) • hand
rękodzieła pl ren-ko-*jye*-wa crafts
rękodzielnictwo ⓝ ren-ko-jyel-*neets*-fo
handicraft
robić *ro*-beech do • make
rodzice pl ro-*jee*-tse parents
rodzina ⓕ ro-*jee*-na family
rok ⓜ rok year
rolnik ⓜ *rol*-neek farmer
Rosja ⓕ *ro*-sya Russia
rower ⓜ *ro*-ver bicycle
rozkład jazdy ⓜ ros-kwad *yaz*-di timetable
rozmieniać roz-*mye*-nyach
change (money)
rozumieć ro-*zoo*-myech understand
rozwiedziony roz-vye-*dzo*-ni divorced
różny *roozh*-ni different
ruchliwy rookh-*lee*-vi busy (street, etc)
ryba ⓕ *ri*-ba fish
rybołówstwo ⓝ ri-bo-*woos*-tfo fishing
rynek ⓜ *ri*-nek market • square (town)
rzeka ⓕ *zhe*-ka river
rzeźba ⓕ *zhezh*-ba sculpture

S

samochód ⓜ sa-*mo*-khoot car
samolot ⓜ sa-*mo*-lot airplane
samoobsługowy sa-mo-ob-swoo-*go*-vi
self-service
schronisko górskie ⓝ
skhro-*nees*-ko *goor*-skye mountain lodge
schronisko młodzieżowe ⓝ
skhro-*nees*-ko mwo-jye-*zho*-ve
youth hostel
seks ⓜ seks sex
sekunda ⓕ se-*koon*-da second
ser ⓜ ser cheese
sezon ⓜ *se*-zon season n
siatkówka ⓕ shyat-*koof*-ka volleyball
— **plażowa** pla-*zho*-va beach volleyball
sierpień ⓜ *shyer*-pyen´ August

silnik ⓜ *sheel*·neek *engine*
silny *sheel*·ni *strong*
siostra ① *shyos*·tra *sister*
skarga ① *skar*·ga *complaint*
sklep ⓜ *sklep* *shop*
skóra ① *skoo*·ra *leather • skin*
skręcić *skren*·cheech *turn*
skrzypce pl *skship*·tse *violin*
słaby *swa*·bi *weak*
słodki *swod*·kee *sweet* a
słoneczny *swo*·nech·ni *sunny*
słońce ⓝ *swon'*·tse *sun*
Słowacja ① *swo*·va·tsya *Slovakia*
słownik ⓜ *swov*·neek *dictionary*
słowo ⓝ *swo*·vo *word*
słuchać *swoo*·khach *listen*
słyszeć *swi*·shech *hear*
smaczny *smach*·ni *tasty*
smutny *smoo*·tni *sad*
sobota ① *so*·bo·ta *Saturday*
soczewki kontaktowe pl
  so·chef·kee kon·tak·*to*·ve *contact lenses*
sok ⓜ *sok* *juice*
sos ⓜ *sos* *sauce*
sosna ① *sos*·na *pine (tree)*
sól ① *sool* *salt*
spacerować spa·tse·*ro*·vach *walk*
spać spach *sleep*
spotkać *spot*·kach *meet (get together)*
spotkanie ⓝ spot·*ka*·nye *appointment*
spragniony ⓜ sprag·*nyo*·ni *thirsty*
sprawdzenie ⓝ sprav·*dze*·nye *bill (check)*
sprzątanie ⓝ spshon·*ta*·nye *cleaning*
sprzedawać spshe·*da*·vach *sell*
sprzedawca/sprzedawczyni ⓜ/①
  spshe·*daf*·tsa/spshe·daf·*chi*·nee
  sales assistant
sprzedaż ① spshe·*dash* *sale*
srebro ⓝ *sre*·bro *silver*
stacja ① *sta*·tsya *station*
  — benzynowa ben·zi·*no*·va
  gas station • petrol station
  — kolejowa ko·le·*yo*·va *railway station*
stary *sta*·ri *old*
statek ⓜ *sta*·tek *ship*
stołówka ① sto·*woof*·ka *cafeteria*
stopnie pl *sto*·pnye *degrees (temperature)*
stół ⓜ *stoow* *table*
strona ① *stro*·na *page • side*
strumień ⓜ *stroo*·myen' *stream* n
styczeń ⓜ *sti*·chen' *January*

suchy *soo*·khi *dry* a
Sudety pl soo·*de*·ti *Sudeten mountains*
surowy soo·*ro*·vi *raw*
suszony soo·*sho*·ni *dried*
suszyć *soo*·shich *dry (clothes)*
Sylwester ⓜ sil·*ves*·ter *New Year's Eve*
syn ⓜ *sin* *son*
sypialnia ① si·*pyal*·nya *bedroom*
szachy pl *sha*·khi *chess*
szampan ⓜ *sham*·pan *champagne*
szampon ⓜ *sham*·pon *shampoo*
szary *sha*·ri *grey*
szatnia ① *shat*·nya
  changing room • cloakroom
szczepienie ⓝ shche·*pye*·nye *vaccination*
szczęśliwy shchen·*shlee*·vi *happy • lucky*
szczotka ① *shchot*·ka *brush (general)*
szczyt ⓜ *shchit* *peak (mountain)*
szeroki she·*ro*·kee *wide*
szklanka ① *shklan*·ka *glass (drinking)*
Szkocja ① *shko*·tsya *Scotland*
szkoła ① *shko*·wa *school*
szosa ① *sho*·sa *highway*
szpital ⓜ *shpee*·tal *hospital*
szprycha ① *shpri*·kha *spoke*
Sztokholm ⓜ *shtok*·kholm *Stockholm*
sztuka ① *shtoo*·ka *art • play (theatre)*
szukać *shoo*·kach *look for*
Szwajcaria ① shvai·*tsar*·ya *Switzerland*
Szwecja ① *shve*·tsya *Sweden*
szybki *shib*·kee *fast*
szynka ① *shin*·ka *ham*

Ś

ścieżka ① *shchyesh*·ka *footpath • path*
ślub ⓜ *shloob* *wedding*
śmieci pl *shmye*·chee *garbage*
śniadanie ⓝ shnya·*da*·nye *breakfast*
śnieg ⓜ *shnyeg* *snow*
śpiwór ⓜ *shpee*·voor *sleeping bag*
środa ① *shro*·da *Wednesday*
środek ⓜ *shro*·dek *centre*
środowisko ⓝ shro·do·*vees*·ko
  environment
świat ⓜ *shfyat* *world*
światło ⓝ *shvyat*·wo *light*
świeca ① *shvye*·tsa *candle*
świekra ① *shwyek*·ra
  mother-in-law (husband's mother)
świeży *shfye*·zhi *fresh*

świę‌to ⓝ *shvyen·*to **holiday**
świę‌towanie ⓝ shvyen·to·*va·*nye **celebration**
świę‌ty *shvyen·*ti **saint**
świt ⓜ shveet **dawn**

T

tak tak **yes**
taksówka ⓕ tak·*soof·*ka **taxi**
także *tak·*zhe **also**
tam tam **there**
tani *ta·*nee **cheap**
taryfa ⓕ ta·*ri·*fa **fare** n
teatr ⓜ *te·*atr **theatre**
telefon ⓜ te·*le·*fon **telephone**
— **komórkowy** ko·*moor·ko·*vi **cell phone · mobile phone**
— **publiczny** poob·*leech·*ni **public phone**
telefonować te·le·fo·*no·*vach **telephone**
telegram ⓜ te·*le·*gram **telegram**
teleobiektyw ⓜ te·le·o·*byek·*tif **zoom lens**
telewizor ⓜ te·le·*vee·*zor **TV**
ten ⓜ ten **this (one)** pron
tenis ⓜ *te·*nees **tennis**
teraz *te·*ras **now**
teściowa ⓕ tesh·*chyo·*va **mother-in-law (wife's mother)**
teść ⓜ teshch **father-in-law**
też tesh **too (also)**
tlen ⓜ tlen **oxygen**
tłumacz/tłumaczka ⓜ/ⓕ *twoo·*mach/ *twoo·mach·*ka **interpreter · translator**
tłusty ⓜ *twoos·*ti **fat** a
to ⓝ to **this**
toaleta ⓕ to·a·*le·*ta **toilet**
torba ⓕ *tor·*ba **bag**
torebka ⓕ to·*rep·*ka **handbag**
towarzysz ⓜ to·*va·*zhish **companion**
tramwaj ⓜ *tram·*vai **tram**
trasa ⓕ *tra·*sa **route**
— **podróży** po·*droo·*zhi **itinerary**
trochę *tro·*khe **little (quantity)**
trolejbus ⓜ tro·*ley·*boos **trolley-bus**
trudny *trood·*ni **difficult**
turysta ⓜ too·*ris·*ta **tourist**
tutaj *too·*tai **here**
twardy *tfar·*di **hard (not soft)**
twój tfooy **your** inf sg
ty ti **you** inf sg

tydzień ⓜ *ti·*jyen' **week**
tylko *til·*ko **only**
tylny *til·*ni **rear (location)** a
tył ⓜ tiw **back (position)**
typ ⓜ tip **type**
typowy ti·*po·*vi **typical**

U

ubezpieczenie ⓝ oo·bes·pye·*che·*nye **insurance**
ubranie ⓝ oo·*bra·*nye **clothing**
ucho ⓝ *oo·*kho **ear**
uchodźca ⓜ oo·*khoj·*tsa **refugee**
uczucia oo·*choo·*chya **feelings**
uczucie ⓝ oo·*choo·*chye **feeling (physical)**
Ukraina ⓕ oo·kra·*ee·*na **Ukraine**
ulica ⓕ oo·*lee·*tsa **street**
umieć *oo·*myech **can (know how to)**
Unia Europejska ⓕ *oo·*nya ew·ro·*pey·*ska **European Union**
uniwersytet ⓜ oo·nee·*ver·*si·tet **college · university**
upadać oo·*pa·*dach **fall (down)**
upał ⓜ *oo·*pow **heat**
uprawomocniać oo·pra·vo·*mots·*nyach **validate**
urodziny pl oo·ro·*jee·*ni **birthday**
urwisko ⓝ oor·*vee·*sko **cliff**
usta pl *oos·*ta **mouth**
użyteczny oo·zhi·*tech·*ni **useful**
używany oo·zhi·*va·*ni **secondhand**

W

w v **in · within (time)**
wadliwy vad·*lee·*vi **faulty**
waga ⓕ *va·*ga **weight**
wagon restauracyjny ⓜ *va·*gon res·tow·rat·*siy·*ni **dining car**
wagon sypialny ⓜ *va·*gon si·*pyal·*ni **sleeping car**
wakacje pl va·*ka·*tsye **holidays · vacation**
walizka ⓕ va·*lees·*ka **suitcase**
Warszawa ⓕ var·*sha·*va **Warsaw**
wartość ⓕ *var·*toshch **value (price)**
warzywo ⓝ va·*zhi·*vo **vegetable**
wasz vash **your** inf pl
ważny *vazh·*ni **important**
wąż ⓜ vonzh **snake**

wcześnie *vchesh*-nye *early*

wczoraj *fcho*-rai *yesterday*

wegetarianin ⓜ ve-ge-tar-*ya*-neen *vegetarian*

wegetariański ve-ge-tar-*yan*'-skee *vegetarian*

wejście ⓝ *veysh*-chye *entry • gate (airport, etc)*

wejść veyshch *enter*

wentylator ⓜ ven-ti-*la*-tor *fan (machine)*

wewnątrz *vev*-nontsh *inside* adv

wędrować ven-*dro*-vach *hike*

wędrówka ① ven-*droof*-ka *hiking*

wiadomości pl vya-do-*mosh*-chee *news*

wiadomość ① vya-*do*-moshch *message*

wiatr ⓜ vyatr *wind*

widok ⓜ *vee*-dok *view*

wieczór ⓜ *vye*-choor *evening*

wiedzieć *vye*-jyech *know (be aware of)*

wiek ⓜ vyek *age*

Wielkanoc ① *vyel*-ka-nots *Easter*

wieś ① vyesh *village*

wieża ① *vye*-zha *tower*

więcej *vyen*-tsey *more*

większy *vyenk*-shi *bigger*

Wigilia ① vee-*gee*-lya *Christmas Eve*

Wilno ⓝ *veel*-no *Vilnius*

wina ① *vee*-na *fault (someone's)*

winda ① *veen*-da *elevator • lift*

winnica ① vee-*nee*-tsa *vineyard*

wino ⓝ *vee*-no *wine*

wiosna ① *vyos*-na *spring (season)*

wirus ⓜ *vee*-roos *virus*

wiza ① *vee*-za *visa*

wkrótce *fkroot*-tse *soon*

wliczony ⓜ *vlee*-cho-ni *included*

właściciel/właścicielka ⓜ/① vwash-*chee*-chyel/vwash-chee-*chyel*-ka *landlord/lady • owner*

Włochy pl *vwo*-khi *Italy*

włosy pl *vwo*-si *hair*

wnuk/wnuczka ⓜ/① vnook/*vnooch*-ka *grandchild*

woda ① *vo*-da *water*
— **mineralna** mee-ne-*ral*-na *mineral water*
— **po goleniu** po go-*le*-nyoo *aftershave*
— **z kranu** z *kra*-noo *tap water*

wodoodporny vo-do-od-*por*-ni *waterproof*

wodospad ⓜ vo-do-*spad* *waterfall*

wojna ① *voy*-na *war*

wojsko ⓝ *voy*-sko *military*

woleć *vo*-lech *prefer*

wolny *vol*-ni *free (available) • free (not bound) • slow*

wódka ① *vood*-ka *vodka*

wózek ⓜ *voo*-zek *trolley*
— **inwalidzki** een-va-*leets*-kee *wheelchair*
— **spacerowy** spa-tse-*ro*-vi *stroller*

wpuszczać *fpoosh*-chach *admit (let in)*

wracać *vra*-tsach *return*

wrzesień ⓜ *vzhe*-shyen' *September*

wschód ⓜ vskhood *east* n
— **słońca** *swon*'-tsa *sunrise*

wspaniały ⓜ vspa-*nya*-wi *great (fantastic)*

współpracownik/ współpracowniczka ⓜ/① fspoow-pra-*tsov*-neek/ fspoow-pra-tsov-*neech*-ka *colleague*

wstęp ⓜ fstemp *admission (price)*

wszy pl vshi *lice*

wszystko *fshist*-ko *everything*

wścieklizna ① fshchyek-*leez*-na *rabies*

wtorek ⓜ *vto*-rek *Tuesday*

wtyczka ① *ftich*-ka *plug (electricity)*

wy vi *you* inf pl

wybierać vi-*bye*-rach *choose*

wybrzeże ⓝ vi-*bzhe*-zhe *coast*

wychodzić vi-*kho*-jeech *go out*

wycieczka ① vi-*chyech*-ka *tour*

wycierać vi-*chye*-rach *dry (oneself)*

wygodny vi-*go*-dni *comfortable*

wygrać vi-grach *win*

wyjście ⓝ *viysh*-chye *exit*

wyłączony vi-won-*cho*-ni *excluded*

wymiana ① vi-*mya*-na *exchange*

wymieniać vi-*mye*-nyach *exchange*

wynająć vi-*na*-yonch *rent*

wynajmować vi-nai-*mo*-vach *hire*

wypadek ⓜ vi-*pa*-dek *accident*

wyprzedany vi-pshe-*da*-ni *booked out*

wysiadać vi-*shya*-dach *get off (bus, train)*

wysoki vi-*so*-kee *high • tall*

wyspa ① *vis*-pa *island*

wystawa ① vis-*ta*-va *exhibition*

wysyłać vi-*si*-wach *send*

wzgórze ⓝ *vzgoo*-zhe *hill*

Z

z z *from* • *with*
za za *after* • *behind* • *too (much)*
— **granicą** gra·nee·tsom *abroad*
zabawa za·ba·va *fun*
zabawny za·bav·ni *funny*
zachód ⓜ za·khood *west*
— **słońca** swon'·tsa *sunset*
zaczynać za·chi·nach *start*
zagranica ⓕ za·gra·nee·tsa *overseas*
zagraniczny za·gra·nee·chni *foreign*
zajęty za·yen·ti *busy* • *engaged*
zakład ⓜ za·kwad *bet*
zakładać się za·kwa·dach shye *bet*
zakonnica ⓕ za·ko·nee·tsa *nun*
zakupy pl za·koo·pi *shopping*
zamawiać za·ma·vyach *order* v
zamek ⓜ za·mek *castle* • *lock*
zamężna ⓕ za·men·zhna *married (of woman)*
zamknięty zam·knyen·ti *closed* • *locked* • *shut*
zamykać za·mi·kach *close*
— **na klucz** na klooch *lock*
zapałki pl za·pow·kee *matches (for lighting)*
zapłata ⓕ za·pwa·ta *payment*
zapomnieć za·pom·nyech *forget*
zapoznać za·poz·nach *meet (first time)*
zapraszać za·pra·shach *invite*
zarabiać za·ra·byach *earn*
zaręczony za·ren·cho·ni *engaged (to be married)*
zaręczyny pl za·ren·chi·ni *engagement (to marry)*
zastrzyk ⓜ zast·shik *injection*
zatłoczony za·two·cho·ni *crowded*
zatrzymać za·tshi·mach *stop (prevent)*
zawrotny za·vrot·ni *dizzy*
zawsze zaf·she *always*
ząb ⓜ zomb *tooth*
zdjęcie ⓝ zdyen·chye *photo*
zdrowie ⓝ zdro·vye *health*

zegar ⓜ ze·gar *clock*
zegarek ⓜ ze·ga·rek *watch*
zepsuty zep·soo·ti *broken down* • *corrupt* • *spoiled (food)*
zespół ⓜ zes·poow *band (music)*
zezwolenie ⓝ ze·zvo·le·nye *permit*
zęby pl zem·bi *teeth*
zgodzić się zgo·jeech shye *agree*
zgubiony zgoo·byo·ni *lost*
zielony zhye·lo·ni *green*
Ziemia ⓕ zhye·mya *Earth*
ziemia ⓕ zhye·mya *land*
zima ⓕ zhee·ma *winter*
zimno ⓝ zhee·mno *cold (temperature)* n
zimny zheem·ni *cold* a
zjazd ⓜ zyazd *downhill*
złoto ⓝ zwo·to *gold*
zły ⓜ zwi *angry* • *bad* • *wrong*
zmęczony zmen·cho·ni *tired*
zmiana ⓕ zmya·na *change*
znać znach *know (be acquainted with)*
zniżka ⓕ zneesh·ka *discount*
zwierzę ⓝ zvye·zhe *animal*
zwolennik ⓜ zvo·le·neek *supporter (politics)*
zwrot pieniędzy ⓜ zvrot pye·nyen·dzi *refund*
zwyczaj ⓜ zvi·chai *custom*
zwyczajny zvi·chai·ni *ordinary*

Ż

żaden zha·den *neither* • *none*
żart ⓜ zhart *joke*
żeński zhen'·skee *female*
żołądek ⓜ zho·won·dek *stomach*
żołnierz ⓜ zhow·nyezh *soldier*
żółty zhoow·ti *yellow*
żona ⓕ zho·na *wife*
żonaty zho·na·ti *married (of man)*
żubr ⓜ zhoobr *bison*
żubrówka ⓕ zhoo·broof·ka *bison vodka*
życie ⓝ zhi·chye *life*
życzyć zhi·chich *wish*
żyć zhich *live (life)*
żydowski zhi·dof·skee *Jewish*

FINDER

The topics covered in this book are listed below in Polish. Show this page to your Polish friends if you're having trouble understanding them.

FINDER